Teacher's Handbook

Stage 2

By Sue Reed and Liz Webster

William Collins' dream of knowledge for all began with the publication of his first book in 1819. A self-educated mill-worker, he not only enriched millions of lives, but also founded a flourishing publishing house. Today, staying true to this spirit, Collins books are packed with inspiration, innovation and practical expertise. They place you at the centre of a world of possibility and give you exactly what you need to explore it.

Collins. Freedom to teach.

Published by Collins

An imprint of HarperCollins*Publishers* Ltd.

77–85 Fulham Palace Road
Hammersmith
London
W6 8JB

Browse the complete Collins catalogue at
www.collinseducation.com

Text © HarperCollins*Publishers* Limited 2014

Design and illustration © HarperCollins*Publishers* Limited 2014

10 9 8 7 6 5 4 3 2 1

ISBN: 978-0-00-753714-3

British Library Cataloguing in Publication Data

A Catalogue record for this publication is available from the British Library.

Authors: Liz Webster and Sue Reed

Commissioning Editor: Sarah Loader

Managing Editor: Helen Terrington

Series designer: Linda Miles, Lodestone Publishing Limited

Series illustrator: Emily Skinner

Printed and bound by Hung Hing, China.

Contents

Hello from the authors

Dear colleagues,

We are thrilled to be able to present to you our dynamic phonics programme, Song of Sounds.

We are Headteacher and Deputy Head at Aldingbourne Primary School in West Sussex, a highly successful and happy village school with 220 pupils from reception to Year 6. Our intake is 'broadly average' with a mixture of socio-economic backgrounds.

Aldingbourne was rated Outstanding in all areas in its last 2 Ofsted inspections (2006 and 2009), with the 2009 report stressing that 'the high quality of teaching...combined with an inventive curriculum results in pupils being creative writers (and) avid readers', that the 'excellent provision (of the Early Years Foundation Stage teaching) ensures that children get off to a flying start and they make rapid progress in all areas of learning'. We are very proud of our school, not only of its achievements, but also its atmosphere of fun and creativity, which we have worked hard to establish.

Both of us have a vast range of teaching experience, having taught all primary ages. We are both Foundation Stage specialists and Sue currently teaches full-time in the Reception class at our school. We have developed Song of Sounds over the last 10 years in a bid to ensure our children get the best possible start to their reading and writing journey, leaving Reception and Year 1 classes with a firm grip on phonics. Children continue this journey throughout the school, building on their word and sentence level skills and blossoming into confident readers and writers.

The rigorous teaching of systematic synthetic phonics is at the core of *Song of Sounds*. Children learn the 42 basic sounds and 27 complex and alternative spellings, and how to blend words for reading and segment words for writing at an impressive rate. Alongside this, they enjoy a range of decodable readers that they can easily sound-blend to ensure success and inspire confidence, as well as games and practical activities to put their phonics skills into practice.

Perhaps our school's results in the National Curriculum's Year 1 statutory Phonics Screening Check are the best evidence of the programme's success: Aldingbourne enjoyed an impressive 87% success rate in 2012 versus a national average of 58%. 7 children out of 30 scored full marks, with 24 out of 30 passing the test. In 2013, the results were similar, with an 86% success rate versus a national average of 69%. 55% of children at Aldingbourne scored either 39 or 40 out of 40.

We passionately believe that, although systematic, there's no reason why the teaching of phonics has to be dull or predictable. Through *Song of Sounds* we have worked hard to create a phonics scheme that is creative, lively and fun. Our programme has as its core ingredient a song that children love to sing and learn the actions to. Our approach is multi-sensory and our programme is packed full of exciting games and activities through which the children have endless opportunities to apply their new skills and embed their learning. There are optional opportunities for you to teach in role as we have created a cast of characters that make letters and sounds all the more appealing.

By following *Song of Sounds*, you will not only be overwhelmed by the success rates in your class or school, but will see first-hand how phonics can truly be a fun and rewarding part of the curriculum for both child and teacher alike.

Regards,

Liz Webster and Sue Reed

Introduction

Systematic synthetic phonics teaches children to read and write by introducing the 42 basic and 17 complex phonemes sounds (phonemes) and their written equivalents (graphemes), blending or synthesising those sounds together to make full words and segmenting them to spell words correctly.

Systematic synthetic phonics has been the recommended approach to learning to read for some time, as noted in the Rose Review (2006) and the Clackmannanshire Report (2006). Both reports showed overwhelming evidence for the use of synthetic phonics in the teaching of reading, reporting that the reading skills of children who followed a pure synthetic phonics approach were more advanced than those of their peers who employed different reading techniques.

Key objectives of systematic synthetic phonics

To:

- teach grapheme-phoneme correspondences (GPCs) at a quick pace (around one a day)
- immediately teach how to blend sounds into complete words for reading e.g. the phonemes /c/ /a/ /t/ blend together to make the word 'cat',
- immediately teach how to segment words into their individual phonemes for writing e.g. the word 'bus' segments into the phonemes /b/ /u/ /s/
- teach key irregular words (tricky words), noting which parts of the words can be blended phonically and which are irregular, e.g. the, I, me, we
- use decodable texts to ensure children apply phonics knowledge to read at an age-appropriate level.

Grapheme-phoneme correspondence

Establishing the relationship between a phoneme (a letter sound) and its corresponding grapheme (the written equivalent) is the first step to success in any phonics programme.

Phonemes are not the same as the letter name (e.g. the letter "s" makes the phoneme sound 'sss' as opposed to its letter name 'es') and are not introduced in alphabetical order; the first phonemes covered (/s/ /a/ /t/) make more simple 2 (CV) and 3 (CVC) letter words than any other phonemes, and are considered the easiest phonemes for children to access first as they are common and feature in a lot of children's names.

Some phonemes are pronounced the same but are spelt differently, for example /ay/ and /ai/. In systematic synthetic phonics programmes these are not all taught simultaneously. Sounds with more than one way of being written are taught first in one form only, for example, the sound /ay/ ('day') is introduced first, with the alternatives

/ai/ ('rain') and /a-e/ ('cake') being taught later as /ay/ makes easier words for Reception level children to decode and use, e.g. 'day' and 'play'. The only exception is /c/ and /k/ as children tend to arrive at school with knowledge of these two letters having been taught them in nursery.

Table 1: Phoneme list

BASIC PHONEMES	COMPLEX PHONEMES	
	DIGRAPHS (2 letter graphemes)	**TRIGRAPHS** (three letter graphemes)
s	qu	igh
a	ch	air
t	sh	are
p	th	
i	ng	
n	ay	
m	ee	
d	ow	
g	oo	
o	oo	
c	ar	
k	or	
e	er	
u	ou	
r	oy	
h	oi	
b	ai	
f	a-e	
l	ea	
j	e-e	
v	ie	
w	i-e	
x	oa	
y	o-e	
z	ew	
	u-e	
	ur	
	ir	
	au	
	aw	
	ow	

Blending sounds

Blending is the process of saying the phonemes in a word and then running them together to decode the word, e.g. the phonemes /c/ /a/ /t/ make the word 'cat'. Like all other phonics skills, this technique improves with practice, and is easier when sounds are said quickly together (to orally blend them and 'voice' a word).

Blending is the first stage of reading full words as letters are no longer seen in isolation from one another. Rather than a 'look and say' approach, in which children learn to recognise words by sight, through blending they apply their decoding skills to the phonemes they have been taught in a range of different combinations, equipping them with the skill set to read any word. For example, with the graphemes /t/, /a/, /p/ and /s/, children can make the words 'tap', 'pat', 'taps', 'pats', 'sat' and 'sap'.

Once children have mastered blending simple phonemes, they can move on to blending words containing digraphs and trigraphs. To do this successfully they must recognise digraphs as grouped letters, which together represent one sound, rather than as separate phonemes. e.g. to read 'moon', they need to recognise the /oo/ and not read /o/ and /o/. Sound buttons can be used to help scaffold words for children.

Sound buttons

Sound buttons are a key visual clue to children learning to blend and segment words. When a word is written, each phoneme is identified by a "sound button" (dot) underneath it; when a teacher points at a sound button, children say the phoneme on its own; when a teacher sweeps their hand under the word, children blend the phonemes to read the whole word. To denote digraphs and trigraphs, a long thin 'sound button' highlights that two or three letters make one sound.

Segmenting sounds

To begin to write independently children must be able to hear the individual phonemes in words to write the corresponding graphemes. Segmenting is the opposite of blending; to write the word 'dog' a child needs to be able to identify and segment the word into the three separate phonemes /d/ /o/ and /g/.

Some sound combinations are more difficult for children to segment than others, particularly as the children move past CVC words onto CCVC words e.g. the n in 'went' and the l in 'belt' are difficult to hear as they merge with the final letter of the word. Again, sound buttons can be used to help children at first, as they can see how many phonemes they should be listening for in a word.

Reading and writing irregular words

Some words cannot be blended or segmented correctly by listening for the phonemes alone, as they contain phonemes that are irregular in their pronunciation. For example, the word 'was' contains an /a/ that makes an 'o' sound and an /s/ that makes a 'z' sound. Children should try and decode words in the first instance by recognising the decodable/regular sounds, learning to recognise irregularities and then self-correcting; in this instance, the /w/ is still decodable while the /a/ and /s/ are not.

These are called the 'tricky words' as they contain irregular spelling and are 'tricky' to decode. Once children can read these words, they can learn to spell them too.

Using decodable texts

As part of a rigorous phonics programme, decodable texts provide children with the opportunity to apply and practise their phonics skills with appropriate reading material. By working through texts that are matched to their phonic ability, children can practise decoding in a 'real book' environment and gain confidence in their reading skills whilst teachers can monitor their progress and identify potential difficulties. A range of high-quality readers on diverse themes and topics across both fiction and non-fiction is critical to ensuring books are relevant and meaningful, increasing children's engagement, comprehension and enjoyment.

Song of Sounds

Song of Sounds is a multi-component, multi-sensory, systematic synthetic phonics programme. Teacher-led, hands-on and interactive, it contains a huge variety of games and activities that reinforce learning and a daily phonics session that has music and movement at its core to embed knowledge and understanding, and to ensure children enjoy the phonics learning process.

The programme ensures fluency by the end of Year 1 by immediately and quickly beginning to teach the 42 basic phonemes. By the end of Reception, these should be secure and then in Year 1 the same process is used for complex sounds and alternative spellings.

From week 2 in Reception, *Song of Sounds* teaches children how to begin to read and write words and sentences using their knowledge of the phonemes they have learned through the processes of blending and segmenting. Letter formation is taught alongside GPCs to ensure handwriting skills are also developed and correct letter formation is achieved.

Teaching the programme

The programme consists of daily phonic sessions, four of these lasting 15 minutes each and one weekly session lasting 2 hours, on the basis that giving children the opportunity to consolidate and apply their phonics skills at the end of the week reinforces learning.

The programme's short sessions are aimed at the rigorous teaching of synthetic phonics skills. At the beginning, this focuses on teaching a different phoneme every day, and blending and segmenting using this new phoneme. Once children have learned all their phonemes, these sessions focus on revision, letter names and word-building.

During weekly sessions, children play games and engage in practical activities all based around them developing and applying their reading and writing skills and increasing confidence in their phonic ability. Weekly lessons not only embed what children have learned during the week; they also revisit previously taught phonemes to ensure children are constantly reinforcing what they have learnt through the whole programme. Suggestions are made in the weekly session overviews to teach in role as a variety of fun characters such as Felicity the Phoneme Fairy to ensure lessons are fun and exciting.

The song

The programme is based around a song which embeds GPCs by matching each phoneme with its written equivalent, a picture and corresponding action. The song is introduced on the first day of school and sung every day. The visual, auditory and kinaesthetic elements of the song enable all types of learners to learn phonemes at a rapid rate. Whilst the programme teaches phonemic awareness by introducing phonemes in order of difficulty, the song introduces phonemes alphabetically.

The song begins with the 26 letters of the alphabet. It is useful to begin with these as it helps children to remember the order of the alphabet later on. The song then moves on to digraphs. Similar digraphs have been placed in the song together e.g. /sh/, /ch/ and /th/ and the first set of long vowels /ay/, /ee/, /igh/, /ow/ and /oo/. This is deliberate to help children make the link between these sets of graphemes.

The Stage 2 song groups graphemes that make the same sound together, e.g. /ai/, /ay/ and /a-e/. Again, this helps children to make the link between these graphemes which is another strategy for helping to remember them.

From the children's first day at school, the song should be sung every day all the way through. This means that while you tackle each GPC individually and systematically in the daily sessions, singing the whole song enables more able children in the class to access all GPCs from the very beginning of the programme. This avoids a monotonous, go-slow approach and broadens the children's phonic experience. The classroom frieze is ordered in the same order as the songs as a visual reminder of the song order.

Teaching irregular words

Tricky words are not taught until Week 13, so that children have a good grasp of the regular rules of phonics before they tackle words that are irregular.

Words that can be blended, i.e. that are phonetically regular, are known in Song of Sounds as 'green words' as green symbolises 'go' whilst red, for tricky words, symbolises 'stop and think'. These 'red' words are taught explicitly in daily and weekly sessions, in which the teacher identifies the regular and irregular parts of the word and gives children advice on how to tackle them. The words are then displayed in the classroom to allow constant reference.

The programme teaches children to apply decoding skills to irregular as well as regular words where possible, by identifying the 'green' and 'red' parts of a word and provides techniques to help remember irregular words, such as mnemonics e.g. remembering how to spell the word because through the phrase 'big elephants can always understand small elephants' or using auditory techniques, such as saying the word as it looks e.g. 'was' instead of 'wos'. A total of 64 irregular words are taught.

Big Cat Phonic readers

As children learn to blend and segment phonemes, they are encouraged to read from a selection of Collins Big Cat Phonic readers. These are high-quality books by a huge range of authors and allow children an authentic experience of reading fiction and non-fiction whilst they practise their decoding skills. The readers are levelled, which ensures children are reading material that is appropriate to their phonic knowledge. Books are mapped through the programme; each weekly lesson teaches or revises a list of target phonemes and readers are suggested for further reading that contain the target phonemes for that week. As well as applying and improving their decoding skills, children also begin to see tricky words in context, allowing children to make judgements on when to decode a word and when to recognise it as tricky, which also helps to reinforce spelling.

A whole-class approach

The programme's daily session starters and weekly carpet sessions, during which children learn new phonemes, are designed to be delivered to the whole class. This ensures an inclusive approach, as the class works together to acquire new skills, led by the class teacher. In contrast to withdrawing children from the class to be grouped with a variety of ages and support staff, a whole-class approach means that children's confidence and self-esteem is high. This is because children are taught alongside their peers and are assessed by their own experienced class teacher who knows them and can effectively differentiate. Carpet sessions cater for differing abilities within the class as they begin by teaching the easier skills and move on to more complex teaching by the end, thus catering for every child whilst teaching the whole class together. Once children have acquired skills together in these progressive sessions, they can then be separated out into differentiated groups to take part in the practical activities of each weekly session, to practise and apply the skills that the class has learnt together at their own particular level.

Differentiation

Not all children will acquire phonic skills at the same rate and some children will need more support than others, and others will need extra challenges to keep them learning at the rate that is right for them. Also, there will be a discrepancy in children's phonic knowledge on entering school. In order to support this, children are assessed on entering the programme and placed in differentiated groups. Each practical activity in the weekly sessions is carefully differentiated, with support and challenge tips offered where appropriate, and children are constantly monitored to ensure they are working at the correct level.

Peer-to-peer interaction is encouraged through the use of a pairing system in which children are paired with a 'chatting chum'. 'Chatting chums' are carefully paired, e.g. a less-able child may be placed with a more-able child, therefore supporting the less-able child and challenging the more-able child as they explain their phonics knowledge to their peer.

Alternatively, two less-able children can be paired so that they can receive extra help from a teacher or teaching assistant during practical activities, or two more-able children can be paired and given extension activities to push them further. Each weekly consolidation session is divided up into games, each of which has its own differentiation capacity, and as the games are played by small groups around the classroom, differentiation is subtle enough that children are unaware of clear ability grouping.

Assessment

Regular diagnostic and formative assessment is a key feature of the programme and helps not only to monitor children's progress but also to identify key areas for revision. Children are diagnostically assessed on entering school, then at specific points throughout the programme (roughly halfway through each term, depending on individual schools' holiday schedules); these more formal assessments should be carried out on a one-to-one basis by a teacher or teaching assistant. The findings of these assessments help teachers to plan carefully to meet class needs and also identify any children who need further support or extension work. Formative assessment ideas are presented in each weekly session guide, mostly through small group observation during games and activities. Through using both diagnostic and formative assessment and having the opportunity to work with every child in a small group every week, the teacher has an accurate understanding of each child's achievement's and needs.

Year One Phonics Screening Check

In England, all Year 1 pupils in state-funded schools must undertake a statutory Phonics Screening Check towards the end of the school year to ensure they are decoding at the appropriate level. Children are asked to decode 40 words under one-to-one test conditions with a teacher or teaching assistant.

The word list contains a combination of real and 'nonsense' words, the latter being included to ensure that children are using phonics skills to decode words and not recognising words by sight. To pass, children must score at least 32 out of 40. Children who fail in Year 1 are expected to retake the test at the end of Year 2.

The test became statutory in 2012 and test results are publicly reported annually by the Department for Education. Results are used to inform internal intervention in schools and reported to Local Education Authorities, which then feed into National Statistics. If children fail the test in Year 1, their results are flagged and a plan of action developed.

Song of Sounds prepares children for the test by immersing them in decoding from their very first week in Reception class. Strong decoding and blending skills enable application to any word – real or nonsense, therefore preparing children for all reading, including the check.

Home/School links

Parents can offer invaluable support to the programme at home if they understand the objectives and contents of it. These can be introduced through an introductory parents' meeting at the beginning of Reception in which they are introduced to the programme's key goals and contents, including the song, which they can sing at home with their children to reinforce the work that children do in the classroom. Various homework options are also identified throughout the programme.

Table 2: List of components

COMPONENT	USE	PURPOSE
Teacher Handbook	By teachers before starting the programme and thereafter for daily and weekly phonics planning	To provide teachers with the methodology behind the synthetic phonics approach, a clear outline of the Song of Sounds programme and a complete planning tool for teaching phonics every day
Audio CD	As part of daily and weekly sessions to sing along to the Song of Sounds song with the whole class or in groups	To reinforce song words and actions. Particularly helpful for auditory learners.
Flashcards	Initially to teach GPCs, then to revise and reinforce GPCs in daily and weekly sessions, and intermittently in between	To teach GPCs with the aid of visual clues

COMPONENT	USE	PURPOSE
Picture cards	To reinforce the teaching of phonemes in daily sessions, and in various games and activities throughout the programme	To teach GPCs with the aid of visual clues
Green word cards	As part of daily and weekly phonics sessions in both whole class and group activities	To practise blending and segmenting words, phrases and short sentences with the aid of sound buttons
Tricky word cards	As part of daily and weekly tricky word sessions in both whole class and group activities	To practise reading and spelling irregular tricky words
Phoneme stars	Used in numerous games and activities throughout the programme	To revise, consolidate and apply children's knowledge of GPCs
Classroom frieze	As a visual aid for the classroom	To display each GPCs visually in the classroom and to reinforce GPCs
Lotto game	By small groups in various weekly sessions	To revise, consolidate and apply children's knowledge of GPCs
Phoneme finder sheet	As an aid for writing, and during various games and activities in weekly sessions	To aid independent writing and GPC recognition
Resource CD	As part of each weekly session	To provide teachers with all IWB and printable resources necessary to teach every weekly session
Decodable readers	Independent or group reading during a lesson or as homework	To practise blending and segmenting skills at the appropriate level; to apply phonics skills to levelled readers

Song of Sounds scheme overview

Stage 2

WEEK	DAILY SESSIONS	WEEKLY SESSION*	WEEKLY LEARNING OBJECTIVES
1	**ASSESSMENT WEEK 1**	**ASSESSMENT WEEK 1**	to assess each child's phonic ability on a one-to one basis
2	Tricky words	Tricky word practice	to practise reading and spelling tricky words
3	Stage 1 revision /ay/, /ai/, /a-e/	Felicity the Phoneme Fairy	to learn to discriminate between the /ay/, /ai/ and /a-e/ graphemes; to practise blending and segmenting words containing /ay/, /ai/ and /a-e/
4	/ee/, /ea/, /e-e/	A letter from Perfect Pete	to learn to discriminate between the /ee/, /ea/ and /e-e/ graphemes; to practise blending and segmenting words containing /ee/, /ea/ and /e-e/
5	/igh/, /ie/, /i-e/	Introducing Croc	to learn to discriminate between the /igh/, /ie/ and /i-e/ graphemes; to practise blending and segmenting words containing /igh/, /ie/ and /i-e/
6	/ow/, /oa/, /o-e/	The O coat	To learn to discriminate between the /ow/, /oa/ and /o-e/ graphemes; to practise blending and segmenting words containing /ow/, /oa/ and /o-e/
7	/oo/, /ew/, /u-e/	A royal appearance	to learn to discriminate between the /oo/, /ew/ and /u-e/ graphemes; to practise blending and segmenting words containing /oo/, /ew/ and /u-e/
8	Tricky words come, some, said, have, any, many	Tricky words	to practise reading and spelling tricky words
9	/ay/, /ai/, /a-e/, /ee/, /ea/, /e-e/, /igh/, /ie/, /i-e/, /ow/, /oa/, /o-e/	Felicity's problem	to understand vowels and consonants and their importance
10	/oo/, /ew/, /u-e/	Long and short vowels	to understand the difference between long and short vowel phonemes
11	Long vowel digraph revision	Long vowel revision	to understand the difference between long and short vowel phonemes
12	**ASSESSMENT WEEK 2**	**ASSESSMENT WEEK 2**	to assess each child's phonic ability on a one-to one basis

WEEK	DAILY SESSIONS	WEEKLY SESSION*	WEEKLY LEARNING OBJECTIVES
13	Tricky words oh, again, one, once, there, their, little, ask	Tricky words	to practise reading and spelling tricky words
14	/er/, /ir/, /ur/	Flower power	to learn to discriminate between the /er/, /ir/ and /ur/ graphemes; to practise blending and segmenting words containing /er/, /ir/ and /ur/
15	/or/, /aw/, /au/	Sort your ors	to learn to discriminate between the /or/, /au/ and /aw/ graphemes; to practise blending and segmenting words containing /or/, /au/ and /aw/
16	/ou/, /ow/	Croc returns	to learn to discriminate between the /ou/ and /ow/ graphemes; to practise blending and segmenting words containing /ou/ and /ow/
17	/oy/, /oi/	The noisy boy	to learn to discriminate between the /oy/ and /oi/ graphemes; to practise blending and segmenting words containing /oy/ and /oi/
18	/air/, /are/	Felicity's favourite phoneme	to learn to discriminate between the /air/ and /are/ graphemes; to practise blending and segmenting words containing /air/ and /are/
19	Tricky words when, what, why, which, where, were, who, how	Tricky words	to practise reading and spelling tricky words
20	Phoneme revision, reading and writing green cards, reading and writing sentences	Felicity returns	to assess each child's phonic ability on a one-to one basis
21	CVC words, words with adjacent consonants	Meet the wordbuilder	to practise reading and spelling a range of CVC and CCVC and CVCC words
22	CCVCC words	The wordbuilder returns	to practise reading and spelling a range of CVC & CCVC/CVCC and CCVCC words
23	Words with two and three syllables	Sally Syllable	to discriminate syllables in multi-syllabic words
24	**ASSESSMENT WEEK 3**	**ASSESSMENT WEEK 3**	to assess each child's phonic ability on a one-to one basis

WEEK	DAILY SESSIONS	WEEKLY SESSION*	WEEKLY LEARNING OBJECTIVES
25	Tricky words of, off, house, because, looked, called	Tricky words	to practise reading and spelling tricky words
26	Phoneme revision, reading and writing green cards, reading and writing sentences	Alphabetical order	to use letter names and to develop an understanding of the order of the alphabet
27	Letter names	Upper and lower case	to be able to match lower and upper case letters and begin to be able write lower and upper case graphemes
28	Letter names, alphabetical order and upper and lower case letters	Alphabetical order	to understand what a dictionary is and what it is used for; to begin to develop the skills needed to use a dictionary effectively
29	Phoneme revision, reading and writing green cards, reading and writing sentences	Felicity returns	to practise blending and segmenting all phonemes learned so far
30	Real and nonsense words without sound buttons	Phonics screening test	to blend and read a mixture of real and nonsense words; to carry out phonics screening test

*All previously taught phonemes are revised every week in addition to those listed being introduced for the first time.

Song of Sounds song

We can sing a song of sounds, skip to my lou my darling.

May I play ay ay ay

Train in the rain ai ai ai

Bake a cake a-e a-e a-e

Skip to my lou my darling

Busy busy bee ee ee ee

Beans in your dreams ea ea ea

Perfect Pete e-e e-e e-e

Skip to my lou my darling

Soar up high igh igh

Lazy lie in ie ie ie

In a while crocodile i-e i-e i-e

Skip to my lou my darling

Throw the snow ow ow ow

Goat on a boat oa oa oa

Phone home o-e o-e o-e

Skip to my lou my darling

Zoom to the moon oo oo oo

New jewels ew ew ew

A huge cube u-e u-e u-e

Skip to my lou my darling

Flower in a shower er er er

If you're hurt see a nurse ur ur ur

Girl in a whirl ir ir ir

Skip to my lou my darling

It's a horse of course or or or

Naughty in autumn au au au

It's an awful claw aw aw aw

Skip to my lou my darling

Mouse in a house ou ou ou

Clown upside down ow ow ow

Boy with a toy oy oy oy

Skip to my lou my darling

Don't be noisy oi oi oi

Hairy fairy air air air

Share if you care are are are

Skip to my lou my darling

Now we've sung our song to you, you can learn to blend sounds too.

Blending helps you read and write so sing this song all day and night.

Song actions

Stage 2

PHONEME	GRAPHEME EXPLANATION	ACTION
ay	hold your arms out with palms up as if asking a question	
ai	tuck your elbows in and move your arms like a train	
a–e	hold a mixing bowl with one arm and stir with the other	
ee	make tiny wings like a bumblebee and flap very fast	
ea	point with your fingers to your head and make circles with your fingers to indicate dreams	
e–e	put your hands under your chin and look angelic	

PHONEME	GRAPHEME EXPLANATION	ACTION
igh	point up high	
ie	put your hands together under your cheek and close your eyes as if sleeping	
i–e	use your arms to snap like a crocodile	
ow (throw)	mime throwing snowballs	
oa	use your fingers to make pointy goat horns and indicate waves with your hand	
o–e	use your hand to make a phone shape and put it to your ear	

PHONEME	GRAPHEME EXPLANATION	ACTION
oo (moon)	rush your hand up quickly (as if zooming) and point to the moon	
ew	point to your neck, as if showing off a necklace	
u–e	use your hands to draw a box shape in the air	
oy	use your thumbs to mime playing a games console/remote control toy	
oi	put your hands over your ears	
or	pretending to sit on a horse, put one hand behind your back, one hand on the reins and ride	

23

PHONEME	GRAPHEME EXPLANATION	ACTION
aw	stretch and point your fingers on one hand to make a scary claw	
au	wag your finger as if telling someone off and then flutter fingers as if leaves falling from the trees	
er	waggle your fingers like rain	
ur	put your fists to your eyes and pretend to cry	
ir	put your hands above your head as if a ballerina doing a whirl and spin	
ou	put your hands over your head to make a roof	

PHONEME	GRAPHEME EXPLANATION	ACTION
ow (clown)	bend your arms over to the side	
air	put your hands on your head to show your messy hair	
are	overlap your hands on your chest to show that you are caring	

English National Curriculum: Early Years Foundation Stage

PRIME AREAS OF LEARNING		
Communication and language development		
ELG 01	Listening and attention	✓
ELG 02	Understanding	✓
ELG 03	Speaking	✓
Physical development		
ELG 04	Moving and handling	✓
ELG 05	Health and self-care	
Personal, social and emotional development		
ELG 06	Self-confidence and self-awareness	✓
ELG 07	Managing feelings and behaviour	✓
ELG 08	Making relationships	✓
SPECIFIC AREAS OF LEARNING		
Literacy development		
ELG 09	Reading	✓
ELG 10	Writing	✓
Mathematical development		
ELG 11	Numbers	✓
ELG 12	Shape, space and measures	
Understanding of the world		
ELG 13	People and communities	
ELG 14	The world	
ELG 15	Technology	✓
Expressive arts and design		
ELG 15	Exploring and using media and materials	✓
ELG 16	Being imaginative	✓

Please visit www.collins.co.uk/category/international for international curricula.

English National Curriculum: Year 1

READING – WORD READING	
Pupils should be taught to:	
apply phonic knowledge and skills as the route to decode words	✓
respond speedily with the correct sound to graphemes (letters or groups of letters) for all 40+ phonemes, including, where applicable, alternative sounds for graphemes	✓
read accurately by blending sounds in unfamiliar words containing GPCs that have been taught	✓
read common exception words, noting unusual correspondences between spelling and sound and where these occur in the word	✓
read words containing taught GPCs and –s, –es, –ing, –ed, –er and –est endings	
read other words of more than one syllable that contain taught GPCs	✓
read words with contractions [for example, I'm, I'll, we'll], and understand that the apostrophe represents the omitted letter(s)	
read books aloud, accurately, that are consistent with their developing phonic knowledge and that do not require them to use other strategies to work out words	✓
reread these books to build up their fluency and confidence in word reading	✓

READING – READING COMPREHENSION	
Pupils should be taught to:	
develop pleasure in reading, motivation to read, vocabulary and understanding by: • listening to and discussing a wide range of poems, stories and non-fiction at a level beyond that at which they can read independently • being encouraged to link what they read or hear read to their own experiences • becoming very familiar with key stories, fairy stories and traditional tales, retelling them and considering their particular characteristics • recognising and joining in with predictable phrases • learning to appreciate rhymes and poems, and to recite some by heart • discussing word meanings, linking new meanings to those already known	✓

understand both the books they can already read accurately and fluently and those they listen to by: • drawing on what they already know or on background information and vocabulary provided by the teacher • checking that the text makes sense to them as they read and correcting inaccurate reading • discussing the significance of the title and events • making inferences on the basis of what is being said and done • predicting what might happen on the basis of what has been read so far	✓
participate in discussion about what is read to them, taking turns and listening to what others say	✓
explain clearly their understanding of what is read to them	✓

WRITING – HANDWRITING

Pupils should be taught to:

sit correctly at a table, holding a pencil comfortably and correctly	✓
begin to form lower case letters in the correct direction, starting and finishing in the right place	✓
form capital letters	✓
form digits 0–9	✓
understand which letters belong to which handwriting families and to practise these	✓

WRITING – COMPREHENSION

Pupils should be taught to:

write sentences by: • saying out loud what they are going to write about • composing a sentence orally before writing it • sequencing sentences to form short narratives • re-reading what they have written to check that it makes sense	
discuss what they have written with the teacher or other pupils	
read aloud their writing clearly enough to be heard by their peers and the teacher	

WRITING – VOCABULARY, GRAMMAR AND PUNCTUATION

Pupils should be taught to:	
develop their understanding of the concepts set out in English appendix 2 by: • leaving spaces between words • joining words and joining clauses using 'and' • beginning to punctuate sentences using a capital letter and a full stop, question mark or exclamation mark • using a capital letter for names of people, places, the days of the week, and the personal pronoun 'I' • learning the grammar for year 1 in English appendix 2	✓
use the grammatical terminology in English appendix 2 in discussing their writing	

Please visit www.collins.co.uk/category/international for international curricula.

Collins Big Cat Phonic Readers

Decodable Fiction

Pink A / Band 1A

Nip! Nip!	In a Pit	Pam Naps	Dip in!
978-0-00-733096-6	978-0-00-733488-9	978-0-00-742190-9	978-0-00-750787-0

Pink B / Band 1B

Rat Naps	Sam the Nut	No, Sid, No!	Sit in It
978-0-00-733287-8	978-0-00-733499-5	978-0-00-742192-3	978-0-00-750789-4

Red A / Band 2A

Muck It Up!	Ant and Snail	Cats and Dogs in a Mess	Puff the Pup	Panda's Band	Pat the Rat	Top Dog
978-0-00-723583-4	978-0-00-723584-1	978-0-00-723582-7	978-0-00-742194-7	978-0-00-742195-4	978-0-00-750791-7	978-0-00-750792-4

Red B / Band 2B

The Mouse and the Monster	Bot on the Moon	We Are Not Fond of Rat!		Goat's Coat	This Is Me, This Is Me	Kat's Wishing Hat
978-0-00-723589-6	978-0-00-723588-9	978-0-00-723590-2	978-0-00-742198-5	978-0-00-742199-2	978-0-00-750795-5	978-0-00-750796-2

Yellow / Band 3

Diggety Dog	Horse Up a Tree	Bart the Shark	The Singing Beetle		Feeling Things	Zeb and Zebra
978-0-00-723595-7	978-0-00-723596-4	978-0-00-723594-0	978-0-00-742202-9	978-0-00-742203-6	978-0-00-750779-5	978-0-00-750780-1

Blue / Band 4

	Mole and the New Hole	Hansel and Gretel	Catching the Moon	The Hat Maker and the Chimps	A Day Out	Bert the Ugly Bug
978-0-00-723601-5	978-0-00-723600-8	978-0-00-723602-2	978-0-00-742206-7	978-0-00-742207-4	978-0-00-750783-2	978-0-00-750784-9

Decodable Non-Fiction

Pink A / Band 1A

 978-0-00-733492-6
 978-0-00-733490-2
 978-0-00-742191-6
 978-0-00-750788-7

Pink B / Band 1B

 978-0-00-733504-6
 978-0-00-733501-5
 978-0-00-742193-0
 978-0-00-750790-0

Red A / Band 2A

 978-0-00-723587-2
 978-0-00-723586-5
 978-0-00-723585-8
 978-0-00-742196-1
 978-0-00-742197-8
 978-0-00-750793-1
 978-0-00-750794-8

Red B / Band 2B

 978-0-00-723592-6
 978-0-00-723593-3
 978-0-00-723591-9
 978-0-00-742200-5
 978-0-00-742201-2
 978-0-00-750777-1
 978-0-00-750778-8

Yellow / Band 3

 978-0-00-723598-8
 978-0-00-723599-5
 978-0-00-723597-1
 978-0-00-742204-3
 978-0-00-742205-0
 978-0-00-750781-8
 978-0-00-750782-5

Blue / Band 4

 978-0-00-723604-6
 978-0-00-723603-9
 978-0-00-723605-3
 978-0-00-742208-1
 978-0-00-742209-8
 978-0-00-750785-6
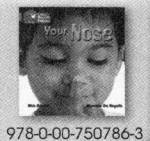 978-0-00-750786-3

An introduction to the daily sessions

Each week of the programme is divided into 4 daily, teacher-led 15 minute sessions, and a 2 hour revision session during which children apply and practise their skills. Daily sessions are taught to the whole class, while weekly lessons are a combination of whole-class teaching and break-out sessions. This structure ensures that children acquire phonic skills at a rapid yet manageable rate via a daily, systematic approach, but also have the opportunity to truly embed their skills by applying them practically in an extended weekly session

What is a daily phonics session?

At the beginning of the programme, daily sessions focus on teaching a different phoneme every day. Once all phonemes have been secured, daily phonics sessions cover specific topics such as syllables, double consonants and letter names, or revise previously-taught work. Each session's target phoneme and learning objectives are clearly outlined at the top of each session's page to help teachers quickly locate the correct lesson.

Daily sessions follow a similar structure every day so that children apply the same systematic approach to securing each phoneme; children are taught a new phoneme and the resulting GPC, then practise reading and writing it and using it in words. This focussed approach helps children to isolate a phoneme and begin to use it successfully before adding it to their list of previously taught phonemes for further practice. This daily repetition aids learning by securing GPCs quickly and effectively. Once phonemes are secured and children move on to exploring tricky words, syllables and word formation, the daily session structure changes slightly, but retains a systematic order to help children progress easily.

All the resources you need to teach these sessions are included in the resource pack and there is a detailed plan for each daily session in the handbook, which follows the same basic structure of teach, practise and review. Through this structure, the teaching point and learning objective of each session is clearly identified, skills are acquired and practised in order for consolidation, and previously acquired skills are revised.

 Teach
e.g. Teach a new grapheme
Teach blending and/or segmentation of phonemes in words

 Practise
e.g. Practise reading and/or spelling with the new phoneme/grapheme

 Revisit and review
e.g. Practise previously learned phonemes and graphemes to embed learning

Whole class approach

In order to provide an inclusive environment where children work together to acquire new skills, a whole-class approach is used to teach the class new phonemes. Daily sessions are short bursts of phonics activity, which are then reinforced by child-initiated learning in weekly sessions. These sessions are led by the children's own class teacher, who can evaluate children's ability level and progression and differentiate accordingly.

Differentiation

Each daily phonics session includes content relevant for each ability group within the class. Each session starts at a level that caters for children with the lowest ability in the class and adds increasingly difficult material to be used with higher-level children as the lesson progresses. Different parts of the sessions are aimed at the different ability groups in the class, but can be accessed by all due to the multi-sensory and fun-filled nature of the lesson. The pace of the session is rapid and the energy level of each session is high, meaning that everyone remains on task for the session. Lower ability children may be supported by their chatting chum or a teaching assistant to ensure they stay involved, whilst the challenging extension activities and tips stretch more able children and keep them motivated.

Assessment

Formative assessment is carried during daily sessions through observation of children as they progress through the lesson. Every daily session includes grapheme recognition, blending and segmenting and reading and writing practice which can be observed during the class. Diagnostic assessment is reserved for weekly sessions, when there is more time to effectively conduct assessments.

GPC, blending, segmenting and writing skills can be observed through carpet session activities such as calling children up to the board to write or read individually, or asking small groups of children or chatting chum pairs to work together to give you the opportunity to assess individuals' performance. Weaknesses in particular skills or gaps in children's learning can then be identified to inform future planning.

An introduction to the weekly session

What is a weekly phonics session?

Weekly sessions are taught over two hours, one day per week, and are designed to help reinforce and embed phonic skills learned during the week, plus to revisit and consolidate previously-taught work. These extended sessions aid children's phonic skills through their practical application to varied activities.

Children play games and engage in practical activities all based around developing their reading and writing skills using all the phoneme/grapheme correspondences learned so far, with a particular emphasis on the phonemes learned over the last week.

The emphasis of these sessions is fun and it through these practical, multi-sensory and memorable sessions that the children truly apply their knowledge and become confident in their phonic ability.

Session structure

Every weekly session follows the same basic structure by including a carpet session, practical activities, plenary and links to Collins Big Cat readers. This structure reflects the systematic nature of the programme and makes planning easy. Learning objectives are provided in clear overview charts in the Teacher's Handbook alongside detailed plans for each weekly session with adaptable ideas offering alternatives for varied teaching styles such as teaching in role and using puppets or props.

Carpet session

The carpet session is delivered to the whole class before they split up into groups for the practical activities. It should last for about 25 minutes and includes a starter and a teaching focus which is clearly identified by the learning objective. The starter outlines the learning objective for each session and is engaging and stimulating so that each session is exciting, meaningful and relevant. Children should have a sound understanding of the aims of the lesson and be ready to participate.

The Song of Sounds song is sometimes sung as part of a carpet session, but care should be taken to avoid the use of the song becoming monotonous – it is more engaging for children to sing the song at different times of the school day in addition to the phonics session, e.g. at registration, at lunchtime, at the end of the school day, than to sing it at the beginning of every daily session. The song can be sung in different ways, too, e.g. using the software to show accompanying phoneme images, singing along to the Song of Sounds CD, silently miming the song actions, singing the phonemes only, using the Song of Sounds flashcards as prompts and so on. Thinking of ways to keep the song fresh and fun is key to keeping children engaged.

During each carpet session, children are guided by the teacher and the use of the Song of Sounds software through revision of the phonemes they have learned through the week. Carpet sessions contain a variety of group games and activities for the class to play together or in pairs to embed phonemes. Once the carpet session is over, children should be divided up into differentiated groups to take part in practical activities, which are games for small groups of children (usually around 5-6 children).

Teaching software

Each weekly session is accompanied by a software presentation. Each presentation is an excellent visual resource for children to engage and interact with, and a guide to the contents of each presentation and how and when to use it is provided in each weekly session overview in the Teacher Handbook. In addition, printable activity sheets are provided to accompany the practical activities and carpet sessions of each weekly session (see Practical Activities section below).

Chatting chums

During the carpet session, children should work with a 'chatting chum' (a partner for pair work). They should sit next to their chatting chum throughout the whole class starter and work collaboratively.

This ensures that all children engage with the lesson, as rather than being asked to put their 'hands up' to tell the teacher the answer, they discuss the answer with their 'chatting chum' and then the teacher chooses a pair at random to answer the question. Children are more confident to volunteer answers that they have tried out with a partner first. Furthermore, they learn and retain so much more when they have discussed it with someone else.

Chatting chum pairs should be chosen by the teacher and rotated every week or fortnight so that they have the opportunity to work with lots of different partners over the year. An effective way to organise this is a display of the children's photos that you move around to show their pairs.

Choosing effective partnerships is key. It is often beneficial to pair chatting chums by ability e.g. a lower ability child with a higher ability child. The higher ability child can then support the lower ability child, and through 'teaching' their partner will truly embed their own learning. However, this is not the only way to pair children and you may want to consider other factors to keep the pairings interesting for children.

Top tips for choosing chatting chum pairs

- Pair very able children and set them more challenging tasks
- Pair 2 less able children, with a teaching assistant for support
- Pair 2 shy children together to encourage them to talk
- Pair a boy and a girl to encourage positive relationships between genders
- Pair a lively child with a well-behaved (but confident) child so that good behaviour is promoted
- Pair friends together so that like-minded children have the opportunity to share ideas

Practical activities

In every weekly session, there is an activity focused on:

- blending for reading
- segmenting for writing
- handwriting/letter formation practice

All of these skills are developed each week to encourage confidence in all aspects of phonics learning.

Practical activities are multi-sensory, and coded for easy reference as kinaesthetic, visual and auditory to help provide a balance of activities.

Each game or activity should last for 20–25 minutes and children should rotate around them in a carousel system in small differentiated groups until they have completed all of them, either working with yourself, a teaching assistant or a parent helper (you can station an adult at each game to ensure children have help where they need it, or explain the rules of each game and move around groups yourself if you do not have any assistance). Practical ideas for different kinds of games are included as well as ideas for how to produce work in an imaginative way (e.g. on paper/in exercise books, on whiteboards, through drawing, through play etc). They can be used and organised in different ways, according to how you manage your classroom. You may decide to adapt the games, vary the group size, or add in some of your own games and ideas.

Numerous printable resources to accompany each game are provided on a Resource CD. These may include game boards, game cards or other resources to make lessons varied and interesting. To minimise administration for teachers, most printable resources are offered as optional, with alternative options where possible. Alternatively, resources can be reused if they are laminated.

Some activities are designed for a classroom setting, some are outside games and some can be played in a large indoor space such as a hall. When setting up your games, ensure that children are clear on the order of the rotation of games, and that you have enough teaching assistants so that each station is overseen by a responsible adult. If this is not possible, games can be tailored to be played in the classroom.

Differentiation

Children should be carefully divided into differentiated groups before they are sent to complete the practical activities. For each activity, tips are provided to help differentiate each game up or down to challenge more-able children and support those that are less-able. In addition, you may use the same activity in a slightly different way to shift the focus of the group's learning. All of the activities provided are optional and fully adaptable, and thus form part of a fast-paced, dynamic lesson catering for all ability levels.

Plenary

Each weekly session ends back on the carpet for a plenary, which gives the class an opportunity to reflect on the session and its learning objective. The plenary should last around 10–15 minutes, during which children should revisit and review their learning. A plenary idea is included in every lesson plan, and careful observation is instrumental here in assessing the children's progress to inform future planning.

Assessment

Diagnostic assessment takes place 8 times in the programme, when the class teacher should work with one child at a time to carry out a formal assessment using the assessment sheets provided. The results of these assessments should be used to inform your future planning and any possible intervention needed for individual children, for example, moving children to a more appropriate ability group or offering extra support for under-achievers. Assessments results could impact on the pace of delivery of the rest of the programme, and/or which parts of the programme you choose to revise.

Furthermore, the weekly sessions can be used for additional formative assessment through close observation of each child within the group-work structure. The weekly sessions are ideal for formative assessment opportunities as you will have the opportunity to work with every child in the class in a small group setting, and see firsthand how they apply their skills and what they are capable of. Again, this will impact further delivery of the programme and guide you on revision areas, the accuracy of differentiated ability groups and any intervention plans for individual students. Weekly sessions will afford you a more extended opportunity to assess children's skills than the daily ones, in which it is more difficult to monitor individuals' progress as sessions are brief, children are taught in a whole class setting and the focus is on imparting information to children and revising previously-taught work collectively. The nature of the carousel system used during the practical activities enables teachers to choose specific assessment focuses to monitor, for example, you may focus on a reading activity to assess children's ability to blend, or the spelling activity to see which children can segment words for writing.

TEACHING SESSIONS

An Introduction to Song of Sounds: Stage 2

Objective

to assess the children's phonic knowledge and establish any gaps

The importance of revision

Typically, you will be beginning the Song of Sounds Stage 2 at the beginning of Year 1. You may be teaching children who completed Song of Sounds Stage 1, or who are completely new to the programme. Either way, you will need to assess children's phonic ability and what they learned during their phonics lessons, whether that be through Song of Sounds or not, during the previous year.

Therefore, it is important that you begin the programme with some revision and careful assessment, before you move on to new learning. Week 1 of the programme focuses on revising children's knowledge of the GPCs they learned in Stage 1 and their ability to blend for reading and segment for writing. Week 2 focusses on revising all of the tricky words learned in Stage 1. For these revision lessons, you will need to use some resources from the Stage 1 pack, which are all provided as generic assets on your Stage 2 CD.

How to begin...

To make the first phonic session of the year a valuable and exciting session, **for this week only, the weekly phonics session comes at the beginning of the week on Monday rather than at the end of the week**. After that you will continue your daily sessions for the remainder of this week. This is the only week in the programme that follows this format.

From next week onwards, your daily sessions should be the first four lessons of the week. Children will then have plenty of opportunity to practise their new-found phonic skills by applying them in the fun-filled weekly phonics session at the end of every week.

Assessment week 1

Learning objective

to assess each child's phonic ability on a one-to-one basis

Resources

Carpet session

- Week 1: Teach software
- An assessment sheet for each child
- Paper and pencil for each child
- A box addressed to the children (optional: cover in sparkly wrapping paper)
- A letter from Felicity to go inside the parcel (on fancy stationery if you wish)

Assessment

- An assessment sheet for each child

Star sprint

- Song of Sounds phoneme stars
- A large (A2) piece of paper for each team

- Song of Sounds phoneme finder sheets (optional)
- A whistle or bell (optional)
- Hoop (optional)
- A mini whiteboard and pen for each child (optional)

Wordbuilding cards

- CVC, CVCC and CCVC and CCVCC wordbuilding cards (Week 1: AS1-4)
- A mini whiteboard and pen for each child (optional)
- One dice per child (optional)

Revision

- Song of Sounds Stage 1 flashcards (stand-alone resource on Resource CD)

Carpet session

- Gather the children on the carpet.
- Explain to them that you have received a parcel from Felicity the Phoneme Fairy and open it with them to find a letter inside.
- NB: If children used Song of Sounds Stage 1 in Reception, the letter should say that Felicity hopes the children had a lovely summer holiday, and that she can't believe they are so grown up that they are now in Year 1. She also asks how they are getting on with their phonemes. Have they forgotten them over the summer holiday?
- If children are new to Song of Sounds, the letter should introduce Felicity the Phoneme Fairy as the person who is going to help them learn how to read and write through the year.
- The letter should also say that Felicity wants to see how clever the children are and she has sent a special test for them to do with their teacher. She says that if they are really clever, she will teach them some more about phonemes. The letter instructs the teacher to look at the screen.

1
- Use the software to check that children can:

2
- Sing their sounds: pictures from the Song of Sounds flash up for children to sing.

3
- Say their sounds: graphemes flash up for the children to say.

4-7
- Read words – words appear for the children to read.

8-11
- Write words: pictures appear on the screen for the children to write.

> **Software**
> Teach
> **W1**

12 • The presentation finishes by reminding children that today's learning objective is to practise using phonemes to read and write.

Practical activities

Assessment

An assessment activity for you or a teaching assistant to do individually with children

Aim: to assess children's phonic ability at the beginning of Stage 2

How to do:

• Complete part one of the assessment this week (part two is for next week).

• This assessment should take about five minutes per child.

• Sit somewhere quiet with the child so it is easy to concentrate and hear them.

• Follow the instructions on the assessment sheet, always ensuring that you are positive and encouraging. You could offer an optional reward after the assessment.

• Check each child's knowledge of graphemes on the assessment sheet.

• Check that they can blend their sounds for reading and segment their sounds for writing.

• You may find that less-able children are not yet able to blend their sounds for reading or attempting to write words. Ask them to try in case they surprise you – don't worry if they struggle, just move on.

Star sprint

A game for a large group of 10–15 children

Aim: to practise recognising the pictures from the Song of Sounds and writing the corresponding grapheme

How to play:

• Gather the resources.

• This game should be played in a large space such as a hall or playground.

• Scatter Felicity's phoneme stars in a hoop (or pile) on the floor.

• Pin up a large piece of paper for each team.

• Split the class into two or three teams and give each team a starting point so that they are all an equal distance away from the hoop/pile.

• Give the first member of each team a pen.

• On a given signal (whistle, bell or clap) the first member of each team should run to the hoop, pick up a phoneme star and sprint to their large piece of paper. They should then write the correct grapheme on their piece of paper, run back to the hoop and replace the star and run back to their team, passing the pen to the next team member.

• Blow your whistle, ring your bell or clap your hands to stop the game. The team with the most correct graphemes on their sheet is the winning team. There should be no repeat graphemes – if children pick up a duplicate they will need to put it back and get a new card.

> **Support**
> Less-able pupils can use a Song of Sounds phoneme finder to help them.

> **Challenge**
> To challenge more-able pupils, they could write a word on the piece of paper containing that GPC.

Wordbuilding cards

An activity for a small group of 5–10 children

Aim: to practise segmenting words for writing

How to play:

- Print out your CVC, CVCC and CCVC and CCVCC wordbuilding cards.
- Scatter the wordbuilding cards all over the table (start with the CVC words and progress according to the children's ability).
- Ask each child to pick a card and, using the sound buttons to help them, write the word on their whiteboard.
- They should roll their dice to see how many times they should write the word (optional).
- They should then continue choosing cards until they have completed them all. Discuss any misconceptions.

Support

Give less-able children a Song of Sounds phoneme finder to help them. Alternatively, choose a word to work on as a group, helping the children to hear the sounds in the word.

Challenge

Ask more-able children to write a sentence containing the word.

Revision

Gather the children back on the carpet. Play "Knock down". Stand the children up in groups of 5–6, one group at a time. Show the group one phoneme, using the Song of Sounds Stage 1 flashcards. The first child to say the sound remains in the game, the other children sit down. Repeat with each group until you have a winner from each. Repeat with the winning children. Play "Knock down" again until you have a winner.

Now read...

If you used Song of Sounds Stage 1 in Reception, choose a range of Collins Big Cat Phonics readers that will test how much children have retained since the end of the Reception year. If you are new to the programme, make your selection of appropriately-levelled readers based on the results of this session's assessment.

Assessment week 1

Learning objective

to revise all phonemes learned so far from Stage 1

Starter

- Gather children on the carpet.
- Sit children with their chatting chums.
- Explain to children that this week they are going to practise everything they learned in Reception with Felicity the Phoneme Fairy, so that she will be really impressed with them and teach them more. NB: If you did not use Stage 1 in Reception, skip this reference to Felicity and introduce her when she "arrives" in the Week 1 weekly session.
- Using the IWB version of the stage 1 Song of Sounds, sing the song all the way through with the class. The children should perform all the actions they know as they go along.

Main lesson

- Play "Sound tennis". Children should sit so they are facing their chatting chums. One child says a sound, e.g. /s/, then the other child should say a sound, e.g. /t/. They should keep going backwards and forwards (like a game of tennis) until one of them falters. Then they should start again. Encourage children to look around the classroom at the Song of Sounds classroom frieze or poster for help. If you did not use Song of Sounds Stage 1 in Reception, you may want to devise your own assessment for this week to gauge phonics ability. The Stage 1 song and flashcards are included on the Stage 2 Resource CD to aid you in assessing children's levels.
- Next play "Song tennis". This time, choose a chatting chum pair to stand at the front of the class. Pick one of the children to sing a phrase from the Song of Sounds, e.g. "busy busy bee ee ee ee" – their partner should listen and do the corresponding action. They should then swap over and keep going, singing different parts of the song and performing the different actions.

Revision

Finish this session with some flashcard work using the Song of Sounds Stage 1 flashcards on the Stage 2 resource CD. Ask the class to do the actions to the song silently as you show them the flashcards one at a time. As you produce the grapheme side, let them say the different sounds.

Assessment week 1

Learning objective

to practise reading and blending graphemes to read words from Stage 1

Resources

- Song of Sounds Stage 1 flashcards (stand-alone resource on Resource CD)
- A lolly stick for each child in the class with their name written on (optional)
- Pencil and paper for each child

Starter

- Remind children that this week they are practising everything they have learned so that Felicity will be impressed with them and teach them something new. NB The children will also be learning some alternate graphemes for phonemes already taught, e.g. /ay/, /ai/ and /a-e/.
- Explain that children are going to practise recognising letters and reading words.
- Use your flashcard pack to play "Speed sounds". Show the class the flashcards one at a time, grapheme-side up, getting faster and faster. As children see the grapheme they should say the sound.

Main lesson

- Sit children with their chatting chums.
- Write eight green words on the board adding sound buttons underneath: book, fan, dad, frost, milk, roof, say, twist. Give children two minutes to work with their chatting chums to blend the letters and read the words together.
- Choose a child (you can do this by drawing a lolly stick out of the pot at random). That child should stand up with their chatting chum and model to the class how to read the word. Discuss any errors. Repeat until all the words have been discussed.
- The whole class should then read the words together. Do this by asking children to say the sounds as you press the sound buttons and then blend the sounds together as you sweep your hand underneath the word.

Revision

Finish this session by putting three green sentences on the board: "The shark has sharp teeth.", "I need a torch in a storm.", "The boy enjoys his toy." Challenge the chatting chums to work together to read the sentences. Ask a child to demonstrate reading a sentence, then ask the whole to class read it too. Repeat for each sentence.

Assessment week 1

Learning objective

to practise writing individual graphemes

Resources

- Song of Sounds Stage 1 flashcards (stand-alone resource on Resource CD)
- Mini whiteboards and pens for each chatting chum pair
- Stage 1 Song of Sounds phoneme finders finder sheets (stand-alone resource on Resource CD)

Starter

- Remind children that this week they are practising everything they have learned so that Felicity will be impressed with them and teach them more.
- Explain that they are going to practise recognising letters and reading words.
- Use your flashcard pack to play "Speed sounds". Show the class the flashcards one at a time, grapheme-side up, getting faster and faster. As children see the grapheme they should say the sound.

Main lesson

- Sit children with their chatting chums and give each pair a mini whiteboard and pen.
- Reveal one of your flashcards, picture-side up, and ask the children to sing the corresponding part of the song and write the correct grapheme on their whiteboards. Repeat.
- Finally, challenge the children to listen to three words and write the common sound. You should begin with the easier initial sounds, such as /r/: ring, robot, rabbit, and progress to harder sounds within words, such as /ar/: car, park, farm. Ensure that you emphasise the common sound so they can hear it.

Support

Give less-able children a Song of Sounds phoneme finder so that they can find the correct letter and copy it.

Challenge

More-able children could write all three words.

Revision

Ask the children to work in pairs. Challenge them to take it in turns to silently write a grapheme on the floor/desk in front of them for their partner to guess. Repeat several times taking turns. To make it harder, you could challenge them to write a grapheme on their partner's back with their finger for them to guess.

Assessment week 1

Learning objective

to segment words into phonemes

Resources

• n/a

Starter

- Gather children on the carpet.
- Remind them that this week they are practising everything they have learned so that Felicity will be impressed with them and teach them more.

Main lesson

- Explain that today they are going to practise counting the phonemes in words by playing a game called "Phoneme fingers".
- Use words of one syllable that are phonetically regular and include only the sounds children have learned so far, such as and, leg, tent, shark, stamp.
- Call out a word. The children must quietly count the phonemes in the word, such as /a/-/n/-/d/, /l/-/e/-/g/, /t/-/e/-/n/-/t/, /sh/-/ar/-/k/, /s/-/t/-/a/-/m/-/p/. They should then put the corresponding number of fingers up on their hand but keep their answer hidden from the other children, and you. At the same time, get your fingers ready – but also hidden so children cannot see them.
- Then say "Ready, steady, phoneme fingers." Both you and the children should reveal your fingers to show the answer.
- You should then count the phonemes in the word together by counting on your fingers: e.g. /sh/-/ar/-/k/ = three.
- This activity is perfect for assessment because you can instantly scan your class to see who is consistently correct and who makes mistakes.
- Repeat multiple times.

Revision

Explain to children that if they can play "Phoneme fingers" they can write, because when you write you just listen to a word, count the phonemes and write the correct letters. Model this with two final words by writing the words on the board as you count out the phonemes.

Target tricky words: "I", "the", "he", "she", "we", "be", "me"

Learning objective

to practise reading and spelling tricky words

Resources

- Song of Sounds tricky word cards: he, the, he, she, we, be, me
- Mini whiteboards and pens for each chatting chum pair
- A red whiteboard pen for each chatting chum pair

Starter

Introducing tricky words

- Explain that today children are going to practise some of the tricky words that you learned last year.
  NB: the tricky words in this lesson were taught in Stage 1 but are also included in the Stage 2 word cards and so can be taught from scratch in this lesson if your class is new to the programme.

- Before you show the tricky word cards, ask if they can remember what makes some words trickier than others (they don't follow Felicity's phoneme rules).

- Hold up the flashcards – and ask children why these words are red and spiky. Elicit that they are red because, like a red traffic light, red means stop and you need to "stop and think" about them , and they are spiky to signify that they are tricky words.

Main lesson

Read tricky words

- Show children the tricky word "I".
- Explain that it is tricky because it sounds like "soar up high igh igh igh". However, /igh/ is a phoneme that you hear in words and "I" is a word on its own. Whenever you hear the word "I" it looks like this.
- Show the tricky word "the".
- Ask them to identify what is tricky about this word. Elicit that the /th/ doesn't sound like "thorns in my thumb th th th" and the "e" sounds like an /u/.
- Show children the remaining Song of Sounds tricky word cards: "he", "she", "we", "be", "me".
- Ask them to identify what is tricky about all of these words. Elicit that the "e" sounds like "busy busy bee ee ee ee". We must remember that all of these words only have one "e". Point out that in these words the "e" is saying its letter name rather than sounding like the phoneme.

Write tricky words

- Sit children with their chatting chums.
- Give each pair a red pen and a mini whiteboard.
- Call out one of the tricky words and ask each pair to work together to spell the word. They could then draw a spiky red shape round the tricky part of the word.

Revision

Tell children that you will keep testing them to see if they can remember the words because they are so tricky. Throughout the day, keep producing the tricky word cards and asking children to read them on sight. Repeat continually throughout the day.

Target tricky words: "no", "go", "to", "you"

Learning objective

to practise reading and spelling tricky words

Resources

- Song of Sounds tricky word cards: no, go, to, you
- Mini whiteboards and pens for each chatting chum pair
- A red whiteboard pen for each chatting chum pair

Starter

Introducing tricky words

- Gather the children on the carpet.
- Explain that today they are going to practise some of the tricky words that they learned last year. NB: the tricky words in this lesson were taught in Stage 1 but are also included in the Stage 2 tricky word cards, so can be taught from scratch in this lesson if your class is new to the programme.
- Before you show children the tricky word cards, ask if they can remember what makes some words trickier than others (they don't follow Felicity's phoneme rules).
- Hold up the flashcards – ask why these words are red and spiky (they are red because, like a red traffic light, red means stop and you need to "stop and think" about them, and they are spiky to signify that they are tricky words).

Main lesson

Read tricky words

- Show children the tricky words "no" and "go".
- Ask them to identify what is tricky about these words, e.g. the "o" in both words sounds like "throw the snow ow ow ow". We must remember that it is just an "o". Point out to the children that in these words the "o" is saying its letter name rather than following the phoneme sound.
- Show children the tricky words "to" and "you".
- Ask them to identify what is tricky about both of these words. They should recognise that in "to" the "o" sounds like "zoom to the moon oo oo oo". Explain that although there is a word "too", which means "as well", this "to" only has one "o". Give some examples of sentences in which you might find "to" and "too". Also, in "you" the "ou" at the end also sounds like "zoom to the moon oo oo oo" but in fact it is spelled "ou". Discuss the fact that it looks like "mouse in a house ou ou ou" but it does not make the /ou/ sound, it makes an /oo/ sound.

Write tricky words

- Sit children with their chatting chums.
- Give each pair a red pen and mini whiteboard.
- Call out one of the tricky words and ask each pair to work together to spell the word. They should then draw a spiky red shape around the tricky part of the word.

Revision

Tell children that you will keep testing them to see if they can remember the words because they are so tricky. Throughout the day, keep producing the tricky word cards and asking children to read them on sight. Repeat continually throughout the day.

Target tricky words: "was", "saw"

Resources

- Song of Sounds tricky word cards: was, saw
- A whiteboard and green and red pens for each chatting chum pair

Starter

- Gather the children on the carpet.
- Explain that today children are going to practise some of the tricky words that they learned last year.
  NB: the tricky words in this lesson were taught in Stage 1 but are also included in the Stage 2 tricky word cards so can be taught from scratch in this lesson if your class is new to the programme.
- Before you show the tricky word cards, ask if they can remember what makes some words trickier than others (they don't follow Felicity's phoneme rules).
- Hold up the flashcards – ask why these words are red and spiky (they are red because, like a red traffic light, red means stop and you need to "stop and think" about them, and they are spiky to signify that they are tricky words).

Main lesson

Read tricky words

- Show the children the tricky word "was".
- Ask children to identify the green bit of this word: the "w" is fine as it obeys Felicity's phoneme rules and makes the correct sound. Ask children to identify the tricky bits of this word. Elicit that the "a" is tricky as it sounds like an /o/, and the "s" is tricky because it sounds like a /z/.
- Show children the tricky word "saw".
- Ask them to identify the green bit of this word: the "s" is fine as it obeys Felicity's phoneme rules and makes the correct sound. Ask children to identify the tricky bit of this word: the "aw" sounds like "it's a horse of course or or or".
- Show that "was" is "saw" backwards. This will help them to remember to pay extra attention to both words.

Write tricky words

- Sit children in chatting chum pairs.
- Give each pair a red pen, a green pen and a whiteboard.
- Call out one of the tricky words and ask each pair to work together to spell the word using the green pen for the green bit of the word and the red pen for the tricky part of the word.
- Call out some of the other words they have learned this week. Can they write the green bits and red bits of the word? Go round the class and check their answers.

Revision

Tell children that you will keep testing them to see if they can remember the words because they are so tricky. Throughout the day, keep producing the tricky word cards and asking children to read them on sight. Repeat continually throughout the day.

Target tricky words: "my", "they", "all", "are"

Learning objective

to practise reading and spelling tricky words

Resources

- Song of Sounds tricky word cards: my, they, all, are
- Mini whiteboards and red and green pens for each chatting chum pair

Starter

Introducing tricky words

- Gather the children on the carpet.
- Explain that today they are going to practise some of the tricky words that they learned last year. Note that the tricky words in this lesson were taught in Stage 1 but are also included in the Stage 2 tricky word cards, so can be taught as new in this lesson if your class is new to the programme.
- Before you show the tricky word cards, ask if they can remember what makes some words trickier than others, i.e. they don't follow Felicity's phoneme rules.
- Hold up the flashcards – ask why these words are red and spiky (they are red because, like a red traffic light, red means stop and you need to "stop and think" about them, and they are spiky to signify that they are tricky words).

Main lesson

Read tricky words

- Show children the tricky word "my".
- Ask children to identify the green bit of this word: the "m" is fine as it obeys Felicity's phoneme rules and makes the correct sound. Ask them to identify the tricky bit of this word: the "y" is tricky as it sounds like "soar up high igh igh igh".
- Show children the tricky word "they".
- Ask them to identify the green bit of this word: the "th" is fine as it obeys Felicity's phoneme rules and makes the correct sound. Ask children to identify the tricky bit of this word: the "ey" is tricky as it sounds like "may I play ay ay ay".
- Show children the tricky word "all".
- Ask them to identify the green bit of this word: the "ll" is fine as it obeys Felicity's phoneme rules and makes the correct sound. Ask children to identify the tricky bit of this word: the "a" is tricky as it sounds like "it's a horse of course or or or".
- Show children the tricky word "are".
- Ask them to identify the green bit of this word: the "ar" is fine as it obeys Felicity's phoneme rules and makes the correct sound. Ask children to identify the tricky bit of this word: the "e" is tricky as you can't hear it. Explain this is called a "silent e." We just have to remember that it's there.

Write tricky words

- Sit children in chatting chum pairs.
- Give each pair a red pen and a green pen and a whiteboard.
- Call out one of the tricky words and ask each pair to work together to spell the word using the green pen for the green bit of the word and the red pen for the tricky part of the word.
- Call out some of the other words you have learned this week. Can they write the green and the red bits of the word? Go round the class and check their answers.

Revision

Tell children that you will keep testing them to see if they can remember the words because they are so tricky. Throughout the day, keep producing the tricky word cards and asking children to read them on sight. Repeat continually throughout the day.

Target skill: tricky word practice

Learning objective

to practise reading and spelling tricky words

Resources

Carpet session

- Week 2: Teach software
- Tricky word cards: I, the, he, she, we, be, me, go, no, to, was, saw, my, you, they, all, are
- Printable green words from Song of Sounds Stage 1 (stand-alone resource on Resource CD)
- Three coloured cards or a coloured fan (blue, purple, green) for each child
- A Tricky Trevor costume, toy or letter (optional)

Tricky word splat

- Splat game (Week 2: Teach software slides 13-15)
- Two chairs

- Tricky word cards from carpet session
- Two fly swatters (optional)

Spot it

- Tricky word cards from carpet session
- Wordsearches (on Resource CD)
- A mini whiteboard pen or a pencil for each child

Tricky time

- Tricky word cards from carpet session
- A timer
- A mini whiteboard and pen for each child

Revision

- Tricky word cards from carpet session

Carpet session

- Gather the resources.
- Sit children in their chatting chum pairs.

1
- This session has the option of teaching in role as Tricky Trevor, a wise man with grey hair and a walking stick. Alternatively, you can use a Tricky Trevor teddy or receive a letter enclosing the tricky words.
- Remind children that you/Trevor are/is an incredibly clever person and that is why you have come here today, to teach them some more tricky words.

> **Software**
> Teach
> **W2**

- From your briefcase/bag produce a selection of green words and tricky words of your choice. Ask children to tell you the difference between "green" words and "tricky" words.

2
- Explain that before you teach the children any more "tricky words" this year, you would like to check that they can remember all the "tricky words" they have learned so far. Press play on the software. The tricky words that children learned on Trevor's last three visits will appear – check that they can read them.

3-6
- Using the software, reveal the different groups of words. Ask children to identify the tricky parts of each set of words and offer advice to help them remember the words.

7-11
- Play "Trevor's trick". Show three different versions of a word, only one of which is the correct spelling, for example, "igh", "I", "iy". Children must work with their chatting chums to choose the correct spelling. Point to each word and ask them to put their hands up when you point to the word that they think is spelled correctly. Alternatively, issue children with fans made up of 3

different colours which match the colours on the screen. Ask them to identify the correctly-spelled word and hold up the corresponding colour on their fan.

12 • Revise the learning objective before dividing the children into differentiated groups and sending them to their practical activities.

Practical activities

Tricky word splat

A game for a group of 6–10 children

Aim: to practise reading tricky words at speed

How to play:

- Gather the resources.
- Display the software version of the game or pin tricky word cards on a board or wall.
- Split the class into two teams.
- In front of each team, place a chair facing away from the IWB.
- Ask a child from each team to take it in turns to sit on the chair (so they have their back to the whiteboard), holding their fly swatter.
- Sing or say a tricky word. The children should get up from their chairs and race to splat the correct tricky word.
- The first to splat the correct tricky word wins a point for their team. Children should take it in turns.

Support
Hold the tricky word card up as you say the word so that less-able children can visually match the tricky word.

Challenge
More-able children could play the game and then practise calling out tricky words for each other to write on a whiteboard. They could also reinforce their learning by drawing a spiky red shape round the tricky part of the word

Spot it

A game for a group of 5–6 children

Aim: to practise reading and spelling tricky words

How to play:

- Gather the resources.
- Gather children round a table.
- Display the tricky word cards near the table.
- Give each child a mini whiteboard pen or a pencil.
- Put the wordsearches in the middle of the table. Most children should choose the trickier side of the wordsearch.
- Each wordsearch has a tricky word at the top. Make sure that children can read the word and ask them to find it five times in the wordsearch.
- The children should search for all five words in their wordsearch. If they finish, they can rub the wordsearch clean and choose a different one.

Support
Less-able children should choose the easier side of their wordsearch.

Challenge
Take the displayed tricky words away so that children have to remember how to spell them in order to find them.

Tricky time

An activity for a group of 5–10 children

Aim: to practise writing tricky words and spelling them correctly

How to play:

- Gather the resources.
- Give each child a mini whiteboard and pen.
- Set the timer to 30 seconds or one minute.
- Call out a tricky word.
- Children should see how many times they can write that word on their whiteboards in the given time.

Support
Display the tricky word card as you say the word for less-able children to copy if they need to

Challenge
Ask more-able children to write a sentence containing the tricky word.

Revision

Play "Pass the tricky word". Sit children in a circle and give them tricky word cards. Pass the cards around the ring while singing, to the tune of "London Bridge is Falling Down", "Pass the tricky words around the ring, around, the ring, around the ring, pass the tricky words around the ring, what do they say?" The children holding the tricky words should stand up and say the word, and the others should repeat it. Play several times.

Now read...

There are two ways that you can use Collins Big Cat Phonics readers for revision here; either choose specific tricky words to cover, or ask children to pick a reader and spot as many tricky words as they can. Tricky words are listed in the back of each reader as "Fast words".

Introducing Song of Sounds: Stage 2

Learning objective

to familiarise children with Song of Sounds: Stage 2

Starter

Introducing Song of Sounds

- Gather the children on the carpet.
- Explain that you have received a parcel. Open it and read the letter from Felicity the Phoneme Fairy.
- The letter congratulates children on their achievements to date and tells them that from now on they will be learning even more difficult sounds. It explains that there is a new song for children to learn this year. It also says that once they have learned the song, Felicity will check to see how they are getting on, and that she has sent some treats for the classroom.
- Look inside the box and pull out the Song of Sounds classroom frieze, CD and flashcards, and show them to the children.

 Resources:

- A parcel from Felicity the Phoneme Fairy including:
  - A letter from Felicity the Phoneme Fairy
  - Week 3: Teach software
  - Song of Sounds flashcards
  - Song of Sounds classroom frieze

Main lesson

- Sing the song all the way through with children (don't worry about the actions yet – just look at the pictures and sing.)
- As you begin to sing the song, notice with the children that some of the graphemes make the same sound but are made up of different letters.
- Suggest that they should sing the song every day to practise it.

Revision

Later in the day, put the Song of Sounds classroom frieze up around your classroom and look at it together.

Target phoneme: /ay/

Learning objective

to learn to say, read and write /ay/

Resources:

- Song of Sounds flashcard: ay
- Song of Sounds picture cards: hay, play, tray
- Song of Sounds green words: day, stay

Starter

Sing /ay/

♪ **Song text:** "may I play ay ay ay"

- Sing the Song of Sounds (Stage 2) all the way through.
- Explain that this week children are going to be learning about different graphemes that make the /ay/ sound.
- Explain that today children are going to practise reading and writing the /ay/ sound that they have already learned.
- Show the class the "ay" flashcard and sing "may I play ay ay ay".
- Remind children of the action and ask them to perform it.

Main lesson

Say /ay/

- Remind children how to say /ay/ – "say /ay/ to me, say /ay/ to your friend, say /ay/ to the ceiling, say /ay/ to the floor, to the book corner" etc.
- Show children the "ay" picture cards and ask them to repeat the words after you say them, using the "I say, you say" technique so they can hear the /ay/ sound in the words: e.g. hay, play, tray.

Read /ay/

- Show children the grapheme side of the card and remind them what an "ay" looks like.
- Hide the flashcard behind your back – if you bring it out and show the picture side they must sing "may I play ay ay ay". If you bring it out and show the grapheme side they must say /ay/. Bring the card out in different ways from either side of your body.

Write /ay/

- Remind children how to form an "ay" on the board using the explanation "go round the apple, down and flick" and "go down and around, down the yoyo's string and add a curl".
- Ask children to follow you and sky-write the "ay" grapheme – don't forget that you need to write backwards when facing the children.

- Ask them to stand next to their chatting chums, and to write an "ay" on their partner's back and then swap over. They should start off by writing a small "ay" and then get bigger.

Blend /ay/

- Using the Song of Sounds green words "day" and "stay", practise reading and blending the graphemes to make the word. Do this by asking children to say the sounds as you press the sound buttons and then blend the sounds together as you sweep your hand underneath the word.

Revision

At different points during the day, produce your "ay" flashcard and ask children to sing the song, do the actions and/or say the sound. Remind them that this week they will be learning different graphemes for the phoneme /ay/.

Target grapheme: /ai/

Learning objective

to learn to say, read and write /ai/

Resources

- Song of Sounds flashcard: ai
- Song of Sounds picture cards: snail, train, rain
- Song of Sounds green words: tail, paint

Starter

Sing /ai/

♪ **Song text:** "train in the rain ai ai ai"

- Gather the children on the carpet.
- Sing the Song of Sounds song (Stage 2) all the way through.
- Explain that today they are going to a learn a new grapheme.
- Show the class the "ai" flashcard and sing "train in the rain ai ai ai".
- Show children the song action and ask them to perform it.

Main lesson

Say /ai/

- Point out to children that /ai/ makes exactly the same sound as the /ay/ in "may I play ay ay ay".
- Show them how to say /ai/. Let them say it to each of their fingers and finally look at you and say /ai/.
- Show children the "ai" picture cards and ask them to repeat the words after you using the "I say, you say" technique so they can hear the /ay/ sound in the word e.g. snail, train, rain.

Read /ai/

- Explain that although this grapheme makes the same sound as "may I play ay ay ay", it looks different.
- Show children the grapheme side of the card and explain what an /ai/ looks like.
- Hide the flashcard behind your back – if you bring it out and show the picture side they must sing "train in the rain ai ai ai". If you bring it out and show the grapheme side they must say /ai/. Bring the card out in different ways from either side of your body.
- Explain that, unlike "may I play ay ay ay", you never see "ai" at the end of a word.

Write /ai/

- Show children how to form an "ai" on the board using the explanation "Go round the apple, down and flick" and "Go down the insect's body, add a flick for his tail and a dot for his head".
- Ask them to follow you as you sky-write the "ai" grapheme – don't forget you need to write backwards.

- Ask children to sit down on the carpet with their chatting chums. Ask one child from each pair to write an "ai" on the carpet in front of them. Ask their chatting chums to check their formation and then swap so that the second child writes the grapheme.

Blend /ai/

- Using the green words "tail" and "paint", practise reading and blending the graphemes to make the words. Do this by asking them to say the sounds as you press the sound buttons and then blend the sounds together as you sweep your hand underneath the word.

Revision

Add the "ai" flashcard to the "ay" flashcard that you taught yesterday. Show the class the flashcards, one at a time, picture-side up, and ask them to sing each sound. Then ask them to do the correct actions silently as you show them the flashcards. As you produce the grapheme side, let them say both (identical) sounds. Repeat continually throughout the day.

Target grapheme: /a-e/

Learning objective

to learn to say, read and write /a-e/

Resources

- Song of Sounds flashcard: a-e
- Song of Sounds picture cards: cake, whale, snake
- Song of Sounds green words and sentences: make, shape, Stay and play a game in the rain.

Starter

Sing /a-e/

♪ **Song text:** "bake a cake a-e a-e a-e"

- Gather the children on the carpet.
- Sing the Song of Sounds song (Stage 2) all the way through.
- Explain that today they are going to a learn a new grapheme.
- Show the class the "a-e" flashcard and sing "bake a cake a-e a-e a-e".
- Show them the action and ask them to perform it

Main lesson

Say /a-e/

- Point out that this phoneme makes the same sound as "may I play" and "train in the rain", but it looks different.
- Show them how to say /a-e/ – they should take turns saying /a-e/ as you point to them.
- Show children the "a-e" picture cards and ask them to repeat the phonemes after you, using the "I say, you say" technique so they can hear the /a-e/ sound in the words: cake, whale, snake.

Read /a-e/

- Show children the grapheme side of the card and explain what an "a-e" looks like.
- Explain that although the "a" and "e" make a sound together, they are not next to each other in the word. There is another letter in-between. Write a word on the board, for example, bake and explain that the "a" and the "e" are holding hands behind the other letter. Together they make the sound /a-e/.
- Hide the "a-e" flashcard behind your back – if you bring it out and show the picture side they must sing "bake a cake a-e a-e a-e"; if you bring it out the grapheme side they must say /a-e/. Bring the card out in different ways from either side of your body and try and catch them out.

Write /a-e/

- Show children how to form an "a-e" on the board using the explanation "Go round the apple, down and flick" and "Go round the elephant's head and add his curly trunk".
- Draw a dash between the two letters and explain that this shows there is another letter in-between. Draw a curvy line joining the "a" and the "e" together to visually demonstrate that it is those two letters together that make the /a-e/ sound.
- Ask children to stand up and follow you with their fingers as you sky-write the "a-e" grapheme – don't forget you need to write backwards.
- Ask them to use their hand as a "pad" and their finger as a "pencil" and practise writing "a-e".

Blend /a-e/

- Using the green word cards "make" and "shape", practise reading and blending the graphemes to make the words. Using the green sentence "Stay and play a game in the rain", discuss the different /ay/, /ai/ and /a-e/ words, then practise blending each word individually and then the whole phrase.

Revision

Add the "a-e" flashcard to the "ay" and "ai" cards you have already taught. Show the class the picture flashcards and ask them to sing each sound. Ask them to do the actions to the song silently as you show the flashcards. Repeat continually throughout the day.

Felicity the Phoneme Fairy

Target graphemes: /ay/, /ai/, /a-e/

Learning objective

to learn to discriminate between the /ay/, /ai/ and /a-e/ graphemes; to practise blending and segmenting words containing /ay/, /ai/ and /a-e/

Resources:

Carpet session

- Week 3: Teach software
- Song of Sounds flashcards: ai, ay and a-e
- Objects or picture cards in a bag that contain the ay, ai or a-e phoneme, such as tray, clay, train, snail, plane, snake (enough for each child/pair)
- Mini whiteboards and pens for each chatting chum pair
- A fairy/wizard outfit and wand, or a fairy toy, or a letter (optional)
- Glitter to reward children with a fairy sparkle on their cheeks
- Three hoops (optional)

Ay on a tray

- Song of Sounds phoneme finders (one per child)
- A tray with 10 ay, ai and a-e objects

- Mini whiteboards and pens for each child

Play the snake game

- Word cards
- A snake game board for each child (Week 3: AS1, 2-4)
- A feely bag or box
- Counters

Train track handwriting

- A train track handwriting card (Week 3: AS3)
- Song of Sounds flashcards: ay, ai and a-e
- A pen for each child (a whiteboard pen if you have laminated the card)

Revision

- Song of Sounds phoneme finders (one per child)
- A tray with 10 ay, ai and a-e objects
- Mini whiteboards and pens for each child

Carpet session

- Gather the children on the carpet.
- This lesson has the option of teaching in role as Felicity the Phoneme Fairy. If you would prefer not to, you could use a puppet or receive a letter from Felicity and read it out to the class, or simply use the software as part of a normal session.
- Depending on the option you have chosen, enter the classroom dressed as Felicity, or hold up your puppet or letter.
- Introduce yourself or your puppet to the children or explain that you have received a letter from Felicity. Revise the term "phoneme".
- Ask children if they received Felicity's parcel at the beginning of the week.

- Ask the children if they have been practising the song. Sing the song with them all the way through, demonstrating the actions too.

1
- Tell the children that you know that they have been learning all about the different /ay/ sounds this week. Produce the "ay", "ai" and "a-e" flashcards and ask them to sing the song and do the actions for each one.
- Suggest that children play a game to see if they can tell the difference between words that contain /ay/, /ai/ and /a-e/.
  - Sit the children in a circle.
  - Put three hoops in the middle of the circle and label them with the "ay", "ai" and "a-e" flashcards. Alternatively, you could put three flashcards down on the floor. Give each child an /ay/, /ai/ or /a-e/ object or picture card from the bag. Play some music. Children should put their object into the correct hoop or next to the correct flashcard. Discuss any misconceptions.

- Now sit the children in their chatting chum pairs.

2
- Using the software, reveal three /ay/, /ai/ and /a-e/ words for children to read. Sound buttons will also appear to help them. The children should work with their chatting chums to see if they can read the words. Ask them to read a word at a time, and reveal the picture to accompany each word.

Software
Teach
W3

3–5
- Give each chatting chum pair a mini whiteboard and pen. Use the software to reveal three pictures. Ask children to work with their chatting chums to decide which /ay/, /ai/ or /a-e/ is in each of the three words. They should write it on their whiteboards. Show the correct answer as you reveal the words.
- To challenge children further, ask them to write all three words on their whiteboards.

6
- Finish the session by revising the learning objective before beginning the practical activities.

Practical activities

 Ay on a tray

A game for a small group of 6–8 children

Aim: to practise segmenting words for writing containg /ay/, /ai/ and /a-e/ and choosing the correct grapheme

How to play:
- Gather the resources.
- Place ten items with /ay/, /ai/ or /a-e/ spellings on a tray.
- Give children one minute to look at the items on the tray.
- Ask them to close their eyes and, while their eyes are closed, remove an object.
- Ask children to open their eyes and work out which object is missing.
- They should then write the name of the object on their whiteboards, thinking carefully about whether it is an /ay/, /ai/ or /a-e/ word.

Support
Less-able pupils should say what is missing and work together to spell the word on their whiteboards.

Challenge
More-able pupils should compete to be the first child to spell the word correctly. One point should be awarded to the winner.

Play the snake game

An activity for a small group of 5–6 children

Aim: to practise blending words for reading containing /ay/, /ai/ and /a-e/

How to play:

- Gather the resources.
- Before the game, put your word cards into a feely bag or box and give each child a playing board and counters.
- Children should take it in turns to pull a word card out of the bag or box.
- They should read the word and cover the correct picture on their playing board with a counter.
- The first to cover all the pictures is the winner.
- If a child pulls out a word that they have already covered, they must miss a turn. If they pull a snake card out, they must take a counter off their board.

Train track handwriting

A game for a small group of 6–8 children

Aim: to practise correct formation of the /ay/, /ai/ and /a-e/ graphemes

How to play:

- Give each child in the group a train track handwriting card and pen.
- Hold up the "ay" flashcard and sing the song, do the actions and/or say the sound with the children.
- Model writing the grapheme using a cursive style.
- Children should then practise their cursive handwriting along the train track.
- Repeat for /ai/ and /a-e/.

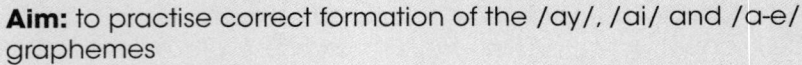

Support

Help less-able children to read the words through oral blending.

Challenge

Ask more-able children to read the words independently. You could also ask them to think of another word containing the same /ay/, /ai/ or /a-e/ sound.

Revision

Gather the children back on the carpet. Replay the "ay on a tray game" as a whole class.

Now read...

This Is Me And This Is Pip, *Red, Band 2B*

Hand Play, *Yellow, Band 3*

Target phoneme: /ee/

Learning objective

to learn to say, read and write /ee/

Resources

- Song of Sounds flashcard: ee
- Song of Sounds picture cards: bee, sheep, tree
- Song of Sounds green words: feet, teeth

Starter

Sing /ee/

♪ **Song text:** "busy busy bee ee ee ee"

- Sing the Song of Sounds all the way through.
- Explain that this week you are going to be learning about different graphemes that make the /ee/ sound.
- Explain that today children are going to practise the /ee/ sound that they have already learned before learning some new ones.
- Show the class the "ee" flashcard and sing "busy busy bee ee ee ee".
- Remind the class of the action and ask them to perform it together.

Main lesson

Say /ee/

- Remind children how to say /ee/ – ask them to whisper /ee/, sing /ee/, shout /ee/, smile /ee/.
- Show children the "ee" picture cards and ask them to repeat after you, using an "I say, you say" technique, so they can hear the /ee/ sound in the words: bee, sheep, tree.

Read /ee/

- Show children the grapheme side of the card and remind them what an "ee" looks like.
- Hide the flashcard behind your back – if you bring it out and show the picture side they must sing "busy busy bee ee ee ee". If you bring it out and show the grapheme side, they must say /ee/. Bring the card out in different ways from either side of your body.

Write /ee/

- Show children how to form an "ee" on the board using the explanation "Go round the elephant's head and add his curly trunk" twice.
- Ask children to follow you and sky-write the "ee" grapheme – don't forget you need to write backwards.
- Ask the children to write an "ee" on each of their fingers.

Blend /ee/

- Using the Song of Sounds green words "feet" and "teeth", practise reading and blending the graphemes to make the word. Do this by asking children to say the sounds as you press the sound buttons, and then blend the sounds together as you sweep your hand underneath the word.

Revision

Add the "ee" flashcard to the stack you have already taught. Show the class the flashcards one at a time, picture-side up and ask them to sing each sound in a whisper, until they see the "busy busy bee" flashcard, when they should sing it out loudly. Repeat a few times. Ask the class to do the actions to the song silently as you show them the flashcards. As you produce the grapheme side, let them whisper the different sounds until they see the "ee", and then shout it. Repeat continually throughout the day.

Target grapheme: /ea/

Learning objective

to learn to say, read and write /ea/ and to recognise that it is an alternative grapheme to /ee/ and /e-e/

Resources

- Song of Sounds flashcard: ea
- Song of Sounds picture cards: seal, peas, leaf
- Song of Sounds green words: eat, read

Starter

Sing /ea/

♪ **Song text:** "beans in your dreams ea ea ea"

- Gather the resources.
- Gather the children on the carpet.
- Sing the Song of Sounds all the way through.
- Explain that today they are going to a learn a new grapheme.
- Show the class the "ea" flashcard and sing "beans in your dreams ea ea ea".
- Show the children the action and ask the class to perform it together.

Main lesson

Say /ea/

- Point out that it makes exactly the same sound as "busy busy bee ee ee ee".
- Show children how to say /ee/ – say /ea/ with a happy face, angry face, sad face.
- Show children "ea" picture cards and ask them to repeat after you, using an "I say, you say" technique, so they can hear the /ee/ sound in the words: seal, peas, leaf.

Read /ea/

- Explain that although this grapheme makes the same sound as "busy busy bee ee ee ee", it looks different.
- Show children the grapheme side of the card and explain what an "ea" looks like.
- Hide the flashcard behind your back – if you bring it out and show the picture side they must sing "beans in your dreams ea ea ea". If you bring it out and show the grapheme side they must say /ea/. Bring the card out in different ways from either side of your body.

Write /ea/

- Show children how to form an "ea" on the board using the explanation "Go round the elephant's head and add his curly trunk" and "Go round the apple, down and flick".
- Ask children to follow you and sky-write the "ea" grapheme – don't forget you need to write backwards.
- Ask children to write a tiny "ea" in the air, then repeat getting increasingly bigger.

Blend /ea/

- Using the Song of Sounds green words "eat" and "read", practise reading and blending the graphemes to make the words. Do this by asking children to say sounds as you press the sound buttons, and then blend the sounds together as you sweep your hand underneath the word.

Revision

Add the "ea" flashcard to the stack you have already taught. Use a piece of card to cover your flashcard pack. Reveal a flashcard very slowly by moving the card downwards. As soon as they know what it is, children should sing it. Reveal the whole flashcard to see if they are right. Repeat the slow reveal game but this time let them do the actions as you reveal the flashcards. As you produce the grapheme side, can they say the different sounds? Repeat continually throughout the day.

Target grapheme: /e-e/

Learning objective

to learn to say, read and write /e-e/ and to recognise that it is an alternative grapheme to /ee/ and /ea/

Resources

- Song of Sounds flashcard: e-e
- Song of Sounds picture cards: Pete, concrete, athlete
- Song of Sounds green words: even, these

Starter

Sing /e-e/

🎵 **Song text:** "perfect Pete e-e e-e e-e"

- Gather children on the carpet.
- Sing the Song of Sounds all the way through.
- Explain that today they are going to a learn a new grapheme.
- Show the class the "e-e" flashcard and sing "perfect Pete e-e e-e e-e".
- Show them the action and ask the class to perform it together.

Main lesson

Say /e-e/

- Point out to children that it makes exactly the same sound as "busy busy bee ee ee ee" and "beans in your dreams ea ea ea".
- Show them how to say /ee/ – ask them to say the /ee/ sound ten times with their eyes closed.
- Show the "e-e" picture cards and ask children to repeat after you, using an "I say, you say" technique, so they can hear the /e-e/ sound in the words: Pete, concrete, athlete.

Read /e-e/

- Explain that although this grapheme makes the same sound as "busy busy bee ee ee ee" and "beans in your dreams ea ea ea", it looks different.
- Show the grapheme side of the card and explain what an "e-e" looks like.
- Explain that the "e" and the "e" are not even next to each other in the word. There is another letter between them. They are holding hands behind the other letter and together they make the sound /ee/.
- Hide the flashcard behind your back – if you bring it out and show the picture side they must sing "perfect Pete e-e e-e e-e", if you bring it out and show the grapheme side they must say /ee/. Bring the card out in different ways from either side of your body.

Write /e-e/

- Show children how to form an "e-e" on the board using the explanation, "Go round the elephant's head and add his curly trunk" twice.
- Draw a dash between the two letters and explain that this shows that there is another letter in-between. Draw a curvy line joining the "e" and the "e" together to demonstrate that it is those two letters together that make the /ee/ sound.
- Ask children to follow you and sky-write the "e-e" grapheme – don't forget you need to write backwards.
- Ask them to look up to the ceiling and write an "e-e" in the air.

Blend /e-e/

- Using the Song of Sounds green words "even" and "these", practise reading and blending the graphemes to make the words. Do this by asking them to say the sounds as you press the sound buttons, and then blend the sounds together as you sweep your hand underneath the word.

Revision

 Add the "e-e" flashcard to the stack of flashcards you have already taught. Ask the children to sit in a circle. Give out the flashcards to random children round the circle. Play the Song of Sounds CD and pass the flashcards round the circle. When you stop the music, children holding flashcards should sing the corresponding parts of the song. Repeat many times, asking them to sing the song, do the actions or say the sounds. As you produce the grapheme side, let them say the different sounds. Repeat continually throughout the day.

Target graphemes: /ee/, /ea/, /e-e/

Learning objective

to revisit the graphemes /ee/, /ea/ and /e-e/

Resources

* Song of Sounds flashcards: ee, ea, e-e
* Song of Sounds picture cards: bee, sheep, tree, seal, peas, leaf, Pete, concrete, athlete
* Song of Sounds green sentence: It is a complete treat for Pete to eat sweets.

Starter

* Gather children on the carpet.
* Sing the Song of Sounds all the way through.
* Explain that today they are going to practise all the /ee/ sounds they have learned this week.

Main lesson

Sing /ee/, /ea/ and /e-e/

* Show the class the "ee", "ea", and "e-e" flashcards and sing the correct parts of the song as you show each card. Ask the children to perform the actions at the same time.

Say /ee/, /ea/ and /e-e/

* Remind children that all of these make exactly the same sound.
* Ask them to smile and say /ee/ as you show them each flashcard, picture-side up.
* Display all the picture cards on the board. Point to a few at random and, using the "I say you say technique", ask children to repeat the word after you, stressing the /ee/ sound.

Read /ee/, /ea/ and /e-e/

* Remind children that although they all make the same sound, they look different.
* Hold up the "busy busy bee" flashcard, picture-side up. Ask if they can remember what it looks like. Choose a child to tell you what letters make the grapheme. Turn the flashcard over to show the grapheme and display it on the board.
* Repeat for "beans in your dreams" and "perfect Pete".

Blend /ee/, /ea/ and /e-e/

* Using the Song of Sounds green sentence "It is a complete treat for Pete to eat sweets", practise blending each word individually and then the whole phrase. Do this by asking children to say the sounds as you press the sound buttons, and then blend the sounds together as you sweep your hand underneath the word. Go through the whole phrase, then go back and point to each word for children to read.

Introduce "my"

* Write the word "mummy" on the board and circle the "y" at the end of the word.
* Ask children what sound this grapheme usually makes, e.g. /y/ in yellow yo yo y y y.
* Explain that sometimes when it is at the end of a word it makes an /ee/ sound and give some more examples, e.g. daddy, fairy, bunny, baby.

Revision

 Sit children in chatting chum pairs. On the board display your three graphemes and all the picture cards. Ask children to work with their chatting chums to discuss which words contain which grapheme. Discuss with children and check that they are correct by revealing the grapheme on the reverse of each picture card. Move the picture cards next to the correct grapheme.

A letter from Perfect Pete

Target phonemes: /ee/, /ea/, /e-e/

Learning objective

to learn to discriminate between the /ee/, /ea/ and /e-e/ graphemes; to practise blending and segmenting words containing /ee/, /ea/ and /e-e/

Resources

Carpet session

- Week 4: Teach software
- Mini whiteboards and pens for each chatting chum pair

Read Pete's letter

- A copy of the letter for each child or pair in the group (Week 4: AS1)
- A dice labelled ee, ea, e-e, y, a tricky word shape and a picture of Perfect Pete (Week 4: AS2)
- A mini whiteboard pen for each child (if letter is laminated), or a pen or pencil

Pete's perfect 10

- Perfect 10 IWB game
- A mini whiteboard and pen for each child (optional)

Pete's perfect pencil control

- Paper and pencil for each child
- Song of Sounds flashcards: ee, ea and e-e

Revision

- Song of Sounds flashcards: ee, ea and e-e

Carpet session

- Gather the children on the carpet.
- In this lesson, you have the option of teaching in role as Perfect Pete, a friendly boy in a sensible jumper. If you do not wish to do this, teach the lesson normally, repeating Perfect Pete's message to the children.

1. • Explain to children that Perfect Pete has heard that they have been learning about the different /ee/ sounds this week and he has sent them a message.

> **Software**
> Teach
> **W4**

2. • Play the software to reveal a letter from Pete. Read it to the children.

3–6. • Pete challenges the children to close their eyes and listen for /ee/, /ea/ and /e-e/ sounds. How many can they hear? Read the letter again while the children close their eyes and listen. Discuss how many sounds they counted. Ask them how many they can see. Is it the same number as they could hear? Circle the sounds together on the letter on the IWB.

- Sit the children in their chatting chum pairs.

7. • Use the software to play "How many /ee/s can you see?" The screen shows a selection of pictures, some of them /ee/, /ea/ and /e-e/ pictures. The children should talk to their chatting chums to decide which words contain an /ee/, /ea/ or /e-e/. Reveal the answers.

8. • Give each chatting chum pair a mini whiteboard and pen. Repeat the above activity using slide 8, this time asking them to write the words. Discuss any misconceptions.

9. • Revise the learning objective before you divide the children into their differentiated groups to begin their practical activities.

Practical activities

Read Pete's letter

A game for a small group of 6–8 children

Aim: to identify words containing /ee/, /ea/ and /e-e/ and blend them for reading

How to play:
- Gather the resources.
- Give each child a copy of Pete's letter and a pen or pencil.
- Children should take it in turns to roll the dice and if it lands on /ee/, /ea/ or /e-e/, they should search Pete's letter for a word with that grapheme and circle it.
- If it lands on ee, /ea/, /e-e/ or /y/, they should find a word in the letter that has the /ee/ sound in it, e.g. "me".
- If it lands on a picture of Perfect Pete, they can circle one of each.
- The child with the most words circled at the end of the game is the winner.

> **Support**
> Less-able children can spot the words visually rather than reading.

> **Challenge**
> More-able children should read the word out loud before circling it.

Pete's perfect 10

An activity for a group of 5–10 children

Aim: to practise segmenting words for writing containing /ee/, /ea/ and /e-e/ and choosing the correct grapheme

How to play:
- Gather the resources.
- Display the first slide of the Perfect 10 IWB game. The slide shows 10 pictures for /ee/, /ea/ or /e-e/.
- Give children one minute to look carefully at the slide and remember as many as they can.
- They should then write down as many as they can remember, thinking carefully about which /ee/ sound is in them.
- Discuss the children's answers and spellings.

> **Support**
> Ask less-able children to recall orally as many pictures as they can. Then, as a group, ask the children to identify, e.g. a word with "busy busy bee ee ee ee" in, and all write it together with you supporting them by saying the sounds.

> **Challenge**
> Encourage more-able children to focus on the correct /ee/ sound in each word.

Pete's perfect pencil control

An activity for a small group of 6–8 children

Aim: to practise correct formation of the /ee/, /ea/ and /e-e/ graphemes

How to play:
- Hold up the "ee" flashcard and sing the song, do the actions and/or say the sound with the children.
- Model writing the grapheme using a cursive style.
- Children should then practise their cursive handwriting and see if they can write a perfect 10 of each grapheme.
- Repeat for /ea/ and /e-e/.

Revision

Play "Phoneme fingers" with a selection of /ee/, /ea/ and /e-e/ words. Say the word and give children 10 seconds to work out how many phonemes are in the sentence. Ask them to reveal their answers by holding up the corresponding number of fingers. When you reveal the answer, ask them to identify which /ee/ sound is in the word by using their letter names.

Now read...

The Singing Beetle, *Yellow, Band 3*

Target phoneme: /igh/

Learning objective

to learn to say, read and write /igh/

Resources

- Song of Sounds flashcard: igh
- Song of Sounds picture cards: fight, light, night
- Song of Sounds green words: might, fright

Starter

Sing /igh/

♪ **Song text:** "soar up high igh igh igh"

- Gather the children on the carpet.
- Sing the Song of Sounds all the way through.
- Explain that this week they are going to be learning about different graphemes that make the /igh/ sound.
- Explain that today they are going to practise the /igh/ sound that they have learned already, before going on to learning some new sounds.
- Show the class the "igh" flashcard and sing "soar up high igh igh igh".
- Remind them of the action and ask the class to perform the action.

Main lesson

Say /igh/

- Remind children how to say /igh/ – say /igh/ in a variety of voices, such as high-pitched or deep.
- Show children the "igh" picture cards and ask them to repeat after you, using an "I say, you say" technique, so they can hear the /igh/ sound in the words: fight, light, night.

Read /igh/

- Show children the grapheme side of the card and remind them what an "igh" looks like.
- Hide the flashcard behind your back – if you bring it out and show the picture side they must sing "soar up high igh igh igh", if you bring it out and show the grapheme side they must say /igh/. Bring the card out in different ways from either side of your body.

Write /igh/

- Show children how to form an /igh/ on the board using the explanation "Go down the insect's body, add a flick for his tail and a dot for his head" and "Go round the goat's tummy, down and round his tail" and "Start at the top, go down, back up half way, over the hat and flick".
- Ask children to follow you and sky-write the "igh" grapheme – don't forget you need to write backwards.
- Ask children to write "igh" on their arm – they should start at their shoulder and write "igh" many times, all the way to their fingertips.

Blend /igh/

- Using the Song of Sounds green words "might" and "fright", practise reading and blending the graphemes to make the word. Do this by asking children to say the sounds as you press the sound buttons, and then blend the sounds together as you sweep your hand underneath the word.

Revision

Add the "igh" flashcard to the stack you have already taught. Show the class the flashcards one at a time, picture-side up and ask them to sing each sound. Give a selection of flashcards, including /igh/, to some children and ask them to come to the front of the class – they should take it in turns to either sing/do the action or say the sound in front of the class. They can then give their flashcard to another child so they can have a turn. Repeat until every child in the class has had a turn. As you produce the grapheme side, let them say the different sounds. Repeat continually throughout the day.

Target grapheme: /ie/

Learning objective

to learn to say, read and write /ie/ and to recognise that it is an alternative grapheme to /igh/ and /i-e/

Resources

- Song of Sounds flashcard: ie
- Song of Sounds picture cards: pie, tie, lie
- Song of Sounds green words: untie, cries

Starter

Sing /ie/

♪ **Song text:** "lazy lie in ie ie ie"

- Sing the Song of Sounds all the way through.
- Explain that today they are going to a learn a new grapheme.
- Show the class the "ie" flashcard and sing "lazy lie in ie ie ie".
- Show the action and ask the class to perform it together.

Main lesson

Say /ie/

- Point out that it makes exactly the same sound as "soar up high igh igh igh".
- Show children how to say /igh/ – say /igh/ to me, say /igh/ to your friend, say /igh/ to the ceiling, say /igh/ to the floor, /igh/ to the IWB etc.
- Show children "ie" picture cards and ask them to repeat after you, using an "I say, you say" technique, so they can hear the /igh/ sound in the words: pie, tie, lie.

Read /ie/

- Explain that although this grapheme makes the same sound as "soar up high igh igh igh", it looks different.
- Show the grapheme side of the card and explain what an "ie" looks like.
- Hide the flashcard behind your back – if you bring it out and show the picture side they must sing "lazy lie in ie ie ie"; if you bring it out and show the grapheme side they must say /e/. Bring the card out in different ways from either side of your body

Write /ie/

- Show children how to form an "ie" on the board using the explanation "Go down the insect's body, add a flick for his tail and a dot for his head" and "Go round the elephant's head and add his curly trunk".
- Ask children to follow you and sky-write the "ie" grapheme – don't forget you need to write backwards.
- Ask the children to write an "ie" on their partner's back. Write a big "ie" and a small "ie" and swap over.

Blend /ie/

- Using the Song of Sounds green words "untie" and "cries", practise reading and blending the graphemes to make the words. Do this by asking children to say the sounds as you press the sound buttons, and then blend the sounds together as you sweep your hand underneath the word.

Revision

Add the "ie" flashcard to the stack you have already taught. Display last week's flashcards, together with "ie", in different places round the classroom. Point to a flashcard and ask children to all point and sing the song. Repeat several times. Point to a flashcard and ask children to all point and do the action. Repeat several times. Point to a flashcard and ask children to all point and say the sound. Repeat several times. Now you should sing the song, do the actions, say the sound and see if the children can point to the correct flashcard. Can they do it with their eyes closed?

Target grapheme: /i-e/

Learning objective

to learn to say, read and write /i-e/ and to recognise that it is an alternative grapheme to /igh/ and /ie/

Resources

- Song of Sounds flashcard: i-e
- Song of Sounds picture cards: kite, dive, five
- Song of Sounds green word cards: like, smile

Starter

Sing /i-e/

♪ **Song text:** "in a while, crocodile i-e i-e i-e"

- Gather the children on the carpet.
- Sing the Song of Sounds all the way through.
- Explain that today they are going to a learn a new grapheme.
- Show the class the "i-e" flashcard and sing "In a while, crocodile i-e i-e i-e". Show them the action and ask them to perform it together.

Main lesson

Say /i-e/
- Point out that it makes the same sound as "soar up high igh igh igh"/ "lazy lie in i-e i-e i-e".
- Show children how to say /igh/. Ask them to say /igh/ to each of their fingers and finally look at you and say the /igh/ sound.
- Show the "i-e" picture cards and ask children to repeat after you, using an "I say, you say" technique, so they can hear the /igh/ sound in the words: kite, dive, five.

Read /i-e/
- Explain that although this phoneme makes the same sound as "soar up high", it looks different.
- Show children the grapheme side of the card and explain what an "i-e" looks like.
- Explain that the "i" and the "e" are not next to each other. There is another letter between them. They are holding hands behind the other letter and together they make the sound /igh/.
- Hide the flashcard behind your back – if you bring it out and show the picture side they must sing "In a while, crocodile i-e i-e i-e"; if you show the grapheme side they must say /igh/.

Write /i-e/

- Sit children with their chatting chums. Show them how to form an "i-e" on the board using the explanation "Go down the insect's body, add a flick for his tail and a dot for his head" and "Go round the elephant's head and add his curly trunk".
- Draw a dash between the two letters and explain that this shows that there is another letter in-between. Draw a curvy line joining the "i" and the "e" together to visually demonstrate that it is those two letters together that make the /i-e/ sound.
- Ask children to follow you and sky-write the "i-e" grapheme, then ask them to work with their chatting chum to write an "i-e". Don't forget you need to write backwards.

Blend /i-e/
- Using the Song of Sounds green words "like" and "smile", practise reading and blending the graphemes to make the words. Do this by asking children to say the sounds as you press the sound buttons, and then blend the sounds together as you sweep your hand underneath the word.

Revision

Add the "ie" flashcard to those you have already taught. Ask a child to pick a number between one and five. Turn over that number of cards and sing the sound you reach. Repeat.

Target graphemes: /igh/, /ie/, /i-e/

Learning objective

to revisit the graphemes /igh/, /ie/ and /i-e/

Resources

- Song of Sounds flashcards: igh, ie, i-e
- Song of Sounds picture cards: fight, light, night, pie, tie, lie, kite, dive, five
- Song of Sounds green sentence: I like to lie in bed at night.
- Song of Sounds tricky word cards: I, my

Starter

- Gather the children on the carpet.
- Sing the Song of Sounds all the way through.
- Explain that today they are going to practise all the /igh/ sounds they have learned this week.

Main lesson

Sing /igh/, /ie/ and /i-e/

- Show the class the "igh", "ie", "i-e" flashcards and sing the relevant parts of the song as you show each card. Ask the children to perform the actions at the same time.

Say /igh/, /ie/ and /i-e/

- Remind the children that all of these make exactly the same sound.
- Ask the children to say /igh/ as you show them each flashcard, picture-side up.
- Display all the picture cards on the board. Point to a few at random and, using the "I say, you say" technique", ask children to repeat the word after you, stressing the /igh/ sound. Remind children of the tricky words that make the /igh/ sound: "my" and "I".

Read /igh/, /ie/ and /i-e/

- Sit children with their chatting chums.
- Remind children that although they all make the same sound, they look different.
- Hold up the "soar up high" flashcard, picture-side up. Ask if they can remember what it looks like. Choose a child to tell you what letters make the grapheme. Turn the flashcard over to show the grapheme and display the card on the board. Repeat for "lazy lie in" and "in a while, crocodile".
- On the board, display your three graphemes and all the picture cards. Ask children to work with their chatting chums to discuss which words contain which grapheme.
- Discuss with children and check that they are correct by revealing the grapheme on the reverse.
- Move the picture cards next to the correct grapheme.

Blend /igh/, /ie/ and /i-e/

- Using the Song of Sounds green sentence "I like to lie in bed at night", practise blending each word individually and then the whole phrase. Do this by asking the children to say the sounds as you press the sound buttons and then blend the sounds together as you sweep your hand underneath the word. Go through the whole phrase, then go back and point to each word for children to read.
- Explain to the children that sometimes when "y" it is at the end of a word it makes an /igh/ sound.
- Give some more examples, such as sky, cry.

Introducing Croc

Target phonemes: /igh/, /ie/, /i-e/

Learning objective

to learn to discriminate between the /igh/, /ie/ and /i-e/ graphemes; to practise blending and segmenting words containing /igh/, /ie/ and /i-e/

Resources

Carpet session

- Week 5: Teach software
- A puppet or soft toy of your choice (we are using a crocodile)
- A mini whiteboard and pen for each chatting chum pair

I spy

- igh, ie and i-e objects hidden round the school or classroom
- Magnifying glasses (optional)

Snap up a word

- A set of igh word cards with sound buttons (Week 5: AS1)

- Six crocodile cards (Week 5: AS2)
- An empty water tray or washing up bowl
- A sock for each child (optional)

Tick tock handwriting

- Song of Sounds flashcards: igh, ie and i-e (Week 5: AS1, 2-4)
- A small bag
- Paper or exercise book for each child
- A pencil for each child
- A spinner or dice with different time limits on the faces: 10 seconds, 20 seconds, 30 seconds, 1 minute

Revision

- Mini whiteboard and pen for each chatting chum pair

Carpet session

- Gather children on the carpet.
- Ask children which graphemes they have been learning about this week, (/igh/, /ie/ and /i-e/, which all make the /igh/ sound).
- Explain that you have brought an /igh/ expert with you today to meet the children.
- Bring out your puppet or soft toy and explain that his name is, for example, "Croc" and that he is an expert in the phoneme /igh/ as the sound is in his full name, crocodile. Draw their attention to the /igh/ sound in the word crocodile.
- Explain that he is just a baby and, although he can talk, he can't say whole words yet so it might be difficult for the children to understand him.
- Ask the puppet a series of questions. The puppet will talk in sound-talk and the children should blend the words together to reveal what he is saying. See below for some sample sentences:
  - "What is your name?" "C-r-o-c"
  - "How old are you?" "(one)" "w-u-n"
  - "Where do you live?" "p-o-n-d"
  - "What do you like to do in the pond?" "s-n-a-p, s-w-i-m"
  - "What is your favourite colour?" "g-r-ee-n"
  - "What do you like to eat?" "f-i-sh", "c-r-a-b"
  - You should congratulate the children on being able to understand Croc.

Software
Teach
W5

- Explain that Croc knows we are learning about words with the /igh/ sound, and he would like to say some /igh/ words and see if they can understand what he is saying. Croc should say a few /igh/ words, such as high, pie, time, fight, lie, five, in sound-talk. Again, children should blend the words together to reveal what he is saying.
- Explain that it is time for Croc to go but he is leaving them some games to play to help them practise the /igh/ sounds. Croc says "bye bye" in sound-talk and you should put him away.
- **2** Use the software to play "I spy". When you press play, a selection of pictures appear on the screen. Every time children see a picture that contains the /igh/ sound, they should shout /igh/.
- **3** On the next screen, a series of graphemes appear on the screen in the same way. Every time children see an "igh", "ie" or "i-e" grapheme, they should shout /igh/.
- Sit children in their chatting chum pairs.
- **4-8** Play "Time to write". Give each chatting chum pair a mini whiteboard and pen, and play the software. A picture of Croc will appear on the screen. In his mouth is a picture of an /igh/ word, for example, pie. Ask children which /igh/ sound is in pie and how they write it. They should write the word as many times as they can before Croc eats it. Repeat several times.
- **9** Revise the session learning objective before beginning the practical activities.

> **Support**
> Provide a Song of Sounds phoneme finder for less-able children and give clues, e.g. this one has "lazy lie in ie ie ie" in it.

Practical activities

I spy
A game for a group of 6–8 children

Aim: to identify target phonemes and discuss whether they contain an /igh/, /ie/ or /i-e/

How to play:
- Gather the resources.
- Before the lesson, position your /igh/, /ie/ and /i-e/ objects round the school.
- Give each child or pair a magnifying glass (optional).
- Ask them to walk around the environment, which can be the classroom, playground or the whole school, and every time they see an /i/ object, they should look at it with their magnifying glass or look closely at it together and make a mental note of what they have seen.
- Get together as a group and discuss what the class saw.

> **Challenge**
> Ask more-able children to write down what they found on their walk.

Snap up a word
An activity for a group of 5–6 children

Aim: to practise blending words for reading containing /igh/, /ie/ and /i-e/

How to play:
- Gather the resources.
- Give each child a sock to represent a crocodile, or ask them to make a snapping mouth with one hand.
- Put the word cards and Croc cards in the empty water tray or washing-up bowl face down.
- Children should take it in turns to use their "Croc" to snap up a word. If they can read the word, they can keep it. However, if they "snap up" a Croc card they must put another card back. The child with the most cards at the end of the game is the winner.

> **Support**
> Say the sounds for the less-able children to help them blend.

> **Challenge**
> Encourage more-able children to read as independently as possible.

Tick tock handwriting

An activity for a group of 5–10 children

Aim: to practise the correct formation of the /igh/, /ie/ and /i-e/ graphemes

How to play:

- Gather the resources.
- Put the "igh", "ie" and "i-e" flashcards in a small bag.
- Ask a child to pick out a grapheme from the bag and ask the group to say it in unison.
- Demonstrate how to write the grapheme correctly in cursive handwriting.
- Spin the spinner or roll a dice to decide the length of time the children have to write that sound as many times as they can. Repeat this activity multiple times.

Challenge

Include the /igh/, /ie/ and /i-e/ Song of Sounds picture cards in the bag and ask children to write the corresponding word.

Revision

Give each chatting chum pair a mini whiteboard and pen. Ask them to write down as many /igh/, /ie/ and /i-e/ objects that they can remember seeing on their hunt around the school. Brainstorm as a class and make a giant list modelling the correct spelling.

Now read...

Rock Out!, *Yellow, Band 3*

The Singing Beetle, *Yellow, Band 3*

Target phoneme: /ow/

Learning objective

to learn to say, read and write /ow/

Resources

- Song of Sounds flashcard: ow
- Song of Sounds picture cards: snow, mow, row
- Song of Sounds green words: show, throw

Starter

Sing /ow/

♪ **Song text:** "throw the snow ow ow ow"

- Gather the children on the carpet.
- Sing the Song of Sounds all the way through.
- Explain that this week they are going to be learning about different graphemes that make the /ow/ sound.
- Tell the class that they are going to practise the /ow/ sound they have learned before going on to learn some new ones.
- Show the class the "ow" flashcard and sing "throw the snow ow ow ow".
- Remind the class of the action and ask them to perform it together.

Main lesson

Say /ow/

- Remind children how to say /ow/ – they should take turns saying /ow/ as you point to them.
- Show children the "ow" picture cards and ask them to repeat after you using an "I say, you say" technique, so they can hear the /ow/ sound in the words: s-n-ow, r-ow, m-ow.

Read /ow/

- Show children the grapheme side of the card and remind them what an "ow" looks like.
- Hide the flashcard behind your back – if you bring it out and show the picture side they must sing "throw the snow ow ow ow", if you bring it out and show the grapheme side they must say /ow/. Bring the card out in different ways from either side of your body.

Write /ow/

- Show children how to form an "ow" on the board using the explanation "Start at the top and go round the orange" and "Go over the stormy waves – down, up, down, up and flick".
- Ask children to follow you and sky-write the "ow" grapheme – don't forget you need to write backwards.
- Ask them to use their hand as a "pad" and their finger as a "pencil" and practise writing an "ow" several times.

Blend /ow/

- Using the Song of Sounds green words "show" and "throw", practise reading and blending the graphemes to make the word.
- Do this by asking the children to say the sounds as you press the sound buttons, and then blend the sounds together as you sweep your hand underneath the word.

Revision

Add the "ow" flashcard to the stack you have already taught. Show the class the flashcards one at a time, picture-side up, and ask them to sing each sound. Ask the class to do the actions to the song silently as you show them the flashcards. As you produce the grapheme side, let them say the different sounds. Repeat continually throughout the day.

Target grapheme: /oa/

Learning objective

to learn to say, read and write /oa/ and to recognise that it is an alternative grapheme to /ow/ and /o-e/

Resources

- Song of Sounds flashcard: oa
- Song of Sounds picture cards: goat, boat, moat
- Song of Sounds green word cards: float, toast

Starter

Sing /oa/

♪ **Song text:** "goat on a boat oa oa oa"

- Gather the children on the carpet.
- Sing the Song of Sounds all the way through.
- Explain that today they are going to a learn a new grapheme.
- Show the class the "oa" flashcard and sing "goat on a boat oa oa oa".
- Show children the action and ask them to perform it together.

Main lesson

Say /oa/

- Point out that it makes exactly the same sound as "throw the snow ow ow ow".
- Show children how to say /oa/ – ask them to whisper /oa/, sing /oa/, shout /oa/.
- Show children "oa" picture cards and ask them to repeat after you, using an "I say, you say" technique, so they can hear the /oa/ sound in the words: goat, boat, moat.

Read /oa/

- Explain that although this phoneme makes the same sound as "throw the snow ow ow ow", it looks different.
- Show the children the grapheme side of the card and explain what an "oa" looks like.
- Hide the flashcard behind your back – if you bring it out and show the picture side they must sing "goat on a boat oa oa oa"; if you bring it out and show the grapheme side they must say /oa/. Bring the card out in different ways from either side of your body

Write /oa/

- Show children how to form "oa" on the board using the explanation "Start at the top and go round the orange" and "Go round the apple, down and flick".
- Ask children to follow you and sky-write the "oa" grapheme – don't forget you need to write backwards.
- Ask the children to write an "oa" on each of their fingers.

Blend /oa/

- Using the Song of Sounds green words "float" and "toast", practise reading and blending the graphemes to make the words. Do this by asking children to say the sounds as you press the sound buttons, and then blend the sounds together as you sweep your hand underneath the word.

Revision

Add the "oa" flashcard to the stack you have already taught. Show the class the flashcards one at a time, picture-side up, and ask them to sing each sound but in a whisper, until they see the "goat on a boat" flashcard when they should sing it out loudly. Repeat a few times. Ask the class to do the actions to the song silently as you show them the flashcards. As you produce the grapheme side let them whisper the different sounds until they see the "oa", when they should shout it. Repeat continually throughout the day.

Target grapheme: /o-e/

Learning objective

to learn to say, read and write /o-e/ and to recognise that it is an alternative grapheme to /ow/ and /oa/

Resources

- Song of Sounds flashcard: o-e
- Song of Sounds picture cards: bone, phone, throne
- Song of Sounds green words: home, joke

Starter

👥 Sing /o-e/

> ♪ **Song text:** "phone home o-e o-e o-e"

- Gather the children on the carpet.
- Sing the Song of Sounds all the way through.
- Explain that today they are going to a learn a new grapheme.
- Show the class the "o-e" flashcard and sing "phone home o-e o-e o-e".
- Show children the action and ask them to perform it together.

Main lesson

👥 Say /o-e/

- Point out that it makes exactly the same sound as "throw the snow ow ow ow" and "goat on a boat oa oa oa".
- Show children how to say /o-e/ – say /o-e/ with a happy face, angry face, sad face.
- Show children the "o-e" picture cards and ask them to repeat after you, using an "I say, you say" technique, so they can hear the /ow/ sound in the words, e.g. bone, phone, throne.

Read /o-e/

- Explain that although this grapheme makes the same sound as "throw the snow ow ow ow" and "goat on a boat oa oa oa", it looks different.
- Show children the grapheme side of the card and explain what an "o-e" looks like.
- Explain that the "o" and the "e" are not next to each other in the word. There is another letter between them. They are holding hands behind the other letter and together they make the sound /ow/.
- Hide the flashcard behind your back – if you bring it out and show the picture side they must sing "phone home o-e o-e o-e", if you bring it out and show the grapheme side they must say /o-e/. Bring the card out in different ways from either side of your body.

Write /o-e/

- Show children how to form an "o-e" on the board using the explanation "Start at the top and go round the orange" and "Go round the elephant's head and add his curly trunk".
- Draw a dash between the two letters and explain that this shows that there is another letter in-between. Draw a curvy line joining the "o" and the "e" together to visually demonstrate that it is those two letters together that make the /o-e/ sound.
- Ask children to follow you and sky-write the "o-e" grapheme – don't forget you need to write backwards.
- Write a tiny "o-e" in the air, then repeat getting increasingly bigger.

Blend /o-e/

- Using the Song of Sounds green words "home" and "joke", practise reading and blending the graphemes to make the words. Do this by asking children to say the sounds as you press the sound buttons, and then blend the sounds together as you sweep your hand underneath the word.

Revision

Add the "o-e" flashcard to the stack you have already taught. Show the class the flashcards one at a time, picture-side up, and sing the corresponding part of the song. If you sing the correct part of the song, children should give you a thumbs up, if you sing the wrong part of the song they should give you a thumbs down. As you produce the grapheme side, say the corresponding sound and ask them to give you a thumbs up if correct and a thumbs down if you're wrong. Finish by all singing and saying the sounds.

Target graphemes: /ow/, /oa/, /o-e/

Learning objective

to revisit the /ow/, /oa/ and /o-e/ graphemes

Resources

- Song of Sounds flashcards: ow, oa, o-e
- Song of Sounds picture cards: snow, mow, row, goat, boat, moat, phone, throne, bone
- Song of Sounds green sentence: It is slow to row the boat home.

Starter

Sing /ow/, /oa/ and /o-e/

- Gather the children on the carpet.
- Sing the Song of Sounds all the way through.
- Explain that today they are going to practise all the /ow/ sounds they have learned this week.
- Show the class the "ow", "oa", "o-e" flashcards and sing the correct parts of the song as you show each card. Ask children to perform the actions at the same time.

Main lesson

Say /ow/, /oa/ and /o-e/

- Remind children that these three graphemes make exactly the same sound.
- Ask them to say /ow/ as you show each flashcard picture-side up.
- Display all the picture cards on the board. Point to a few at random and, using the "I say, you say technique", ask children to repeat the word after you, stressing the /ow/ sound in the word.

Read /ow/, /oa/ and /o-e/

- Remind children that although they all make the same sound, they look different.
- Hold up the "throw the snow" flashcard picture-side up. Ask whether they can remember what it looks like. Choose a child to tell you which letters make the grapheme. Turn the flashcard over to show the grapheme and display it on the board.
- Repeat for "goat on a boat" and "phone home".
- On the board, display the three graphemes and all the picture cards. Ask children to work with their chatting chums to discuss which words contain which grapheme.
- Discuss with children and check that they are correct by revealing the grapheme on the reverse of each picture card.
- Move the picture cards next to the correct graphemes.

Blend /ow/, /oa/ and /o-e/

- Using the green sentence "It is slow to row the boat home", practise blending each word individually and then the whole phrase. Do this by asking children to say the sounds as you press the sound buttons, and then blend the sounds together as you sweep your hand underneath the word. Go through the whole phrase, then go back and point to each word for children to read.

Introduce "oh"

- Write the word "oh" on the board and ask if they have ever seen this word before. Explain that this word also makes the /ow/ sound and it is usually used when someone is surprised. Give a few examples, such as "Oh no", "Oh dear" and "Oh! You made me jump."

The O coat

Target graphemes: /ow/, /oa/, /o-e/

Learning objective

to learn to discriminate between the /ow/, /oa/ and /o-e/ graphemes; to practise blending and segmenting words containing /ow/, /oa/ and /o-e/

Resources

Carpet session

- Week 6: Teach software
- Song of Sounds flashcards: ow, oa and o-e
- A mini whiteboard and pen for each chatting chum pair
- ow, oa and o-e pictures (Week 6: AS1) (optional)
- A coat (optional)

O in a row

- Set of ow, oa and o-e words (Week 6: AS2-4)
- "O in a row" playing board for each child (Week 6: AS5)
- A feely bag
- Six counters

Cards on the coat

- The ow, oa and o-e cards used in the carpet session
- Three coats with ow, oa, o-e fixed on (including the coat from the carpet session)
- Three large pieces of paper
- Three marker pens

Rainbow writing

- Song of Sounds flashcards: ow, oa and o-e
- Pencils or felt tips in the colours of the rainbow
- Paper or exercise books
- A small bag

Revision

- A coat with nothing pinned on
- ow, oa and o-e pictures (Week 6: AS1)
- Clips or safety pins

Carpet session

- Gather the resources.
- Before this session, print the pictures from the resource CD (Week 6: AS1) and fix them to an old coat.
- Sit children with their chatting chums, in a circle.
- **1** Ask children which graphemes they have been learning about this week: "ow", "oa" and "o-e" which all make the /oa/ sound. Put the "ow", "oa" and "o-e" flashcards on the board, grapheme-side up.

> **Software**
> Teach
> **W6**

- **2-3** Explain that to learn about the different "o" sounds, you have brought something to help. Put on your "o" coat, or use software slides 2 and 3 instead.
- Give children three minutes to discuss with their chatting chums the different pictures they can see on your coat and which "o" grapheme they contain – /ow/, /oa/ or /o-e/. Revise that the "o" and the "e" hold hands to make the /ow/ sound.

- Invite each pair to come to the middle of the circle, and choose a picture from your coat. Remove it for them and let them display it on the board next to the correct grapheme. Discuss any misconceptions.

4
- Use the software to show some /ow/ words. Ask children to read the words with their chatting chums. Choose a pair to stand up and read a word to you. Use the software to reveal the correct answer. Repeat for the remaining words.

5–7
- Play "Pick up the phone". Give each chatting chum pair a mini whiteboard and pen. On the software is a phone that rings. Click the button to answer the phone and a picture will appear as the word is said out loud. Children must work with their chatting chums to decide which /ow/ sound is in the word and write the correct grapheme on their whiteboards.

> **Support**
> Give less-able children a Song of Sounds phoneme finder to help them.

- Reveal the correct grapheme, followed by the correct word. Repeat.

8
- Revise the session's learning objective before dividing the children into differentiated groups for the practical activities.

> **Challenge**
> Ask more-able children to write the whole word.

Practical activities

O in a row

A game for a small group of 5–6 children

Aim: to practise blending words for reading containing /ow/, /oa/ and /o-e/

How to play:
- Gather the resources.
- Put your /ow/, /oa/ and /o-e/ words into the feely bag.
- Give each child in the group a playing board and put some counters in the middle of the table.
- Children should take it in turns to pull a word out of the feely bag and read it using the sound buttons to help them.
- They should then identify which "o" grapheme is in the word and cover the corresponding grapheme on their playing board with a counter.
- The first player to get three correct in a row is the winner.

> **Support**
> Help less-able children by orally blending the word.

> **Challenge**
> Encourage more-able children to read at speed without using the sound buttons.

Cards on the coat

An activity for a large group of 10–15 children

Aim: to practise segmenting words for writing containg /ow/, /oa/ and /o-e/ and choosing the correct grapheme

How to play:
- Gather the resources.
- This game should be played in a large space such as a hall or a playground.
- Split the children into three teams and give each team a large piece of paper and a pen.
- Give each team a coat with either /ow/, /oa/ or /o-e/ pinned on.
- Scatter the "ow", "oa" and "o-e" picture cards around the space.
- The first person in each team should put the coat on.
- On a whistle or given signal, (e.g. clap your hands or shout "go") they should run and find a picture card that corresponds with the grapheme on their team's coat. They should bring it back to their teams and write it on their piece of paper.
- Repeat for each team member.
- The first team with five correct words written on their piece of paper is the winner.

> **Support**
> Less-able children could collect the correct pictures to match their graphemes without writing.

> **Challenge**
> More-able children could write their words in a sentence.

Rainbow writing

An activity for a small group of 5–10 children

Aim: to practise the correct formation of the /ow/, /oa/ and /o-e/ graphemes

How to play:

- Put the "ow", "oa" and "o-e" flashcards in a bag.
- Ask one child to pick out a grapheme from the bag. All children must say the grapheme in unison.
- Demonstrate how to write the grapheme correctly in cursive handwriting.
- The children should then practise writing the grapheme seven times, using pens from each colour of the rainbow.

Challenge

Include the ow, oa and o-e picture cards and ask children to write the corresponding word.

Revision

Gather the children on the carpet and ask them to sit with their chatting chums in a circle around you. Put the coat on again, with nothing pinned on it. Give each chatting chum pair a picture. Ask them to discuss which grapheme is in the word. Each chatting chum pair should take it in turns to tell you the correct grapheme and hand it to you so that you can pin it on your coat.

Now read...

Goat's Coat, *Red, Band 2B*

Horse Up a Tree, *Yellow, Band 3*

Target phoneme: /oo/

Learning objective

to learn to say, read and write /oo/

Resources

- Song of Sounds flashcard: oo
- Song of Sounds picture cards: moon, zoo, spoon
- Song of Sounds green words: food, tooth

Starter

Sing /oo/

♪ **Song text:** "zoom to the moon oo oo oo"

- Gather the children on the carpet.
- Sing the Song of Sounds all the way through.
- Explain that this week you are going to be learning about different graphemes that make the /oo/ sound.
- Explain that today they are going to practise the /oo/ sound they have learned before going on to learn some new ones.
- Show the class the "oo" flashcard and sing "zoom to the moon oo oo oo".
- Remind children of the action and ask the class to perform it together.

Main lesson

Say /oo/

- Remind children how to say /oo/ – ask them to say it ten times with their eyes closed.
- Show children the "oo" picture cards and ask them to repeat after you, using an "I say, you say" technique, so they can hear the /oo/ sound in the words: moon, zoo, spoon.

Read /oo/

- Show children of the grapheme side of the card and remind the class what an "oo" looks like.
- Hide the flashcard behind your back – if you bring it out and show the picture side they must sing "zoom to the moon oo oo oo"; if you bring it out and show the grapheme side they must say /oo/. Bring the card out in different ways from either side of your body.

Write /oo/

- Show children how to form an "oo" on the board using the explanation "Start at the top and go round the orange" twice.
- Ask children to follow you and sky-write the "oo" grapheme – don't forget you need to write backwards.
- Ask them to look up to the ceiling and write an "oo" in the air.

Blend /oo/

- Using the Song of Sounds green words "food" and "tooth", practise reading and blending the graphemes to make the word.
- Do this by asking children to say the sounds as you press the sound buttons, and then blend the sounds together as you sweep your hand underneath the word.

Revision

Add the "oo" flashcard to the stack you have already taught. Use a piece of card to cover your flashcard pack. Reveal a flashcard very slowly by moving the card downwards. As soon as they know what it is, the children should sing it. Reveal the whole flashcard to see if they are right. Repeat the slow reveal game but this time let them do the actions as you reveal the flashcards. As you produce the grapheme side, can they say the different sounds? Repeat continually throughout the day.

Target grapheme: /ew/

Learning objective

to learn to say, read and write /ew/ and to recognise that it is an alternative grapheme to /oo/ and /u-e/

Resources

- Song of Sounds flashcard: ew
- Song of Sounds picture cards: jewels, screw, chew
- Song of Sounds green words: new, few

Starter

Sing /ew/

♪ **Song text:** "new jewels ew ew ew"

- Gather the children on the carpet.
- Sing the Song of Sounds all the way through.
- Explain that today they are going to a learn a new grapheme.
- Show the class the "ew" flashcard and sing "new jewels ew ew ew".
- Show the class the action and ask them to perform it together.

Main lesson

Say /ew/

- Point out that it makes exactly the same sound as "zoom to the moon oo oo oo".
- Show children how to say /ew/ – say /ew/ in a variety of voices, such as high-pitched, deep etc.
- Show children "ew" picture cards and ask them to repeat after you, using an "I say, you say" technique, so they can hear the /ew/ sound in the words: jewels, screw, chew.

Read /ew/

- Explain that although this phoneme makes the same sound as "zoom to the moon oo oo oo", it looks different.
- Show the children the grapheme side of the card and explain what "ew" looks like.
- Hide the flashcard behind your back – if you bring it out and show the picture side they must sing "new jewels ew ew ew"; if you bring it out and show the grapheme side they must say /ew/ . Bring the card out in different ways from either side of your body.

Write /ew/

- Show children how to form a "ew" on the board using the explanation "Go round the elephant's head and add his curly trunk" and "Go over the stormy waves – down, up, down, up and flick".
- Ask children to follow you and sky-write the "ew" grapheme – don't forget you need to write backwards.
- Ask them to write "ew" on their arm – they should start at their shoulder and write it lots of times, all the way to their fingertips.

Blend /ew/

- Using the Song of Sounds green words "new" and "few", practise reading and blending the graphemes to make the words. Do this by asking children to say the sounds as you press the sound buttons, and then blend the sounds together as you sweep your hand underneath the word.

Revision

Add the "ew" flashcard to the stack you have already taught. Ask children to sit in a circle. Give out the flashcards to random children around the circle. Play the Song of Sounds CD and pass the flashcards around the circle. When you stop the music, the children holding flashcards should sing the corresponding parts of the song. Repeat lots of times, asking the children either to sing the song, do the actions or say the sounds. As you produce the grapheme side, let them say the different sounds. Repeat continually throughout the day.

Target grapheme: /u-e/

Resources

- Song of Sounds flashcard: u-e
- Song of Sounds picture cards: cube, flute, tube
- Song of Sounds green words: tune, rude

Learning objective

to learn to say, read and write /u-e/ and to recognise that it is an alternative grapheme to /oo/ and /ew/

Starter

Sing /u-e/

> ♪ **Song text:** "A huge cube u-e u-e u-e"

- Sing the Song of Sounds all the way through.
- Explain that today they are going to a learn a new grapheme. Show the class the "u-e" flashcard and sing "A huge cube u-e u-e u-e".
- Show them the action and ask the class to perform it together.

Main lesson

Say /u-e/

- Point out that it makes the same sound as "zoom to the moon" and "new jewels".
- Show children how to say /u-e/ – say /u-e/ to me, say /u-e/ to your friend, say /u-e/ to the ceiling, say /u-e/ to the floor, etc.
- Show children the "u-e" picture cards and ask them to repeat after you, using an "I say, you say" technique, so they can hear the /oo/ sound in the words e.g. cube, flute, tube.

Read /u-e/

- Explain that although this phoneme makes the same sound as "zoom to the moon oo oo oo" and "new jewels ew ew ew", it looks different.
- Show children the grapheme side of the card and explain what "u-e" looks like.
- Explain that the "u" and the "e" are not even next to each other in the word. They are holding hands behind the other letter and together they make the sound /oo/.
- Hide the flashcard behind your back – if you bring it out and show the picture side they must sing "a huge cube u-e u-e u-e"; if you bring it out and show the grapheme side they must say /oo/. Bring the card out in different ways from either side of your body.

Write /u-e/

- Show children how to form a "u-e" on the board using the explanation "Start at the top, go down, round the puddle, back up, down and flick" and "Go round the elephant's head and add his curly trunk".
- Draw a dash between the two letters and explain that this shows that there is another letter in-between. Draw a curvy line joining the "u" and the "e" together to visually demonstrate that it is those two letters together that make the /u-e/ sound.
- Ask children to follow you and sky-write the "u-e" grapheme – don't forget you need to write backwards.
- Ask children to write a "u-e" on their chatting chum's back: a big "u-e" and a small "u-e" and then swap over.

Blend /u-e/

- Using the Song of Sounds green words "tune" and "rude", practise reading and blending the graphemes. Do this by asking the children to say the sounds as you press the sound buttons and then blend the sounds together as you sweep your hand underneath the word.

Revision

Check children's understanding with flashcard practise as for previous lessons. Repeat throughout the day.

Target graphemes: /oo/, /ew/, /u-e/

Learning objective

to revisit the graphemes /oo/, /ew/ and /u-e/

Resources

- Song of Sounds flashcards: oo, ew, u-e
- Song of Sounds picture cards: moon, zoo, spoon, jewels, screw, chew, cube, flute, tube
- Song of Sounds green sentence: I will soon play a tune with my new flute.

Starter

- Gather the children on the carpet.
- Sing the Song of Sounds all the way through.
- Explain that today they are going to practise all the /oo/sounds they have learned this week.

Main lesson

Sing /oo/, /ew/ and /u-e/

- Show the class the "oo", "ew", "u-e" flashcards and sing the correct parts of the song as you display each card. Ask them to perform the actions at the same time.

Say /oo/, /ew/ and /u-e/

- Remind children that all of these make exactly the same sound.
- Ask them to say /oo/ as you show them each flashcard, picture-side up.
- Display all the picture cards on the board. Point to a few at random and, using the "I say, you say" technique, ask them to repeat the word after you, stressing the /oo/ sound in the word.

Read /oo/, /ew/ and /u-e/

- Remind children that although they all make the same sound, they look different.
- Hold up the "zoom to the moon" flashcard picture-side up. Ask them if they can remember what it looks like. Choose one child to tell you what letters make the grapheme. Turn the flashcard over to show the grapheme and display it on the board.
- Repeat for "new jewels" and "a huge cube".
- On the board you will have three graphemes and all the picture cards. Ask the children to work with their chatting chums to discuss which words contain which grapheme.
- Discuss with children and check if they are correct by revealing the grapheme on the reverse of each picture card.
- Move the picture cards next to the correct grapheme.

Blend /oo/, /ew/ and /u-e/

- Using the green sentence "I will soon play a tune with my flute", practise blending each word individually and then the whole phrase. Do this by asking children to say the sounds as you press the sound buttons, and then blend the sounds together as you sweep your hand underneath the word. Go through the whole phrase, then go back and point to each word for the children to read.

Introduce /ue/

- Write the word "blue" on the board and circle the /ue/ at the end of the word.
- Explain that in the word blue, the /ue/ at the end also makes an /oo/ sound.
- Explain that there are a few words with the "u" and the "e" not holding hands behind another letter, but standing next to each other and they still make the same /oo/ sound.
- Sound out the word with the children, for example, /b/-/l/-/oo/.
- Give some more examples, such as glue, true, barbecue.

A royal appearance

Target graphemes: /oo/, /ew/, /u-e/

Learning objective

to learn to discriminate between the /oo/, /ew/ and /u-e/ graphemes; to practise blending and segmenting words containing "oo", "ew" and "u-e"

Resources

Carpet session

- Week 7: Teach software
- Song of Sounds flashcards: oo, ew and u-e
- Song of Sounds CD
- Jewellery box (this could be a shoe box covered in gold paper) full of jewels with oo, ew and u-e (optional: laminated)
- A mini whiteboard and pen for each chatting chum pair
- Hoops (optional)
- A queen costume (optional)

Queen runs quickly

- Parts of Song of Sounds classroom frieze of oo, ew and u-e
- List of Song of Sounds green words containing oo, ew and u-e – food/tooth; new/flew; tune/rude
- A "throne" (decorated chair)
- A mini whiteboard and pen for each child
- A crown (optional)

Crown it!

- A Crown it! lotto board for each child (Week 7: AS1)
- oo, ew and u-e word cards (Week 7: AS2–3)
- New jewels cards (Week 7: AS4–8)
- A jewellery box (re-use box from the carpet session) or feely bag
- Yellow counters or crown counters (Week 7: AS9)

Quest to be queen

- Song of Sounds flashcards: oo, ew and u-e
- A piece of paper, exercise book or mini whiteboard for each child
- Yellow pencils, pens or crayons
- A feely bag
- A crown

Revision

- Song of Sounds flashcards: oo, ew and u-e
- Jewels with oo, ew and u-e (Week 7: AS1)
- Three hoops

Carpet session

- Sit children with their chatting chums, in a circle.
- This lesson has the option of teaching in role as the queen in a crown or cape. Alternatively, you could use the software presentation to "meet" the queen.

Software
Teach
W7

1. • Depending on the option you have chosen, enter the classroom dressed as the queen or play the software.

2. • Ask children which graphemes they have been learning about this week ("oo", "ew" and "u-e"). Show the graphemes one-by-one and sing the corresponding parts of the song.

3. • Explain to children that to help them learn about the different sounds, you have brought your new jewels to help.

4. • Show your jewellery box with your "new jewels" in. Alternatively, use the software.

   • In the middle of the circle, place three hoops. In each hoop put one of your "oo", "ew" and "u-e" flashcards. Alternatively, place each flashcard on the floor at a distance from each other.

   • Give each chatting chum pair one of your "jewels" making sure you say the name of the picture as you give it to them, in case it is difficult to recognise. Give the chatting chums one minute to discuss which grapheme is in their picture.

   • Play The Song of Sounds Audio CD. As the music plays, each chatting chum pair should come and place their "jewel" in the correct hoop (or next to the correct flashcard), according to which grapheme they think their word contains. Discuss any misconceptions.

5. • Use the software to play "The Queen's jewels". On the IWB are pictures of the Queen's jewels with words on. Ask the children to read the words on the jewels. Choose a chatting chum pair to stand up and read a word to you. Use the IWB presentation to reveal the correct answer as the jewel disappears to reveal the picture underneath it. Repeat for the remaining words.

   • Give each chatting chum pair a mini whiteboard and pen.

6. • On the IWB are pictures of the Queen's jewels with pictures of /oo/, /ew/ and /u-e/ words on each jewel. Ask the chatting chum pairs to write the words on the "jewels" on their whiteboards.

   • Reveal the correct words, and repeat.

7. • Revise the session's learning objective before dividing children into their differentiated groups for the practical activities.

Support
Give less-able children a Song of Sounds phoneme finder to help them.

Challenge
Ask more-able children to write the words in a sentence.

Practical activities

Queen runs quickly

A game for a small group of 5–6 children

Aim: to practise segmenting words for writing containg /oo/, /ew/ and /u-e/ and choosing the correct grapheme

How to play:
• Gather the resources.

• Place the /oo/, /ew/ and /u-e/ parts of the Song of Sounds classroom frieze all around the classroom or a large space (hall or playground).

• Give each child a mini whiteboard and a pen.

• Sit on the throne and call out a green /oo/, /ew/ and /u-e/ word made up of the sounds already covered by the children.

• The children should run to the correct /oo/ sound, touch it and race back to write it on their whiteboards. The first to hold up the word written correctly is the winner.

• A crown could be worn by the winning child for the next turn until someone wins it from them.

Support
Less-able children could run and touch the correct grapheme; the first child back is the winner.

Challenge
Move on to more complex words, e.g. computer, kangaroo

Crown it!

A game for a small group of 5-6 children

Aim: to practise blending words for reading containing /oo/, /ew/ and /u-e/

How to play:

- Gather the resources.
- Gather the children around a table.
- Put the word cards and new jewels cards in the jewellery box.
- Place the crown cards or counters in the middle of the table.
- Each child should take a turn to pick out a word card. They should read the card and place a counter over the approriate picture. The object is to cover three pictures in a row. If they pick out a new jewels card they can cover any picture they like. If they cannot read the word they must put it back and miss a turn.

> **Support**
> Read the letters for less-able children to blend orally.

> **Challenge**
> Encourage more-able children to read completely independently.

Quest to be queen

An activity for a small group of 5-10 children

Aim: to practise the correct formation of /oo/, /ew/ and /u-e/

How to play:

- Put the flashcards in the feely bag.
- Give each child a piece of paper, exercise book or mini whiteboard and a royal pen (yellow pencil or pen).
- Place the crown in the middle of the table.
- Pull one of the graphemes out of a feely bag and model writing it on the board in a cursive script using the correct explanation.
- The children write the approriate grapheme and you should decide whose writing is the neatest. The winner can to wear the crown until the next letter is written.
- Repeat the activity using the different graphemes.

> **Challenge**
> Ask more-able children to finish by writing a few words.

Revision

Sit the children in their chatting chum pairs in a circle. Place the three hoops in the middle of the circle with an "oo", "ew" and "u-e" flashcard, or put the flashcards on the floor with sufficient distance between them. Give each chatting chum pair one of the queen's jewels and ask them to sort them again into the correct hoops.

Now read...

Feeling Things, *Yellow, Band 3*

Real Monsters, *Yellow, Band 3*

Rock Out!, *Yellow, Band 3*

Target tricky words: "come", "some"

Learning objective

to practise reading and spelling tricky words

Resources

• Song of Sounds tricky word cards: come, some

Starter

Introducing "come" and "some"

• Explain that today children are going to learn two new tricky words.
• Ask them if they can remember what makes some words trickier than others (they don't follow Felicity's phoneme rules).
• Hold up the flashcards "come" and "some". Ask children why these words are red and spiky (they are red because, like a red traffic light, red means stop and you need to stop and think about them).

Main lesson

Read "come" and "some"

• Show children the tricky word "come" and read it to them.
• Give a few examples of when "come" might be used in sentences, for example, "You can come to my party" and "Come and play my game."
• Display the word "come". Explain that the "c" is not tricky because it makes the /c/ sound and follows Felicity's phoneme rules. Also the "m" is not tricky as it makes the /m/ sound. The "o-e" makes more of an /u/ sound than a typical /o-e/ sound, such as "cone".
• Show the word "some" and explain that this rhymes with "come". Explain that it has exactly the same tricky bit – the "o-e" makes an /u/ sound.

Write "come" and "some"

• Show children how to write the word "come" on the board. As you write each grapheme say it aloud: "c"-"o"-"m"-"e". Draw the sound buttons underneath with a long curvy sound button joining the o-e to make it clear that it is one sound.
• Repeat for "some".

Revision

Tell children that you will keep testing them to see if they can remember the words because they are so tricky. Throughout the day, keep producing the "come" and "some" flashcards and ask children to read them on sight. Repetition is the key.

Target tricky word: "said"

Learning objective

to practise reading and spelling tricky words

Resources

- Song of Sounds tricky word card: said
- Previously-taught Song of Sounds tricky words: come, some

Starter

Introducing "said"

- Gather the children on the carpet.
- Explain that today they are going to a learn a new word.
- Ask children if they can remember what makes some words trickier than others (they don't follow Felicity's phoneme rules).
- Hold up the "said" flashcard – remind children that it is red because, like a red traffic light, red means stop and you need to stop and think about them.

Main lesson

Read "said"

- Show children the tricky word "said" and read it to them.
- Give a few examples of when "said" might be used in sentences, for example, "She said she's not my friend" and "'Ouch,' said the man".
- Display the word "said". Explain that the "s" is not tricky because it makes the /s/ sound and follows Felicity's phoneme rules. The "d" is not tricky either as it makes a /d/ sound. However, the "ai" makes an /e/ sound like "elephants enormous e e e". The tricky bit of "said" is that you have to remember that the "ai" makes the /e/ sound.

Write "said"

- Show children how to write the word "said" on the board. As you write each grapheme, say it out loud: "s"-"a"-"i"-"d".
- Ask children to say "said" phonetically to help them remember how to spell it.

Revision

Add your "said" flashcard to the flashcards you taught during the previous session. Throughout the day, keep producing the flashcards and asking children to read them on sight. Repetition is the key.

Target tricky word: "have"

Learning objective

to practise reading and spelling tricky words

Resources

- Song of Sounds tricky word card: have
- Previously-taught Song of Sounds tricky word cards: come, some, said

Starter

Introducing "have"

- Explain that today they are going to a learn a new word.
- Ask children if they can remember what makes some words trickier than others (they don't follow Felicity's phoneme rules).
- Hold up the "have" tricky word card – remind children that it is red because, like a red traffic light, red means stop and you need to "stop and think" about the word.

Main lesson

Read "have"

- Show children the tricky word "have" and read it to them.
- Give a few examples of when "have" might be used in sentences, for example, "You have the same coat as me" and "I have two cats and a dog".
- Display the word "have". Explain that the "h" is not tricky because it makes the /h/ sound and follows Felicity's phoneme rules. The "v" is not tricky either as it makes a /v/ sound. However, the "a-e" does not make the /a-e/ sound, but instead makes an /a/ sound like "ants on an apple" even though there is an "e" on the end of the word. The tricky bit of "have" is that you have to remember that it has a silent "e" on the end.

Write "have"

- Show children how to write the word "have" on the board. As you write each grapheme, say it out loud: /h/-/a/-/v/ and (whisper) silent /e/. Emphasise the "e" so that the children remember it.

Revision

Add your "have" tricky word card to the tricky word cards you have already taught this week. Throughout the day, keep producing the cards and asking the children to read them on sight. Repetition is the key.

Target tricky words: "any", "many"

Learning objective

to practise reading and spelling tricky words

Resources

- Song of Sounds tricky word cards: any, many
- Previously-taught Song of Sounds tricky word cards: come, some, said, have

Starter

Introducing "any" and "many"

- Explain that today they are going to learn two new words.
- Ask children if they can remember what makes some words trickier than others (they don't follow Felicity's phoneme rules).
- Hold up the "any" and "many" flashcards – remind children that they are red because, like a red traffic light, red means stop and you need to stop and think about them.

Main lesson

Read "any" and "many"

- Show the children the tricky word "any" and read it to them.
- Give a few examples of when "any" might be used in sentences, for example, "I haven't got any more sweets" and "I didn't see any birds".
- Explain that the "a" is tricky because it sounds like an /e/, like "elephants enormous e e e". The "n" is not tricky because it sounds like /n/ and obeys Felicity's phoneme rules. The "y" is tricky as it looks like "yellow yo yo y y y" but in this word it makes the /ee/ sound, as in "mummy".
- Display the word "many" and explain that this rhymes with "any". Explain that it has exactly the same tricky bits – the "a" makes an /e/ sound and the "y" makes an /ee/ sound, as in "mummy".

Write "any" and "many"

- Show children how to write the word "any" on the board. Say each grapheme as you write it: "a"-"n"-"y", "m"-"a"-"n"-"y".
- Repeat for "many".

Revision

Add the "any" and "many" flashcards to the flashcards you have already taught this week. Throughout the day, keep producing the flashcards and asking children to read them on sight. Repetition is the key.

Tricky word practice

Learning objective

to practise reading and spelling tricky words

Resources

Carpet session

- Week 8: Teach software
- Song of Sounds tricky word cards: come, some, said, have, any, many
- A selection of Song of Sounds green words that you have taught so far
- A Tricky Trevor costume, toy or letter (optional)
- Cards of three different colours for each child, or fans with three colours (purple, green, blue)

Tricky aim

- Song of Sounds tricky word cards from carpet session
- Six buckets (they can be the same size or varying sizes)
- A ball for each child

- A spot or hoop for each child to stand on/in (optional)

Tricky spell

- Six large pieces of paper
- Six different mediums, such as red paint, red felt tip, red pastel, red crayon, red chalk, red sand
- A dice with the tricky words from the lesson on (Week 8: AS1)

Tricky time

- Song of Sounds tricky word cards: from carpet session
- A timer
- A mini whiteboard and pen for each child

Homework

- Parent letter (Week 8: AS2)

Revision

- Song of Sounds tricky word cards from carpet session

Carpet session

- Sit children with their chatting chums.
- This lesson has the option of teaching in role as "Tricky Trevor", a wise old man with grey hair and a walking stick. If you do not wish to do this, you could use a Tricky Trevor teddy or receive a letter enclosing the tricky words from Trevor.
- Depending on the option you have chosen, enter the classroom as Tricky Trevor or hold up your teddy or letter.
- Remind children that Trevor is an incredibly clever man and that is why he has come here today, to teach the children some more tricky words.
- From your briefcase/bag produce a selection of green words and tricky words of your choice. Ask the children what the differences between "green" words and "tricky" words are.
- Then from your briefcase/bag produce the tricky word cards that you are going to learn about today. Ask them again if they know why these words are red and spiky.

- Show children the tricky words and ask them to repeat the words after you. Ask them to whisper the words, shout the words, say the words and sing the words.

1-2
- Press play on the software. Using the presentation, reveal the words one at a time. Ask the children to identify the green and tricky parts of each word, and offer advice to help them remember each word.

- Sit the children with their chatting chums.

3-9
- Play "Trevor's trick". Give each child cards of three different colours corresponding to the colours of the words on the software game , or a coloured fan with these colours. Show the three different versions of each word, only one of which is the correct spelling, for example, "said, sed, seid". Children must work with their chatting chums to choose the correct spelling and reveal the card of that colour.

Software Teach **W8**

10
- Revise the session's learning objective before dividing children into their differentiated groups for the practical activities.

Practical activities

Tricky aim

A game for a small group of 5–6 children

Aim: to practise reading tricky words

How to play:
- Gather the resources.
- Attach a tricky word to each of the six buckets.
- Arrange the buckets so that children can see the tricky words.
- Give each child a ball and line them up so that they are standing an equal distance from the buckets.
- Call out a tricky word.
- Children should read the words on the buckets to find the correct word and throw their balls, aiming for the correct bucket.
- If they get their ball in the correct bucket, they win a point. The one with the most points at the end wins.
- Show them which word was correct and revise the tricky bits of the word.

> **Support**
> Give less-able children some clues, e.g. remember the "a" in this word makes an /o/ sound.

> **Challenge**
> Ask children to close their eyes and spell the word on the bucket once they have thrown their ball.

Tricky spell

A game for a small group of 5–6 children

Aim: to practise spelling tricky words using different mediums

How to play:
- Gather the resources.
- Gather your group around a large table.
- Place the six large pieces of paper, each with a different medium next to it, round the table (for example red paint, red crayons).
- Choose one child to roll the "tricky" dice.
- Whichever tricky word it lands on, children should practise writing that word each using a different medium. They should then move around the table writing the word in each medium until each child has used all six.

> **Challenge**
> Take the word away so that more-able children have to remember how to spell it in order to write it.

Tricky time

An activity for a small group of 5–10 children

Aim: to practise spelling tricky words

How to play:

- Gather the resources.
- Give each child a mini whiteboard and pen.
- Set the timer to 30 seconds or one minute.
- Call out a tricky word.
- Children should see how many times they can write that word on their whiteboards in the given time.

Support

Display the tricky word card as you say the word for less-able children to copy if they need to.

Challenge

Ask more-able children to write a sentence containing the tricky word.

Homework (optional)

On the resource CD is a letter for parents that you might choose to send home. The letter explains the concept behind "tricky words" and has the tricky words you have taught today on the reverse for parents to practise reading and spelling with their child.

Revision

Play "Pass the tricky word". Sit children in a circle and give them tricky word cards. Pass the cards round the ring while singing (to the tune of London Bridge is Falling Down) "Pass the tricky words around the ring, around the ring, around the ring, pass the tricky words around the ring, what do they say?" Children holding the tricky words should stand up and say the word, and the others should repeat it. Play several times.

Now read...

Peas, Please!, *Yellow, Band 3*

Zog and Zebra, *Yellow, Band 3*

The Small Bun, *Blue, Band 4*

Buzzy Bees, *Blue, Band 4*

Target graphemes: /ay/, /ai/, /a-e/

Learning objective

to revisit the /ay/, /ai/, /a-e/ graphemes

Starter

- Gather the children on the carpet.
- Explain that today children are going to practise the /ay/ phoneme and the graphemes /ay/, /ai/ and /a-e/.

Resources

- The Song of Sounds song IWB version
- Song of Sounds flashcards: ay, ai, a-e
- Song of Sounds picture cards: hay, play, tray, snail, train, rain, cake, whale, snake
- Song of Sounds green word cards: day, stay, tail, paint, make, shape

Main lesson

Time to learn

- Use the "ay", "ai", "a-e" flashcards.
- Begin by showing the picture side of the flashcards. Ask the children to sing them.
- Show the picture side of the flashcards again and ask them to do the actions silently.
- Show them the grapheme side of the flashcards and discuss which letters make up the different "ay" graphemes.

Time to practise

- Ask the children to work with their chatting chums.
- Give each pair an "a" picture card or green word.
- Ask them to discuss which /ay/ sound it contains.
- Sing part of the song and ask the pairs who have a picture or a word with that sound in to stand up.
- Repeat several times, varying the game by sometimes just doing the actions and asking the children to stand up. Get quicker and quicker.
- Display the "a" pictures all over the board and give each chatting chum pair a mini whiteboard and pen.
- Give children a series of writing challenges, for example:
  - Who can write all the /ee/ words the quickest? Or the /ea/ words? Or the /e-e/ words?
  - Write one of each.
  - How many can you write in a minute? 30 seconds? Before the whistle sounds?
  - How quickly can you write them all?

Revision

At different points during the day, produce your "ay", "ai" and "a-e" flashcards and ask children to sing the song, do the actions and/or say the sound. Remind them that this week they will be practising phonemes that have more than one grapheme.

Target graphemes: /ee/, /ea/, /e-e/

Learning objective

to revisit the /ee/, /ea/, /e-e/ graphemes

Starter

- Gather the children on the carpet.
- Explain that today children are going to practise the /ee/ phoneme and the different graphemes /ee/, /ea/ and /e-e/.

Resources

- The Song of Sounds song IWB version
- Song of Sounds flashcards: ee, ea, e-e
- Song of Sounds picture cards: bee, sheep, tree, seal, peas, leaf, Pete, concrete, athlete
- Song of Sounds green word cards: feet, teeth, eat, read, even, these
- A mini whiteboard and pen for each chatting chum pair

Main lesson

Time to learn

- Use the "ee", "ea" and "e-e" flashcards.
- Begin by showing the picture side of the flashcards. Ask children to sing them.
- Show the picture side of the flashcards again and ask them to silently do the actions.
- Show them the grapheme side of the flashcards and discuss which letters make up the different "e" graphemes.

Time to practise

- Ask the children to work with their chatting chums.
- Give each pair an "e" picture card or green word.
- Ask them to discuss which /ee/ sound it contains.
- Sing part of the song and ask the pairs who have a picture or a word with that sound in to stand up.
- Repeat several times, varying the game by sometimes just doing the actions and asking the children to stand up. Get quicker and quicker.
- Display the "e" pictures all over the board and give each chatting chum pair a mini whiteboard and pen.
- Give children a series of writing challenges, for example:
  - Who can write all the /ee/ words the quickest? Or the /ea/ words? Or the /e-e/ words?
  - Write one of each.
  - How many can you write in a minute? 30 seconds? Before the whistle sounds?
  - How quickly can you write them all?

Revision

Display a selection of green words on the board. Give children one minute to read as many words as they can with their chatting chums. Go through each word slowly and then ask them to read the words at speed as you point to them.

Target graphemes: /igh/, /ie/, /i-e/

Learning objective

to revisit the /igh/, /ie/, /i-e/ graphemes

Starter

- Explain that today children are going to practise the graphemes "igh", "ie" and "i-e".

Resources

- The Song of Sounds song IWB version
- Song of Sounds flashcards: igh, ie, i-e
- Song of Sounds picture cards: fight, light, night, pie, tie, lie, kite, dive, five
- Song of Sounds green word cards: might, fright, untie, cries, like, smile
- A mini whiteboard and pen for each chatting chum pair

Main lesson

Time to learn

- Use the "igh", "ie" and "i-e" flashcards.
- Begin by showing the picture side of the flashcards. Ask the children to sing them.
- Show the picture side of the flashcards again and ask them to do the actions silently.
- Show the grapheme side of the flashcards and discuss which letters make up the different "i" graphemes.

Time to practise

- Ask the children to work with their chatting chums.
- Give each pair a picture card or a green word.
- Ask them to discuss which sound it contains.
- Sing part of the song and ask the pairs who have a picture or a word with that sound to stand up.
- Repeat several times, varying the game by sometimes just doing the actions and asking children to stand up. Get quicker and quicker.
- Display the "i" pictures all over the board and give each chatting chum pair a mini whiteboard and pen.
- Give children a series of writing challenges, for example:
  - Who can write all the /igh/ words quickest? Or the /ie/ words? Or the /i-e/ words?
  - Write one of each.
  - How many can you write in a minute? 30 seconds? Before the whistle sounds?
  - How quickly can you write them all?

Revision

Display the Song of Sounds green words on the board. Give children one minute to read as many words as they can with their chatting chums. Go through each word slowly and then ask them to read the words at speed as you point to them.

Target graphemes: /ow/, /oa/, /o-e/

Learning objective

to revisit the /ow/, /oa/, /o-e/ graphemes

Starter

- Explain that today children are going to practise the different graphemes "ow", "oa" and "o-e".

> ### Resources
>
> - The Song of Sounds song IWB version
> - Song of Sounds flashcards: ow, oa, o-e
> - Song of Sounds picture cards: snow, mow, row, goat, boat, moat, bone, phone, throne
> - Song of Sounds green word cards: show, throw, float, toast, home, joke
> - A mini whiteboard and pen for each chatting chum pair

Main lesson

Time to Learn

- Use the "ow", "oa" and "o-e" flashcards.
- Begin by showing the picture side of the flashcards. Ask children to sing them.
- Show the picture side of the flashcards again and ask them to do the actions silently.
- Show the grapheme side of the flashcards and discuss which letters make up the different "o" graphemes.

Time to practise

- Ask the children to work with their chatting chums.
- Give each pair a picture card or a green word.
- Ask them to discuss which "o" grapheme it contains.
- Sing part of the song out loud and ask the pairs who have a picture or a word with that sound in to stand up.
- Repeat several times, varying the game by sometimes just doing the actions and asking different children to stand up. Get quicker and quicker.
- Display the "o" pictures all over the board and give each chatting chum pair a mini whiteboard and pen.
- Give children a series of writing challenges, for example:
  - Who can write all the /ow/ words quickest? Or the /oa/ words? Or the /o-e/ words?
  - Can you write one of each?
  - How many can you write in a minute? 30 seconds? Before the whistle sounds?
  - How quickly can you write them all?

Revision

Finally, display the selection of green words on the board. Give children one minute to read as many words as they can with their chatting chums. Go through each word slowly and then ask them to read the words at speed as you point to them.

Felicity's problem

Learning objective

to understand vowels and consonants and their importance

Resources

Carpet session

- Week 9: Teach software
- Printed labels (Week 9: AS1)
- Enough letters of the alphabet for each child in your class
- A mini whiteboard and pen for each chatting chum pair
- Three different-coloured pens for each child
- A box addressed to the children (optional: covered in wrapping paper)
- A letter from Felicity to go inside the parcel (optional: fancy envelope)
- Two hoops (optional)

Sieve the sand

- Labelled hoops or labels from the carpet session (Week 9: AS1)
- Sandpit

- Plastic letters (as many as possible)
- Sieves

Snip and stick

- A piece of A4 coloured paper for each child in the group
- Assortment of magazines and newspapers
- Scissors
- Glue

Roll and mould

- A dice with the word vowel on three sides and consonant on the other three sides (Week 9: AS2)
- Modelling clay

Revision

- Plastic letters
- A box
- A ball
- Music (optional)

Carpet session

- Sit children with their chatting chums.
- Explain to that you have received a parcel, and open it with them.

1. • The letter tells children that everybody in the letter kingdom is arguing about vowels and consonants and which are more important. Felicity has sent a package to help the children to understand that they are equally important. Her letter explains that today the children are going to learn all about vowels and consonants and why they are both needed in Letter Kingdom, where Felicity lives.

> **Software**
> Teach
> **W9**

2. • The screen says "Let's play a game". In the parcel, Felicity has sent a selection of letters, the 26 letters of the alphabet (duplicate four consonants if you have a class of 30). Sit the children in a circle and give each child a letter. Place two hoops in the middle of the circle and label each hoop "vowel" or "consonant". Alternatively, place the labels a sufficient distance apart so that children can pile their letters together instead of using hoops. On a given signal, ask them to take it in turns to put their letters in the correct hoop. Discuss with children what they notice. Explain that "a", "e", "i", "o" and "u" are vowels and every other letter is a consonant.

3. • Using the software, play "I spy a vowel". Letters will appear on the screen. Children should identify which letters are the vowels and when they spot one they must shout "VOWEL". Repeat for the consonants.

4–7

- Play "Under and over". Give each chatting chum pair a mini whiteboard and three different-colour pens. A word will appear on the board. As a class read the word. Ask children to identify which letters are vowels and which are consonants. Using their whiteboards, ask the pairs to copy the word onto their board, then underline the vowels in one colour and place a small dash over the consonants in the other colour. Press to reveal which letters are which. If children identify "y" as a vowel, tell them that y is a special letter which sometimes works as a consonant (in my, for instance) and sometimes as a vowel.

8

- Invite the children to do some practical activities to practise recognising vowels and consonants.

Practical activities

Sieve the sand

A game for a small group of 5–6 children

Aim: to identify whether letters are vowels or consonants

How to play:
- Gather the resources.
- Hide the plastic letters in the sandpit.
- Put the two labelled hoops next to the sandpit, or two labels spaced apart.
- Invite children, one at a time, to sieve in the sand to try to find as many letters as possible.
- Children should decide whether their letters are vowels or consonants and put them in the correct hoop or pile. Discuss any misconceptions.

> **Support**
> Provide a board with a list of vowels and consonants so less-able children may check their choices.

> **Challenge**
> More-able children could try to create a word from the letters they have sieved from the sandpit.

Snip and stick

A game for a small group of 6–10 children

Aim: to create a vowel or consonant collage, reinforcing which letters are vowels and which are consonants

How to play:
- Gather the resources.
- Give each child a piece of A4 coloured paper.
- Ask children if they would like to make a consonant or a vowel collage picture.
- They should search through magazines and newspapers to find consonants or vowels, cut the letters out and stick them on their piece of paper to create either a vowel collage or a consonant collage.

Roll and mould

An activity for a small group of 5–10 children

Aim: to identify whether letters are vowels or consonants

How to play:
- Gather the resources.
- Give each child a ball of modelling clay.
- Ask children to take it in turns to roll the dice.
- If the dice lands on the word "consonant", each child must make a consonant letter using modelling clay. If it lands on the word "vowel", they should make a vowel letter.
- Once children have made their letters, ask them to practise tracing the letter with their finger over the top.
- Repeat many times.

> **Support**
> Before you begin this activity, work collaboratively with the group to write the alphabet on a whiteboard. Ask the group to help you to identify the vowels and circle them. Ensure this alphabet is visible to the children while they are working.

> **Challenge**
> Ask the children to work independently to identify vowels and consonants.

Revision

Play "Vowel or consonant". Ask children to stand in a circle. Put a selection of letters in a box and put it in the middle of the circle. Play some music (optional) and pass a ball around the ring. When the music stops, the child holding the object should pick a letter from the box and identify whether it is a vowel or a consonant.

Now read...

Choose a mix of Collins Big Cat Phonics readers that contain both short and long vowels. Read through a few readers with children, asking them to point out consonants and long and short vowels, and to discuss the relationship between the two.

Target graphemes: /oo/, /ew/, /u-e/

Learning objective

to revisit the "oo", "ew" and "u-e" graphemes

Starter

- Explain that today children are going to practise the /oo/ phoneme and the different graphemes "oo", "ew" and "u-e".

Resources

- The Song of Sounds song IWB version
- Song of Sounds flashcards: oo, ew, u-e
- Song of Sounds picture cards: moon, zoo, spoon, jewels, screw, chew, cube, flute, tube
- Song of Sounds green word cards: food, tooth, new, few, tune, rude

Main lesson

Time to learn

- Use the "oo", "ew", "u-e" flashcards.
- Begin by showing the picture side of the flashcards. Ask children to sing them.
- Show the picture side of the flashcards again and ask them to do the actions silently.
- Show them the grapheme side of the flashcards and discuss which letters make up the different "u" graphemes.

Time to practise

- Ask children to work with their chatting chums.
- Give each pair an "oo", "ew", "u-e" picture card or green word.
- Ask them to discuss which /oo/ sound it contains.
- Sing part of the song and ask the pairs who have a picture or a word with that sound in to stand up.
- Repeat several times, varying the game by sometimes just doing the actions and asking the children to stand up. Get quicker and quicker.
- Stick the "oo", "ew", "u-e" pictures all over the board and give each chatting chum pair a mini whiteboard and pen.
- Give children a series of writing challenges, for example:
  - Who can write all the /oo/ words quickest? Or the /ew/ words? Or the /u-e/ words?
  - Can you write one of each?
  - How many can you write in a minute? 30 seconds? Before the whistle sounds?
  - How quickly can you write them all?

Revision

Finally stick the selection of green words on the board. Give children one minute to read as many words as they can with their chatting chums. Go through each word slowly and then ask them to read the words at speed as you point to them.

Target skill: revise all graphemes learned so far

Learning objective

to use all graphemes with increased confidence

Resources

- Song of Sounds IWB version
- Song of Sounds flashcards you have taught so far
- Song of Sounds CD
- Whiteboards and pens for each chatting chum pair

Starter

- Gather the children on the carpet.
- Sing the Song of Sounds using the IWB version.

Main lesson

Time to learn

- Explain that today children are going to practise all the sounds they have learned so far in Year 1.
- Show the class the flashcards one at a time, picture-side up, and ask them to sing each sound.
- Ask them to do the actions to the song silently as you show the flashcards.
- As you produce the grapheme side, can they say the different sounds? Ask the class to say them in unison as you get faster and faster.

Time to practise

- Play "Sound circle". Ask children to sit in a circle. From your flashcard pack, choose the "ay", "ee", "igh", "ow", and "oo" flashcards. Give these out randomly to different children around the circle. Play the Song of Sounds CD. As the music plays, children should pass the flashcards round the circle. When the music stops, the children who have the flashcards should stand up and sing the part of the song on their cards, do the corresponding action or say the sound. Repeat a few times. Then replace the flashcards with "ai", "ea", "ie", "oa" and "ew" flashcards and repeat a few times. Finally, repeat with the "a-e", "e-e", "i-e", "o-e", "u-e" flashcards.
- Play "Phoneme families". Choose 15 children to stand in the centre of the circle and give them each a flashcard. They should move around the circle showing the other children their flashcards and saying their phonemes over and over again, for example, /ay/ /ay/ /ay/. When they find someone making the same sound as them, for example, someone with the grapheme /ai/ or /a-e/, they should hold hands. When they have found both of their matching sounds they should sit down as a group. At the end of the game, call out a sound, for example /e/, and the group that has that sound should all jump up. Those in the circle should then go and swap their flashcards with the other children in the circle and play again.
- At the end of the session, stick the flashcards on the board in their groups, for example, "igh", "ie" and "i-e". As you point to each group, the children should say that sound out loud.

Revision

Use your Song of Sounds flashcards throughout the day to reinforce all phonemes.

Target skill: revise all graphemes learned so far

Learning objective

to use all graphemes with increased confidence

Starter

- Gather the children on the carpet.
- Sing the Song of Sounds using the IWB version.

Resources

- Song of Sounds IWB version
- Song of Sounds flashcards you have taught so far
- Song of Sounds picture cards related to short vowels a, e, i, o, u
- Song of Sounds audio CD
- A mini whiteboard and pen for each chatting chum pair
- 5 hoops

Main lesson

Time to learn

- Explain that today children are going to practise all the sounds they have learned so far from the new song.
- Show the class the flashcards one at a time, picture-side up, and ask them to sing each sound.
- Ask the class to silently do the actions to the song as you show them the flashcards.
- As you produce the grapheme side, let them say the different sounds. Ask the class to say them in unison as you get faster and faster.

Time to practise

- Play "Sort the sounds". Ask the class to sit in a circle. In the middle of the circle, place five hoops. In the first hoop put the "a" flashcards, grapheme-side up; in the second hoop put the "e" flashcards grapheme side up and so on. Give each child in the class a picture card for one of the sounds. They should take it in turns to come into the middle of the circle and put their picture cards in the correct hoop. Discuss any misconceptions.
- Play "Phoneme friends". Give half the class a Song of Sounds flashcard and the other half a picture card. Play the Song of Sounds CD – children should move around the room silently showing each other their cards and look for the picture card or flashcard to match their own. When they have found their partner, they become "phoneme friends", and should sit down together. To check their answers, sing the song, and when they hear their part they should stand up and show the class their flashcard and matching picture card. Discuss any misconceptions.

Revision

Use your Song of Sounds flashcards throughout the day to reinforce all phonemes.

Target skill: revise all graphemes learned so far

Learning objective

to use all graphemes with increased confidence

Resources

- Song of Sounds flashcards taught so far
- Song of Sounds green words related to short vowels a, e, i, o, u
- Song of Sounds CD

Starter

- Gather the children on the carpet.
- Show the class the Song of Sounds flashcards one at a time, picture-side up, and ask them to sing each sound.
- Ask the class to do the actions to the song silently as you show them the flashcards.
- As you produce the grapheme side, can they say the different sounds? Ask the class to say them in unison as you get faster and faster.

Main lesson

Time to learn

- Sit children with their chatting chums.
- Explain that today you are going to practise reading some green words that include all the sounds they have learned so far from the new song.

- Stick ten green words on the board (all the words should have a different digraph). Give children three minutes to work with their chatting chums to read as many words as possible, using the sound buttons to help them.
- To check their reading, ask each chatting chum pair to read you a word.

Time to practise

- Play "Higher and lower". Arrange your ten green words in a long vertical line on the board. Choose a word, but don't tell the children what it is. Ask one child to guess the green word. If they get it wrong, you should put a cross next to their incorrect guess and then tell them whether your word is "higher" or "lower" than the one they have just guessed. Keep going until the word is guessed. The winner can come out to the front and this time *they* should choose the word, not you. For each new game, you can swap the green words so that you have new words for children to read. Read all the words together as a class first before beginning a new game.

Revision

Use your Song of Sounds flashcards throughout the day to reinforce all phonemes.

Long and short vowels

Learning objective

to understand the difference between long and short vowel phonemes

Resources

Carpet session

- Week 10: Teach software
- Flags (Week 10: AS1)
- Train conductor costume (optional)

All aboard

- A selection of long and short vowel pictures (Week 10: AS2-6)
- One chair per child, in a circle

The vowel train

- A train playing board for each child (Week 10: AS7-8)

- A selection of long and short vowel pictures (Week 10: AS2-6)
- A feely bag or box

Train track handwriting

- A train track handwriting cards (Week 10: AS9), one for each child
- Long vowel flashcards: ay, ai, a-e, ee, ea, e-e, igh, ie, i-e, ow, oa, o-e, oo, ew, u-e
- A pen or pencil for each child

Revision

- A selection of long and short vowel pictures (Week 10: AS2-6)

Carpet session

- This session has the option of teaching in role as a train conductor. For this, you might wear a blue suit and a cap with a train logo on. Alternatively, use the software and meet a virtual train conductor.

> **Software**
> Teach
> **W10**

- Depending on the option you have chosen, enter the classroom in your costume or press play on the software.
- Explain that you have heard that the children have been busy learning all about vowels. Ask the class to name the vowels.
- [1] Explain that you are train conductor for a train called "The vowel express".
- [2] Explain that there are two different carriages on the train because there are two different kinds of vowels. Explain that one carriage is called the long vowel carriage and the other carriage is called the short vowel carriage.
- [3] Using the software, show the children examples of the short vowels: /a/, /e/, /i/, /o/, /u/ and give examples of words with short vowels in, for example: cat, pen, fish, dog, sun. Show that they belong in the short vowel carriage.
- [4] Then show the children how the long vowels belong in the long vowel carriage, and give examples of words with long vowels, for examplke, spoon, beans and, of course, train.
- Explain to children it is very important that people know what a long vowel is and what a short vowel is, so that the sounds get into the correct carriage.
- Give each chatting chum pair a long vowel flag and a short vowel flag.
- [5] Play "Flag fun". Use the software to show some graphemes and ask the children to wave the correct flag. Press the grapheme to reveal the answer as it flies into the right carriage.
- Repeat the game, but this time just say the phonemes so children have to listen for the vowel.
- [6] Finally, a selection of pictures appears on the screen. Children should take turns to wave the flag according to whether it is a long vowel or short vowel.
- [7] The presentation finishes by inviting children to play some games to practise recognising long and short vowels.

Practical activities

All aboard

A game for a large group of 10+ children

Aim: to discriminate between long and short vowels

How to play:
- Gather the resources.
- This game should be played in a large space.
- Sit the children on chairs in a circle.
- Give each child a card with a long vowel or short vowel picture.
- Ask one child to stand in the middle of the circle without a card.
- Call out either "long vowel" or "short vowel" or a phoneme, for example, /a/, /e/, /f/.
- Those children whose cards correspond with what you have called out should jump up and swap chairs with someone else. The person in the middle should run to get a seat. Whoever is left without a seat remains in the middle for the next turn. If you say "all aboard" *everyone* should swap places.
- After each turn, ask children to swap cards with the person next to them.

The vowel train

A game for a small group of 5–6 children

Aim: to discriminate between long and short vowels

How to play:
- Gather the resources.
- Print out your playing boards and give one to each child.
- Put the picture cards in a feely bag or box.
- Children should take turns to pick a picture and cover the corresponding carriage with the picture. For example, if they pick "dog" they should cover the "o" short vowel grapheme.
- If they haven't got that grapheme on their board, they should give the picture to someone else in the group who does.
- The first to cover all the carriages on their train is the winner.

Train track handwriting

A game for a small group of 6–8 children

Aim: to practise the correct formation of long vowel graphemes

How to play:
- Gather the resources.
- Hold up a long vowel flashcard and sing the song, do the actions and/or say the sound with children.
- Model writing the grapheme using a cursive style.
- Children should then practise their cursive handwriting along the train track card.
- Repeat for further long vowels.

Revision

Gather children on the carpet to play "Voice your vowels". Show the children a long or short vowel picture and ask them to identify whether it has a short or long vowel in it. They should respond by saying "short" or "long". Progress to asking the children to call out the correct phoneme, for example, /a/ or /ee/.

Now read...

Choose a mix of Collins Big Cat Phonics readers that contain both short and long vowels. Read through a few readers with children, asking them to point out long and short vowels and consonants, and to discuss the relationship between them.

Target skill: revise all long vowel digraphs

Learning objective

to use long vowels with increased confidence

Resources

- Song of Sounds flashcards
- Song of Sounds IWB version
- A mini whiteboard and pen for each chatting chum pair

Starter

- Gather the children on the carpet.
- Sing the Song of Sounds using the IWB version.

Main lesson

Time to learn

- Explain that today the children are going to practise all the sounds they have learned so far from the new song.
- Show the class the flashcards one at a time, picture-side up and ask them to sing each sound.
- Ask them to do the actions to the song silently as you show them the flashcards.
- As you produce the grapheme side, can they say the different sounds? Ask the class to say them in unison as you get faster and faster.

Time to practise

- Play "Sound circle". Ask the class to sit in a circle. Give out all 15 long vowel flashcards to random children around the circle. Play the Song of Sounds CD. Children should pass the flashcards around the circle to the music. When the music stops, call out a long vowel, for example, /ay/. Those holding the three flashcards that make that sound should stand up and, in turn, sing the part of the song they are holding. The whole class should join in with the chorus: "Skip to my lou my darling". Repeat lots of times, ensuring that all the long vowels have been covered.

- Move out of the circle. Collect the flashcards and stick them on the board in their groups, for example, "igh", "ie" and "i-e". As you point to each group, children should say that sound out loud.

- Give each chatting chum pair a mini whiteboard and a pen. This time call out a long vowel, for example, /ow/. Ask each chatting chum pair to write on their whiteboard the three ways for writing that long vowel sound – /ow/, /oa/ and /o-e/ – and hold it up.

Support

To support less-able children, leave the flashcards on the board for them to refer to.

Challenge

Challenge more-able children to write them without looking.

Target skill: Revise all long vowel digraphs

Learning objective

to use long vowels with increased confidence

Resources

- Song of Sounds IWB version
- Song of Sounds flashcards
- Song of Sounds picture cards related to long vowels
- A mini whiteboard and pen for each chatting chum pair

Starter

- Gather the children on the carpet.
- Sing the Song of Sounds using the IWB version.

Main lesson

Time to learn

- Explain that today children are going to practise all the sounds they have learned so far from the new song.
- Show the class the flashcards one at a time, picture-side up and ask them to sing each sound.
- Ask them to do the actions to the song silently as you show them the flashcards.
- As you produce the grapheme side, let them say the different sounds. Ask them to say the sounds in unison as you get faster and faster.

Time to practise

- Sit the children with their chatting chums.
- Prior to the lesson, stick around the classroom picture cards related to the long vowels, one per child.
- Give every chatting chum pair a whiteboard and pen.
- Ask one of the chatting chums to go for a walk around the classroom and find a picture card. They should bring it back to their partner and together they should write the word on their whiteboard. Then they should swap over and the second chatting chum should go and find a picture card and they should write that too.
- Go to each chatting chum pair and ask them to show you and read to you the words they have written.
- Collect up the picture cards and muddle them all up and stick them all over the board.
- Give the class a series of challenges – can they write an /ay/ word? An /ee/ word? An /igh/ word? Can they write three /ow/ words using the three different graphemes for /ow/? How many words can they write in a minute? Ensure that both chatting chums have a go at writing.

Target skill: Revise all long vowel digraphs

Learning objective

to use long vowels with increased confidence

Resources

- Song of Sounds flashcards
- Song of Sounds green words related to a, e, i
- Song of Sounds audio CD

Starter

- Gather the children on the carpet.
- Show the class the Song of Sounds flashcards one at a time, picture-side up and ask them to sing each sound.
- Ask them to silently do the actions to the song as you show them the flashcards.
- As you produce the grapheme side, can they say the different sounds? Ask the class to say them in unison as you get faster and faster.

Main lesson

Time to learn

- Sit the children with their chatting chums.
- Explain that today children are going to practise reading some green words that include all the long vowels they have been learning about.
- Display 10 green words on the board (all with a different long vowel digraph). Give children three minutes to work with their chatting chums to read as many words as possible, using the sound buttons to help them.
- To check their reading, ask each chatting chum pair to read you a word. Discuss which long vowel is in each word.

Time to practise

- Play "Conductor of the orchestra". Explain to the class that they are about to become an orchestra. Explain what an orchestra is. Display a green word, which the class will read in unison over and over again until the you display a new green word. Explain that someone in the class will be the "conductor". The conductor of the orchestra will tell you when to show a new word by winking (or blinking). Every time the conductor winks, you must show a new green card for the class to read. Explain that the fun part of this game is that you are going to choose a detective. The detective must try to guess who the conductor is by catching them out.
- Choose one child to be the "detective" and send them out of the room while you choose a conductor. Once everyone is ready, invite the detective back in. They should stand at the front of the class and, while you read the green words, try and guess who is conducting the orchestra by winking at the teacher.
- If they guess correctly, the conductor becomes the detective. If they don't guess correctly, they have to be the detective again.
- Every time you start a new game, choose ten new green words. Read them together as a class before you start the game so that everyone knows what they say.

Target skill: revise all long vowel digraphs

Learning objective

to use long vowels with increased confidence

Starter

- Gather the children on the carpet.
- Show the class the Song of Sounds flashcards one at a time, picture-side up and ask them to sing each sound.
- Ask them to silently do the actions to the song as you show them the flashcards.
- As you produce the grapheme side, can they say the different sounds? Ask the class to say them in unison as you get faster and faster.

Resources

- Song of Sounds flashcards
- Song of Sounds green sentences related to long vowels. Stay and play a game in the rain. It is a complete treat for Pete to eat sweets. I like to lie in bed at night. It is slow to row the boat home. I will soon play a tune with my flute.
- A mini whiteboard and pen for each chatting chum pair

Main lesson

Time to learn

- Sit the children with their chatting chums.
- Explain that today children are going to practise reading some green sentences that include all the long vowels they have been learning about.
- Stick five green sentences on the board. Give children three minutes to work with their chatting chums to see if they can read the sentences, using the sound buttons to help them.
- Read the sentences together as a class.
- Ask them to identify anything in the sentences they found tricky and discuss.

Time to practise

- Leave the sentences on the board. Give each chatting chum pair a whiteboard and pen.
- Give the children a series of challenges, for example:
  - In this sentence can you find one of Tricky Trevor's words and write it on your whiteboard?
  - In this sentence can you write down a word that has a short vowel?
  - In this sentence can you write down a word that has a long vowel?
  - In this sentence can you find three words with different long vowels?
  - Can you write a word that rhymes with row?
- Finish the session by asking children to read the sentences backwards with their chatting chums. As you point to the words out of order, can they read them?

Long vowel revision

Learning objective

to understand the difference between long and short vowel phonemes

Resources

Carpet session

- Week 11: Teach software
- A mini whiteboard and pen for each child
- Train conductor costume (optional)

The long vowel carriage

- Song of Sounds flashcards: long vowels: ay, ai, a-e, ee, ea, e-e, igh, ie, i-e, ow, oa, o-e, oo, ew, u-e
- Song of Sounds CD or other music
- One chair per child

The vowel express

- Song of Sounds phoneme finders

- Picture cards of long-vowel words (reuse from last week's lesson) (Week 10: AS2)
- A train-shaped zig zag book with five pages (optional), or an exercise book for each child
- Pencils

Train track handwriting

- A train track handwriting card (Week 10: AS4) for each child
- Song of Sounds flashcards: long vowels: ay, ai, a-e, ee, ea, e-e, igh, ie, i-e, ow, oa, o-e, oo, ew, u-e
- A pen or pencil for each child

Revision

- Song of Sounds flashcards: long vowels

Carpet session

- Sit the children in their chatting chum pairs.
- This lesson has the option of teaching in role as a train conductor. You could wear a blue suit and cap. Alternatively, use the software and meet a virtual train conductor.
- Depending on the option you have chosen, enter the classroom as a train conductor or press play on the software.

> **Software**
> Teach
> **W11**

1. Remind children that you are a train conductor for a train called "The vowel express" and that there are two different carriages on the train. Ask children if they can remember what the two carriages are for: short vowels and long vowels. Ask them to explain what short vowels and long vowels are and give you some examples.

2. Use the software to sort the graphemes into the short and long vowel carriages. Explain that short vowels are easy because there are only five of them, but the long vowels are more difficult because there are lots of them, so today you have come to help them practise their long vowels.

3. Remind children what the long vowels are and how they have learned three different graphemes for each long vowel sound, for example, /ay/, /ai/ and /a-e/.

4. Ask them to sing the corresponding parts of the song as the long vowel pictures appear.

5. Ask them to say the sounds as the long vowel graphemes appear.

6-10. Give each chatting chum pair a mini whiteboard and pen. A selection of three pictures will appear that contain the same long vowel. Children should work together to decide which long vowel it is and write it on their whiteboards. Ask them to hold their boards up to show you their answers. Repeat for four slides.

11. Revise the session's learning objective before you divide the children into their differentiated groups for the practical activities.

Practical activities

The long vowel carriage

A game for a large group of 10+ children

Aim: to practise reading long vowel graphemes

How to play:
- Gather the resources.
- This game is based on the traditional party game "Musical chairs" and should be played in a large space.
- Place a number of chairs in a line with their backs to each other. The number of chairs should be one fewer than the number of children playing. On each chair, put one of the long vowel flashcards.
- Have some music ready, perhaps the Song of Sounds song.
- Ask the players to stand in a circle around the chairs before the music begins. Once the music starts, they should move in a line around the chairs.
- Stop the music. All players must try to take the seat closest to them. The player left without a chair is eliminated and their chair is removed from the circle. Then ask every child to tell you which long vowel is on their seat, for example, /ai/. If they get it right, they are "in" but if they get it wrong, they are also eliminated and their chair is removed.
- Repeat until you have a winner.

> **Support**
> Less-able children could sing the correct part of the Song of Sounds song rather than read the grapheme.

> **Challenge**
> Ask more-able children to think of a word containing that grapheme.

The vowel express

An activity for a small group of 5–10 children

Aim: to practise segmenting words for writing and choosing the correct long vowel

How to play:
- Gather the resources.
- Give each child a train-shaped zigzag book and exercise book.
- There should be five pages in each book. At the top of each page ask children to write the three different graphemes they have learned for each long vowel sound: ay, ai, a-e, on page 1, ee, ea, e-e on page 2, etc.
- Scatter the picture cards on the table.
- Ask children to choose a picture card and write the word on the correct page in their book.

> **Support**
> Give less-able children a Song of Sounds phoneme finder to help them. Ask less-able children to choose a picture card together and sound the word out together.

> **Challenge**
> Ask more-able children to work independently without a Song of Sounds phoneme finder. They could also move on to putting the words into sentences in their books.

Train track handwriting

A game for a small group of 6–8 children

Aim: to practise correct formation of the long vowel graphemes

How to play:
- Gather the resources.
- Hold up a long vowel flashcard and sing the song, do the actions and/or say the sound with the children.
- Model writing the grapheme using a cursive style.
- Children should then practise their cursive handwriting along the train track card.
- Repeat for further long vowels.

Revision

 Gather the children back onto the carpet. Use your long vowel flashcards. Ask children to collectively call out the correct phoneme as you show the grapheme. Test how quickly they can call out the phonemes.

Now read...

Bot on the Moon, *Red B, Band 2B*

Goat's Coat, *Red B, Band 2B*

Feelings, *Red B, Band 2B*

I Found a Sound, *Red B, Band 2B*

Bart the Shark, *Yellow, Band 3*

Singing, *Yellow, Band 3*

Feeling Things, *Yellow, Band 3*

Your Nose, *Blue, Band 4*

Assessment week 2

Learning objective

to revise all phonemes learned so far

Resources

- The Song of Sounds IWB version
- Song of Sounds flashcards taught so far

Starter

- Gather the children on the carpet.
- Explain that this week they are going to practise *everything* they have learned so far so they can see how well they are doing.
- Using the IWB version of the Song of Sounds, sing the song all the way through with the class. They should perform all the actions they know.

Main lesson

- Play "Song tennis". Choose a chatting chum pair to stand at the front of the class. Pick one of the children to sing a phrase from the Song of Sounds, e.g. "busy busy bee ee ee ee" – their partner should listen and do the corresponding action. They should then swap over and keep going, singing different parts of the song and performing the different actions.
- Play "Sound tennis". Children should sit so they are facing their chatting chums. One child should say a sound, for example, /ay/, and then spell the grapheme they mean using letter names: "a", "y". Their chatting chums should then do exactly the same for a different sound, for example, /i-e/, "i split e". They should keep going backwards and forwards (like a game of tennis). until one of them falters. Then they should start again. Encourage children to look around the classroom at the Song of Sounds classroom frieze or poster for help.

Revision

Finish this session with some flashcard work. Show the class the flashcards one a time and ask them to do the actions silently. As you produce the grapheme side, can they say the different sounds?

Assessment week 2

Learning objective

to practise reading graphemes and blending to read words

Resources:

- Song of Sounds flashcards
- Eight Song of Sounds green words of your choice
- Three Song of Sounds green sentences of your choice
- A lolly stick for each child in the class with their name written on (optional)

Starter

- Remind children that this week they are practising everything they have learned so far so you can see how well they are doing with their phonics..
- Explain that today they are going to practise recognising letters and reading words.
- Use your flashcard pack to play "Speed sounds". Show the class the flashcards one at a time, grapheme-side up, getting faster and faster. As they see the grapheme they should say the sound.

Main lesson

- Sit the children with their chatting chums.
- Display approximately eight green words on the board. Give children two minutes to work with their chatting chums to blend the letters and read the words together.
- Pick a lolly stick out of a pot or bag. Read out the child's name. That child should stand up with their chatting chums and model to the class how to read the word. Discuss any errors. Repeat until all the words have been discussed.
- The whole class should then read the words together. Do this by asking them to say the sounds as you press the sound buttons, and then blend the sounds together as you sweep your hand underneath the word.

Revision

Finish this session by putting three green sentences on the board. Challenge chatting chums to work together to read the sentences. Ask a child to demonstrate reading a sentence, then ask the whole to class read it. Repeat for each sentence.

Assessment week 2

Learning objective

to practise writing individual graphemes

Starter

- Gather children on the carpet.
- Remind them that this week they are practising *everything* they have learned so far so you can see how well they are doing with their phonics.
- Explain that today they are going to practise writing the letters you have been learning about.
- Use your flashcard pack to play "Speed sounds". Show the flashcards one at a time, grapheme-side up, getting faster and faster. As children see the grapheme they should say the sound.

Resources:
- Flashcards of the sounds taught so far
- Mini whiteboards and pens
- Song of Sounds phoneme finders

Main lesson

- Sit the children with their chatting chums and give each pair a mini whiteboard and pen.
- Reveal one of your flashcards picture-side up, and ask children to sing the corresponding part of the song and write the correct grapheme on their whiteboards. Repeat multiple times.
- Finally, challenge children to listen to word as you say them and write the initial sound that they can hear. For example, if you say "sun" they should write an "s". Ensure that you emphasise the initial sound so they can hear it.
- Finally, challenge them to listen to words as you say them and write the long vowel sound that they can hear. For example, if you say they "rain" should write an "ai". Ensure that you emphasise the long vowel sound so they can hear it.

Support
Give less-able children a Song of Sounds phoneme finder so they can find the correct letter and copy it.

Challenge
Encourage more-able children to write the whole word.

Revision

Choose a selection of Collins Big Cat Phonics readers to work through with the class based on the results of this week's assessment.

Assessment week 2

Learning objective

to segment words into phonemes

Starter

- Gather the children on the carpet.
- Remind them that this week they are practising everything they have learned so far so you can see how well they are doing with their phonics.

Main lesson

- Explain that today they are going to practise counting the phonemes in words by playing a game called "Phoneme fingers".
- Use words of one syllable that are phonetically regular and include only the sounds children have learned so far, such as train, hay, moon, throw. Call out a word. They must quietly count the phonemes in the words: /t/-/r/-/ay/-/n/: four. They should then put the corresponding number of fingers up on their hand but keep their answers hidden from the other children, and you. At the same time, get your fingers ready but also hidden so the children cannot see them.
- Then say "Ready, steady, phoneme fingers" and both you and the children should reveal fingers to show the answer.
- You should then count the phonemes in the word together by counting on your fingers, for example, /th/-/r/-/ow/: three. Now the children know their letter names, it is good practice to use these to explain the grapheme, for example, by asking which /ow/ it is ("o, w" using letter names).
- This activity is perfect for assessment because you can instantly scan the class to see who is repeatedly correct or making mistakes.
- Repeat lots of times.

Revision

Explain to children that if they can play "Phoneme fingers" they can write because when you write you just listen to a word, count the phonemes and write the correct letters. Model this with two final words by writing the words on the board as you count out the phonemes.

Assessment week 2

Learning objective

to assess each child's phonic ability on a one to one basis

Resources

Carpet session

- Week 12: Teach software
- An assessment sheet for each child (on the Resource CD)
- A letter from Felicity to go inside the parcel
- A box addressed to the children (optional: covered in pink paper)

Assessment

- An assessment sheet for each child (on the Resource CD)

Star sprint

- Song of Sounds phoneme finders (optional)
- Song of Sounds phoneme stars of phonemes taught so far

- Song of Sounds picture cards that relate to previously-taught graphemes (optional)
- A grapheme to match each phoneme star (magnetic, foam, carpet etc.)
- A whistle or bell (optional)
- Mini whiteboards and pens (optional)

Blending bags

- Picture cards (to be stuck on zip bags) (Week 12: AS1)
- Fifteen zip bags
- Magnetic letters to go inside each bag to spell out the picture on the bag, e.g. s-n-ai-l.
- A mini whiteboard and pen for each child
- Dice (optional)

Revision

- Song of Sounds flashcards that you have already taught

Carpet session

- Gather the resources.
- Gather the children on the carpet.
- Explain that you have received a parcel from Felicity and open it with the children to find an envelope and the assessment sheets.
- The letter asks children how they are getting on with their phonemes and says that Felicity has sent a special test for them to do with their teacher. It instructs the teacher to look at the screen.

[1] • Work through the slides to check that the children can:

[2]   • sing their sounds – pictures from the Song of Sounds flash up for children to sing

[3]   • say their sounds – graphemes flash up for the children to say

[4-8]   • read words – words appear for the children to read

[9-11]   • write words – pictures appear on the screen for the children to write.

[12] • Invite children to play some games to practise using all their sounds.

Software
Teach
W12

Practical activities

Assessment

An assessment activity for the teacher or teaching assistant to do individually with the children.

Aim: to assess individual children's progress so far

How to do:
- This assessment should take about five minutes per child.
- Sit somewhere quiet with each child so it is easy to concentrate and hear them.
- Follow the instructions on the assessment sheet, always ensuring that you are positive and encouraging. You could offer children an optional reward after the assessment.
- Check all children's knowledge of graphemes on the assessment sheet.
- Check whether children can blend their sounds for reading and segment them for writing.
- You may find that less-able children are unable to blend their sounds for reading or attempting to write words. Ask them to try in case they surprise you – don't worry if they struggle, just move on.

Star sprint

A game for a small group of 6–10 children

Aim: to identify the correct grapheme-phoneme correspondences

How to play:
- Play this game in the hall or a large indoor or outdoor space.
- Pin the phoneme stars up all around the space.
- Scatter the graphemes all over the floor.
- On a given signal (e.g. whistle or bell) children should run to a grapheme, pick it up and sprint to the correct star, for example if they pick up an /a-e/ they should sprint to "bake a cake a-e a-e a-e". You should then check they have run to the correct star and discuss any errors.

Blending bags

An activity for a small group of 5–10 children

Aim: to segment words into the correct phonemes and order the graphemes accordingly to match the word

How to play:
- Gather the resources.
- Attach the pictures to the front of the zip bags.
- Scatter the zip bags on a table and give each child a mini whiteboard and pen.
- Children should pick a zip bag, unzip it and take out the letters to see if they can make the picture word on the front with the magnetic letters.
- They should then write this word on their whiteboards.
- Repeat until they have completed all the bags.

Support
Less-able pupils can use a Song of Sounds phoneme finder to help them.

Challenge
Scatter the selection of Song of Sounds picture cards on the floor, grapheme-side up. On a given signal the children should run to a grapheme, pick it up, run to the corresponding star and write the picture word on the whiteboard.

Support
Ask less-able pupils to find the initial letter of their picture and give them a Song of Sounds phoneme finder to help them.

Challenge
More-able pupils could roll a dice and write their word that number of times or put the word in a sentence.

Revision

 Play "Knock down". Stand the children up a in group (six to eight) at a time. Using the Song of Sounds flashcards, show children a grapheme. The first child to say the sound remains in the game, the other children should sit down. Repeat with each group until you have a winner from each. Repeat with the winning children and carry on playing until you have an overall winner.

Now read...

Choose a selection of Collins Big Cat Phonics readers to work through with the class based on the results of this week's assesment.

Target tricky words: "oh", "again"

Learning objective

to practise reading and spelling tricky words

Resources

- Song of Sounds tricky word cards: oh, again

Starter

Introducing "oh" and "again"

- Gather the children on the carpet.
- Explain that today they are going to learn two new tricky words.
- Ask them if they can remember what makes some words trickier than others (they don't follow Felicity's phoneme rules).
- Hold up the "oh" and "again" flashcards – ask children why these words are red and spiky. Remind them that they are red because, like a red traffic light, red means stop. Because they are tricky words, you need to stop and think about them.

Main lesson

Read "oh" and "again"

- Show children the tricky word "oh" and read it to them.
- Give a few examples of when "oh" might be used in sentences, such as "Oh no", "Oh that"s fantastic news".
- Display the word "oh". Tell children that it sounds like the /ow/ long vowel sound that they have been learning about. Explain that you see it often in reading books when characters are surprised and it often has an exclamation mark after it. In this word the "o" and the "h" do not make their usual sounds but together they make /ow/. Practise saying it with the children in a suprised voice.
- Display the word "again" and tell them that this is another long vowel word that does not follow Felicity's phoneme rules. Explain that the "a" is not tricky because it follows Felicity's phoneme rules but the /ai/ is tricky because it does not sound like "train in the rain ai ai ai" but more like "elephants enormous e e e". The "g" and the "n" are not tricky because they make the correct sound. To remember this word, they must remember the tricky /ai/.

Write "oh" and "again"

- Show children how to write the word "oh" on the board. As you write the grapheme, say: "o-h makes /ow/". Practise saying it again with a surprised voice.
- Show them how to write the word "again" the board. As you write each grapheme say the phoneme: /a/-/g/-/ai/-/n/.

Revision

Tell children that you will keep testing them to see if they can remember the words because they are so tricky. Throughout the day keep producing the "oh" and "again" flashcards and asking children to read them on sight. Repeat continually throughout the day.

Target tricky words: "one", "once"

Learning objective

to practise reading and spelling tricky words

Resources

- Song of Sounds tricky word cards: one, once
- Previously-taught Song of Sounds tricky word cards: oh, again

Starter

Introducing "one" and "once"

- Gather the children on the carpet.
- Explain that today they are going to a learn two new words.
- Ask them if they can remember what makes some words trickier than others (they don't follow Felicity's phoneme rules).
- Hold up the "one" and "once" flashcards – remind children that they are red because, like a red traffic light, red means stop. Because they are tricky words, you need to stop and think about them.

Main lesson

Read "one" and "once"

- Show children the tricky word "one" and read it to them.
- Give a few examples of when "one" might be used in sentences, such as "One, two, three, four..." and "One day the princess met a dragon."
- Display the word "one". Explain that the "o" in "one" is the really tricky bit as it does not make its "octopus is orange o o o" sound but instead it makes a /w/ sound like "whales in the water w w w" followed by "umbrellas up u u u". You can hear the /n/ in the word but it also has an "e" on the end which you cannot hear. The tricky bit of "one" is that you have to remember that the "o" makes a /w/ sound and also remember the "e" on the end.
- Show the word "once". Give a few examples of when "once" might be used in sentences, for example "Once upon a time there lived a clever princess," and "Once you have tidied up, you can go out to play." Explain that "once" is tricky in the same ways as "one" but it is even harder, as it has an extra tricky bit. Show the children the "c" in once and explain that it does not make a /c/ sound but rather a /s/ sound.

Write "one" and "once"

- Show children how to write the word "one" on the board. As you write each grapheme, spell it out loud: o-n-e.
- Show them how to write the word "once" on the board. As you write each grapheme spell it out loud: o-n-c-e.

Revision

Add the "one" and "once" flashcards to those you taught yesterday. Throughout the day keep producing the flashcards and asking children to read them on sight. Repeat continually throughout the day.

Target tricky words: "there", "their"

Learning objective

to practise reading and spelling tricky words

Resources

- Song of Sounds tricky word cards: there, their
- Previously-taught Song of Sounds tricky word cards: oh, again, one, once

Starter

Introducing there and their

- Gather the children on the carpet.
- Explain that today they are going to a learn two new words.
- Ask children if they can remember what makes some words trickier than others (they don't follow Felicity's phoneme rules).
- Hold up the "there" and "their" flashcards – remind the children that they are red because, like a red traffic light, red means stop. Because they are tricky words, you need to stop and think about them.

Main lesson

Read "there" and "their"

- Show the children the tricky word "there" and read it to them.
- Give a few examples of when "there" might be used in sentences, for example "Your shoes are over there" and "There is my coat". Explain that /th/ is not tricky because it makes the /th/ sound and follows Felicity's phoneme rules. However "ere" is tricky as here it makes the /air/ sound in "a hairy fairy air air air". The tricky bit of "there" is that you have to remember that the "ere" at the end makes an /air/ sound.
- Display and read the word "their". Explain that this word sounds exactly the same, but it looks different and it has a different meaning. Give a few examples of when "their" might be used in sentences, for example "It is their game" and "Their garden is huge". Explain that this "their" is tricky in the same way as the other "there" but in this word it is "eir" that makes the sound /air/.

Write "there" and "their"

- Show children how to write the word "there" on the board. As you write each grapheme, say it out loud: /th/-/air/. Draw sound buttons underneath to emphasis that the "ere" is all one sound.
- Repeat for "their".

Revision

Add the "there" and "their" flashcard to those you have already taught this week. Throughout the day keep producing the flashcards and asking children to read them on sight. Repeat continually throughout the day.

Target tricky words: "little", "ask"

Learning objective

to practise reading and spelling tricky words

Resources

- Song of Sounds tricky word Song of Sounds flashcards: little and ask
- Previously-taught Song of Sounds tricky word cards: oh, again, one, once, there, their

Starter

Introducing "little" and "ask"

- Gather the children on the carpet.
- Explain that today they are going to learn two new words.
- Ask them if they can remember what makes some words trickier than others: they don't follow Felicity's phoneme rules.
- Hold up the Song of Sounds tricky word cards "little" and "ask" and remind children that the cards are red to signal the need to stop and think.

Main lesson

Read "little" and "ask"

- Show children the tricky word "little" and read it to them.
- Give a few examples of when "little" might be used in sentences, such as "My little brother is three" and "I like it a little bit".
- Explain that the "l" is not tricky because it follows Felicity's phoneme rules. The "i" is not tricky" either and the "t" makes the right sound too, although we do need to remember it is a double "t". The "l" is not tricky but the tricky bit of the word is the "e" on the end of the word that doesn"t make a sound. To remember the word we must remember that the "t" sound is made by two "t"s and the silent "e" on the end.
- Display the word "ask" and read it to the children. Give a few examples of when "ask" might be used in sentences, for example, "Can I ask you to pass the peas?" and "Go and ask Daddy". Explain that the "a" is tricky as it should make the "ants on an apple a a a" sound but it makes the sound "go far in your car ar ar ar". However, this is the only tricky bit in the word because the "s" and the "k follow the phoneme rules and are not tricky.

Write "little" and "ask"

- Show children how to write the word "little" on the board. As you write each grapheme, say it out loud: l-i-tt-le. Whisper the silent "e" at the end and write the "e" very small.
- Show them how to write the word "ask" on the board. As you write each grapheme say it out loud: a-s-k.

Revision

Add the "little" and "ask" flashcards to those you have already taught this week. Throughout the day keep producing the flashcards and asking children to read them on sight. Repeat continually throughout the day.

Tricky words

Learning objective

to practise reading and spelling tricky words

Resources

Carpet session

- Week 13: Teach software
- Tricky word cards: oh, again, one, once, there, their, little, ask (Week 13: ASl)
- Song of Sounds green word cards
- A Tricky Trevor costume or toy
- Three coloured cards or a coloured fan (blue, purple, green) per child

Tricky treasure hunt

- Tricky word cards (Week 13: ASl)
- A bucket for each child
- A whistle (optional)

Tricky spell

- Tricky word cards (Week 13: ASl)

- A range of red and green mediums/ materials, e.g. red and green paper, red and green felt tips, red and green pastels, red and green crayons, red and green chalks, red and green glitter, etc.
- An exercise book for each child

Tricky time

- Tricky word cards (Week 13: ASl)
- A timer
- A mini whiteboard and pen for each child

Homework

- Homework sheet

Revision

- Tricky word cards (Week 13: ASl)

Carpet session

- Gather the resources.
- Sit the children with their chatting chums.
- This lesson has the option of teaching in role as "Tricky Trevor", a wise old man with grey hair, a briefcase or bag and a walking stick. If you do not wish to do this, you could use a Tricky Trevor teddy or receive a letter enclosing the tricky words from a professor.
- Depending on the option you have chosen, enter the classroom as Tricky Trevor or hold up your teddy or letter.
- Remind children that Trevor is an incredibly clever man and that is why he has come here today, to teach children some more tricky words.
- From your briefcase/bag produce a selection of green words and tricky words of your choice. Ask children what the differences between "green" words and "tricky" words are.
- Then from your briefcase/bag produce the tricky word cards that children are going to learn about today. Ask them again if they know why these words are red and spiky.
- Show children the tricky words and ask them to repeat the words after you. Ask them to whisper the words, shout the words, say the words and sing the words.

1-2
- Press play on the software. Reveal the words one at a time. Ask children to identify the green and tricky parts of each word and offer advice to help them remember each word.

3-10
- Play "Trevor's trick". Give each child cards of three different colours corresponding to the colours of the words on the software game. Show the three different versions of each word, only one of which is the correct spelling e.g. said, sed, seid. Children must work with their chatting chums to choose the correct spelling and reveal the card of that colour.

10
- Revise the session's learning objective before dividing children into their differentiated groups for the practical activities.

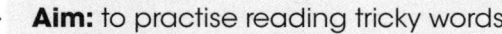

> **Software**
> Teach
> **W13**

Practical activities

Tricky treasure hunt

A game for a small group of 5–6 children

Aim: to practise reading tricky words

How to play:
- Gather the resources.
- This game should be played in a large space (indoors or outdoors).
- Print the tricky words and hide them all around the space.
- Give each child a bucket to collect their "treasure" in.
- On a given signal, they should run around the space collecting as many tricky words as they can find until you signal the end of the game.
- Children should then return to their starting point with their "treasure".
- Listen to each child reading their words individually. Every word they can read earns them a point.
- Scatter the words and begin again. You could also give children different challenges, e.g. the first child to find the word "little" and bring it back wins a point, the first child to find the word "ask" wins a point, the first child to find all eight words wins a point.

> **Challenge**
> Ask more-able children to close their eyes and spell the words.

Tricky spell

An activity for a small group of 5–6 children

Aim: to practise spelling tricky words, identifying the tricky parts of the word

How to play:
- Gather the resources.
- Put the different red and green mediums in the middle of the table for the children to choose from.
- Give each child a tricky word card and ask them to explain the tricky/easy parts of the word.
- Ask the children to use the mediums to represent the word and its tricky parts, for example they might use green chalks for the easy graphemes and draw them small, and red felt tips for the "tricky" letters. They could emphasise them with red glitter and by drawing them larger.
- Encourage children to make all their words as different as possible.

> **Challenge**
> Ask more-able children to write a sentence underneath their large tricky word.

Tricky time

An activity for a small group of 5–10 children

Aim: to practise spelling tricky words

How to play:
- Gather the resources.
- Give each child a mini whiteboard and pen.

> **Support**
> Display the tricky word card as you say the word for less-able children to copy if they need to.

- Set the timer to 30 seconds or 1 minute.
- Call out a tricky word.
- Children should see how many times they can write that word on their whiteboards in the given time.

Challenge
Ask more-able children to write a sentence containing the tricky word.

Homework (optional)

On the resource CD is a letter for parents that you might choose to send home with each child. The letter explains the concept behind tricky words and has the tricky words that you have taught today on the reverse for parents to practise reading and spelling with their child.

Revision

Play "Pass the tricky word". Sit children in a circle and give them tricky word cards. Pass the cards round the circle while singing (to the tune of "London Bridge is Falling Down"), "Pass the tricky words around the ring, around the ring, around the ring, pass the tricky words around the ring, what do they say?" Those holding the tricky words should stand up and say the word, and the other children should repeat it. Play several times .

Now read...

Diggety Dog, *Yellow, Band 3*

Frog or Toad?, *Yellow, Band 3*

The Sun and the Moon, *Yellow, Band 3*

Peas, Please!, *Yellow, Band 3*

Real Monsters, *Yellow, Band 3*

Rock Out!, *Yellow, Band 3*

Hand Play, *Yellow, Band 3*

Feeling Things, *Yellow, Band 3*

The Rainforest at Night, *Blue, Band 4*

Your Nose, *Blue, Band 4*

The Small Bun, *Blue, Band 4*

Buzzy Bee, *Blue, Band 4*

Target phoneme: /er/

Learning objective

to learn to say, read and write /er/

Starter

Sing /er/

♪ **Song text:** "flower in a shower er er er"

Resources

- Song of Sounds flashcard: er
- Song of Sounds picture cards: flower, shower, letter
- Song of Sounds green word cards: never, sister

- Gather the children on the carpet.
- Sing the Song of Sounds all the way through.
- Explain that this week they are going to be learning about different graphemes that make the /er/ sound.
- Explain that today they are going to practise the /er/ sound that they have learned before going on to learning some new ones.
- Show the class the "er" flashcard and sing "flower in a shower er er er".
- Remind them of the action and ask the class to perform it together.

Main lesson

Say /er/

- Remind children how to say /er/ – ask them to say /er/ to each of their fingers, and finally look at you and say the /er/ sound.
- Show them the "er" picture cards and ask them to repeat after you, using the "I say, you say" technique so they can hear the /er/ sound in the word: /f/-/l/-/ow/-/er/, /sh/-/ow/-/er/, /l/-/e/-/tt/-/er/.

Read /er/

- Show children the grapheme side of the card and remind them what an "er" looks like.
- Hide the flashcard behind your back – if you bring it out and show the picture side they must sing "flower in a shower er er er", if you bring it out and show the grapheme side they must say /er/. Bring the card out in different ways from either side of your body.

Write /er/

- Show children how to form an "er" on the board using the explanation "Go around the elephant's head and add his curly trunk" and "Start at the top, go down, back up and over the rabbit's floppy ear."
- Ask them to follow you and sky-write the "er" grapheme – don't forget you need to write backwards.
- Ask them to write an "er" on the carpet with their finger. Ask their chatting chums to check their formation.

Blend /er/

- Using the Song of Sounds green words "never" and "sister", practise reading and blending the graphemes to make the word. Do this by asking children to say the sounds as you press the sound buttons, and then blend the sounds together as you sweep your hand underneath the word.

Revision

Add the "er" flashcard to the stack you have already taught. In front of the children, display a selection of flashcards together with /er/ in different places round the classroom. Point to a flashcard and ask children to all point and sing the song. Repeat a few times. Point to a flashcard and ask them all to point and do the action. Repeat a few times. Point to a flashcard and ask them to all point and say the sound. Repeat a few times. Now you should sing the song, do the actions or say the sound and see if children can point to the correct flashcard. Can they do it with their eyes closed?

Target phoneme: /ir/

Learning objective

to learn to say, read and write /ir/

Resources

- Song of Sounds flashcard: ir
- Song of Sounds picture cards: girl, bird, skirt
- Song of Sounds green word cards: stir, first

Starter

Sing /ir/

♪ **Song text:** "girl in a whirl ir ir ir"

- Gather the children on the carpet.
- Sing the Song of Sounds all the way through.
- Explain that today they are going to a learn a new grapheme.
- Show the class the "ir" flashcard and sing "girl in a whirl ir ir ir".
- Show the class the action and ask them to perform it together.

Main lesson

Say /ir/

- Point out that it makes exactly the same sound as "flower in a shower er er er".
- Show children how to say /ir/ – they should take turns saying /ir/ as you point to them.
- Show them "ir" picture cards and ask them to repeat after you, using the "I say, you say" technique, so they can hear the /ir/ sound in the word, for example, /g/-/ir/-/l/, /b/-/ir/-/d/, /s/-/k/-/ir/-/t/.

Read /ir/

- Explain that although this grapheme makes the same sound as "flower in a shower", it looks different.
- Show children the grapheme side of the card and explain what "ir" looks like.
- Hide the flashcard behind your back – if you bring it out and show the picture side they must sing "girl in a whirl ir ir ir"; if you bring it out and show the grapheme side they must say /ir/. Bring the card out in different ways from either side of your body.

Write /ir/

- Show children how to form an "ir" on the board using the explanation "Go down the insect's body, add a flick for his tail and a dot for his head" and "Start at the top, go down, back up and over the rabbit's floppy ear."
- Ask children to follow you and sky-write the "ir" grapheme – don't forget you need to write backwards.
- Ask them to use their hand as a pad and their finger as a pencil and practise writing an "ir" several times.

Blend /ir/

- Using the Song of Sounds green words "stir" and "first", practise reading and blending the graphemes to make the words. Do this by asking children to say the sounds as you press the sound buttons, and then blend the sounds together as you sweep your hand underneath the word.

Revision

Add the "ir" flashcard to the stack you have already taught. Ask a child to suggest a number between 1 and 10. Turn over that number of flashcards from the pack and sing the flashcard you reach. Repeat lots of times singing, doing the actions or saying the sounds.

Target phoneme: /ur/

Learning objective

to learn to say, read and write /ur/

Resources

- Song of Sounds flashcard: ur
- Song of Sounds picture cards: church, nurse, purse
- Song of Sounds green word cards: hurt, turn

Starter

Sing /ur/

♪ **Song text:** "if you're hurt, see a nurse ur ur ur"

- Gather the children on the carpet.
- Sing the Song of Sounds all the way through.
- Explain that today they are going to a learn a new grapheme.
- Show the class the "ur" flashcard and sing "if you're hurt see a nurse".
- Show them the action and ask the class to perform it together.

Main lesson

Say /ur/
- Point out that it makes exactly the same sound as "flower in a shower er er er" and "girl in a whirl ir ir ir".
- Show children how to say /ur/ – ask them to whisper /ur/, sing /ur/, shout /ur/.
- Show them the "ur" picture cards and ask them to repeat after you, using the "I say, you say" technique, so they can hear the /ur/ sound in the word.

Read /ur/
- Explain that although this phoneme makes the same sound as "flower in a shower er er er" and "girl in a whirl ir ir ir", it looks different.
- Show children the grapheme side of the card and explain what this "ur" looks like.
- Hide the flashcard behind your back – if you bring it out and show the picture side they must sing "If you're hurt, see a nurse ur ur ur", if you bring it out and show the grapheme side they must say /ur/. Bring the card out in different ways from either side of your body.

Write /ur/
- Show children how to form a "ur" on the board using the explanation "Start at the top, go down, around the puddle, back up, down and flick" and "Start at the top, go down, back up and over the rabbit's floppy ear."
- Ask them to follow you and sky-write the "ur" grapheme – don't forget you need to write backwards.
- Ask the children to write a "ur" on each of their fingers.

Blend /ur/
- Using the Song of Sounds green words "hurt" and "turn", practise reading and blending the graphemes to make the words. Do this by asking the children to say the sounds as you press the sound buttons, and then blend the sounds together as you sweep your hand underneath the word.

Revision

Add the "ur" flashcard to the stack of taught flashcards. Show the class the flashcards one at a time, picture-side up, and ask them to sing each sound. Ask them to do the actions to the song silently as you show them the cards. As you produce the grapheme side, let them say the different sounds. Repeat continually throughout the day.

Target phonemes: /er/, /ir/, /ur/

Learning objective

to learn to say, read and write /er/, /ir/ and /ur/

Resources

- Song of Sounds flashcards: er, ir, ur
- Song of Sounds picture cards: flower, shower, letter, girl, bird, skirt, church, nurse, purse
- Song of Sounds green sentence: My sister has a new skirt for church.

Starter

- Gather the children on the carpet.
- Sing the Song of Sounds all the way through.
- Explain that today they are going to practise all the /er/ sounds they have learned this week.

Main lesson

Sing /er/, /ir/ and /ur/

- Show the class the "er", "ir" and "ur" flashcards and sing the correct parts of the song as you show each card. Ask them to perform the actions at the same time.

Say /er/, /ir/ and /ur/

- Remind children that all of these make exactly the same sound.
- Ask them to say /er/ as you show each flashcard picture-side up.
- Stick all the picture cards on the board. Point to a few at random and, using the "I say, you say" technique, ask children to repeat the word after you stressing the /er/ sound in the word.

Read /er/, /ir/ and /ur/

- Sit children in their chatting chum pairs.
- Remind them that although the graphemes all make the same sound, they look different.
- Hold up the "flower in a shower" flashcard picture-side up. Ask children if they can remember what it looks like. Choose one child to tell you which letters make the grapheme. Turn the flashcard over to show the grapheme and stick it on the board.
- Repeat for "girl in a whirl" and "if you're hurt see a nurse".
- On the board, display the three graphemes and all the picture cards. Ask children to work with their chatting chum to discuss which picture cards contain which grapheme.
- Discuss with children and check that they are correct by revealing the grapheme on the reverse of each picture card.
- Put the picture cards next to the correct graphemes.

Blend /er/, /ir/ and /ur/

- Using the green sentence "My sister has a new skirt for church", practise blending each word individually and then the whole phrase. Do this by asking children to say the sounds as you press the sound buttons, and then blend the sounds together as you sweep your hand underneath the word. Go through the whole phrase, then go back and point to each word for them to read.

Introduce /ear/

- Write the word "learn" on the board and circle the /ear/. Sound each grapheme out as you write it: "l"-"e"-"a"-"r"-"n".
- Explain that in the word learn, the /ear/ also makes an /er/ sound.
- Sound out the word with the children: /l/-/ear/-/n/.
- Give some more examples, such as pearl, heard, search.

> **Tip**
> There are four main ways of spelling this vowel sound. There are no rules to help you decide which spelling to use — you have to rely on your visual memory.

Flower power

Target graphemes: /er/, /ir/, /ur/

Learning objectives

to learn to discriminate between the /er/, /ir/ and /ur/ graphemes; to practise blending and segmenting words containing /er/, /ir/ and /ur/

Resources

Carpet session

- Week 14: Teach software
- er, ir and ur picture cards (Week 14: AS1)
- A mini whiteboard and pen for each chatting chum pair

Flower power

- Picture cards used in the carpet session (Week 14: AS1)
- Raindrop cards (Week 14: AS2)
- A flower power playing board for each child (Week 14: AS3)
- A feely bag or box
- Six counters

Flower picking

- er, ir and ur real and nonsense words (Week 14: AS4–6)
- A flower pot for each child (or similar)
- Bin

Fun formation

- er, ir and ur picture cards (Week 14: AS1)
- Song of Sounds flashcards: er, ir, ur
- Paper or exercise books
- Felt tips or pencils in bright colours
- A feely bag

Revision

- Song of Sounds flashcards or all the words learned so far

Carpet session

- Gather the resources.
- Sit children in their chatting chum pairs.
- Before the lesson, scatter enough "er", "ir" and "ur" pictures around the classroom for each chatting chum pair.

1. Tell children that your favourite sound is /er/ because it is in your favourite word: flower, but that spelling words with the /er/ sound is difficult because there are different ways to spell it.

2. Check they know their /er/ sounds, first by asking them to sing them as they see the pictures appear on the screen. Discuss the different graphemes "er", "ir" and "ur".

3. Different graphemes will appear on the screen. Ask children to sing the corresponding part of the song as the graphemes appear.

4. Challenge them to read the words "letter", "shirt" and "burst". Ask them to say the sounds as you press the sound buttons, and then blend the sounds together as you sweep your hand underneath the word.

5. Explain that once you know that /er/, /ir/ and /ur/ all make the /er/ sound, reading words is not tricky. The tricky bit is knowing which /er/ to use when you are writing words. Give each chatting

Software
Teach
W14

chum pair a mini whiteboard and pen. A picture of a purse will appear on the screen, together with the three graphemes. Ask children to discuss with their chatting chums which grapheme makes the /er/ sound in "purse" and to write it on their whiteboards. Ask them to hold up their whiteboards to reveal their answers and discuss.

6-7 • Repeat for "flower" and "skirt".

8 • Reveal the three pictures. Ask children to write all three words on their whiteboards using the correct /er/ grapheme in each word. Reveal the answers and discuss.

9 • Play "Search for an /er/". Ask the children to move around the classroom and search for an /er/, /ir/ and /ur/ picture. You could play some music while they do this. When they have found one, they should come and display it next to the correct grapheme on the board. When everyone has sat down again, discuss any misconceptions.

10 • Revise the session's learning objectives before moving off the carpet to begin the practical activities.

Practical activities

Flower power

A game for a small group of 5–6 children

Aim: to listen to words that contain the /er/, /ir/ and /ur/ graphemes and choose the correct grapheme

How to play:
• Gather the resources.
• Put the picture cards and raindrop cards in a feely bag or box.
• Give each child a playing board.
• Ask them to take it in turns to pull a picture card out of the bag.
• They must decide whether the word is spelled using /er/, /ir/ or /ur/. If they are correct, they cover the correct grapheme on their playing board with a counter.
• However, if they pull out a raindrop card, it rains on their flower and "washes" a counter away.
• The first to cover all their graphemes is the winner.

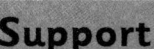

Support
To make this game easier for less-able children, you could use the Song of Sounds picture cards, which have the correct grapheme on the reverse for them to match.

Challenge
Ask more-able children to spell the word out loud to win their counter.

Flower picking

A game for a small group of 5–6 children

Aim: to practise blending real and nonsense words for reading containing /er/, /ir/ and /ur/

How to play:
• Gather the resources.
• Place your /er/, /ir/ and /ur/ words around a large space.
• Stand children in a group and, on a given signal, they should run and pick a word and bring it back to you.
• They should sit in a circle and take it in turns to read their word to you.
• If the word is a real word, such as church, it is a "flower" and they may keep it and put it in their flowerpot.
• If the word is a nonsense word, such as pirt, it is a "weed" and they should put it in the bin.
• The child with the most words in their flower pot at the end of the game is the winner.

Support
Read the letters for less-able children to blend orally.

Challenge
More-able children should be challenged to read completely independently.

Fun formation

An activity for a small group of 5–10 children

Aim: to practise correct formation of the "er", "ir" and "ur" graphemes

How to play:
• Gather the resources.
• Gather the children around a table.

- Give each child a piece of paper or exercise book.
- Put your felt tips or pencils in the middle of the table.
- Put the picture cards in a feely bag.
- Pull one of the picture cards out of the feely bag and discuss which /er/ grapheme is in the word.
- Model writing it on the board in a cursive script using the correct grapheme explanation.
- Ask children to choose a colour and practise writing the appropriate grapheme lots of times.
- Repeat the activity using different picture cards.

Support

Less-able children can use the flashcards instead and sing the song and do the actions prior to writing.

Challenge

Ask more-able children to finish by writing a few /er/ words.

Revision

Use all the Song of Sounds flashcards you have taught so far. Show them grapheme-side up to the children in silence. Every time they see "er", "ir" or "ur", they should say "Flower power". Then hold up one of the flashcards grapheme-side up, e.g. "er", and ask children to call out a word containing that grapheme, e.g. flower. The child who calls the word out first comes to the front and chooses the next flashcard to hold up. Repeat numerous times.

Now read...

Thick and Thin, *Red B, Band 2B*

Birds, *Blue, Band 4*

Gorillas, *Blue, Band 4*

Target phoneme: /or/

Learning objective

to learn to say, read and write /or/

Starter

Sing /or/

♪ **Song text:** "it's horse of course or or or"

- Gather the children on the carpet.
- Sing the Song of Sounds all the way through.
- Explain that this week they are going to be learning about different graphemes that make the /or/ sound.
- Explain that today they are going to practise the /or/ grapheme before learning some new graphemes.
- Show the class the "or" flashcard and sing "It's a horse of course or or or".
- Remind them of the action and ask the class to perform it together.

Main lesson

Say /or/

- Remind children how to say /or/ – say /or/ with a happy face, angry face, and a sad face.
- Show children the "or" picture cards and ask them to repeat after you, using the "I say, you say" technique, so they can hear the /or/ sound in the word, for example, /h/-/or/-/s/, /t/-/or/-/ch/, /f/-/or/-/k/.

Read /or/

- Show the children the grapheme side of the card and remind them what an "or" looks like.
- Hide the flashcard behind your back – if you bring it out and show the picture side they must sing "it's a horse of course or or or", if you bring it out and show the grapheme side they must say /or/. Bring the card out in different ways from either side of your body.

Write /or/

- Show children how to form an "or" on the board using the explanation "Start at the top and go around the orange" and "Start at the top, go down, back up and over the rabbit's floppy ear."
- Ask children to follow you and sky-write the "or" grapheme – don't forget you need to write backwards.
- Ask children to write a tiny "or" in the air, then repeat, getting increasingly bigger.

Blend /or/

- Using the Song of Sounds green words "horn" and "storm", practise reading and blending the graphemes to make the word.
- Do this by asking children to say the sounds as you press the sound buttons, and then blend the sounds together as you sweep your hand underneath the word.

Revision

Add the "or" flashcard to the stack you have already taught. Show the class the flashcards one at a time, picture-side up, and ask them to sing each sound but in a whisper, until they see the "it's a horse of course" flashcard when they should sing it out loudly. Repeat a few times. Ask children to do the actions to the song silently as you show them the flashcards. As you produce the grapheme side, let them whisper the different sounds until they see the "or" when they should shout it. Repeat flashcard work throughout the day.

Target phoneme: /au/

Learning objective

to learn to say, read and write /au/

Resources:
- Song of Sounds flashcard: au
- Song of Sounds picture cards: autumn, pause, sauce
- Song of Sounds green words: haunt, launch

Starter

Sing /au/

♪ **Song text:** "naughty in autumn au au au"

- Gather children on the carpet.
- Sing the Song of Sounds all the way through.
- Explain that today they are going to a learn a new grapheme.
- Show the class the "au" flashcard and sing "naughty in autumn au au au".
- Show them the action and ask the class to perform it together.

Main lesson

Say /au/

- Point out that it makes exactly the same sound as "it's a horse of course or or or".
- Show children how to say /au/ – ask them to say /au/ ten times with their eyes closed.
- Show them the /au/ picture cards and ask them to repeat after you, using the "I say, you say" technique, so they can hear the /au/ sound in the word: /au/-/t/-u/-m/, /p/-/au/-/z/, /s/-/au/-c/-/e/.

Read /au/

- Explain that although this phoneme makes the same sound as "it's a horse of course or or or", it looks different.
- Show children the grapheme side of the card and explain what an "au" looks like.
- Hide the flashcard behind your back – if you bring it out and show the picture side they must sing "naughty in autumn au au au", if you bring it out and show the grapheme side they must say /au/. Bring the card out in different ways from either side of your body.

Write /au/

- Show children how to form an "au" on the board using the explanation "Go around the apple, down and flick" and "Start at the top, go down, around the puddle, back up, down and flick."
- Ask them to follow you and sky-write the "au" grapheme – don't forget you need to write backwards.
- Ask them to look up to the ceiling and write an "au" in the air.

Blend /au/

- Using the Song of Sounds green words "haunt" and "launch", practise reading and blending the graphemes to make the words. Do this by asking children to say the sounds as you press the sound buttons, and then blend the sounds together as you sweep your hand underneath the word.

Revision

Add the "au" flashcard to the stack you have already taught. Show the class the flashcards one at a time, picture-side up, and sing the corresponding part of the song. If you sing the correct part of the song, the children should give you a thumbs-up, if you sing the wrong part of the song the children should give you a thumbs-down. As you produce the grapheme side, say the corresponding sound and ask them to give you a thumbs-up if correct and a thumbs-down if you're wrong. Finish by all singing and saying the sounds.

Target phoneme: /aw/

Learning objective

to learn to say, read and write /aw/

Resources

- Song of Sounds flashcard: aw
- Song of Sounds picture cards: claw, saw, draw
- Song of Sounds green word cards: straw, prawn

Starter

Sing /aw/

> ♪ **Song text:** "it's got an awful claw aw aw aw"

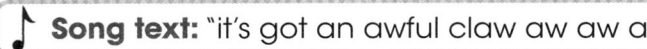

- Gather the children on the carpet.
- Sing the Song of Sounds all the way through.
- Explain that today they are going to a learn a new grapheme.
- Show the class the "aw" flashcard and sing "it's got an awful claw aw aw aw".
- Show them the action and ask the class to perform it together.

Main lesson

Say /aw/

- Point out that it makes exactly the same sound as "it's a horse of course or or or "and "naughty in autumn au au au".
- Show children how to say /aw/ – say /aw/ in a variety of voices, such as deep, high-pitched etc.
- Show them the "aw" picture cards and ask them to repeat after you, using the "I say, you say" technique, so they can hear the /aw/ sound in the words: /c/-/l/-/aw/, /s/-/aw/, /d/-/r/-/aw/.

Read /aw/

- Explain that although this phoneme makes the same sound as "it's a horse of course or or or" and "naughty in autumn au au au", it looks different.
- Show children the grapheme side of the card and explain what "aw" looks like.
- Hide the flashcard behind your back – if you bring it out and show the picture side they must sing "it's got an awful claw aw aw aw", if you bring it out and show the grapheme side they must say /aw/. Bring the card out in different ways from either side of your body.

Write /aw/

- Show children how to form an "aw" on the board using the explanation "Go around the apple, down and flick" and "Go over the stormy waves – down, up, down, up and flick."
- Ask them to follow you and sky-write the "aw" grapheme – don't forget you need to write backwards.
- Ask them to write "aw" on their arm – they should start at their shoulder and write "aw" smaller and smaller, all the way to their fingertips.

Blend /aw/

- Using the Song of Sounds green words "straw" and "prawn", practise reading and blending the graphemes to make the words. Do this by asking children to say the sounds as you press the sound buttons, and then blend the sounds together as you sweep your hand underneath the word.

Revision

Add the "aw" flashcard to the stack you already have. Use a piece of card to cover your flashcard pack. Reveal one flashcard really slowly by moving it downwards. As soon as they know what it is, children should sing it. Reveal the whole flashcard to see if they are right. Repeat the slow reveal game but this time ask them to do the actions as you reveal the flashcards. As you produce the grapheme side, can they say the different sounds? Repeat continually throughout the day.

Target phonemes: /or/, /au/, /aw/

Learning objective

to learn to say, read and write /or/, /au/ and /aw/

Resources

- Song of Sounds flashcards: or, au, aw
- Song of Sounds picture cards: horse, torch, fork, claw, saw, draw, autumn, pause, sauce
- Song of Sounds green sentence: It was an awful storm for August.

Starter

Sing /or/, /au/ and /aw/

- Gather the children on the carpet.
- Sing the Song of Sounds all the way through.
- Explain that today they are going to practise all the /or/ sounds they have learned this week.
- Show the class the "or", "au" and "aw" flashcards and sing the correct parts of the song as you show each card. Ask them to perform the actions at the same time.

Main lesson

Say /or/, /au/ and /aw/

- Remind children that all of these graphemes make exactly the same sound.
- Ask them to say /or/, /au/ and /aw/ as you show them each flashcard, picture-side up.
- Stick all the picture cards on the board. Point to a few at random and, using the "I say, you say" technique, ask children to repeat the word after you, stressing the /or/ sound in the word.

Read /or/, /au/ and /aw/

- Remind children that although they all make the same sound, they look different.
- Hold up the "it's a horse of course" flashcard picture-side up. Ask them if they can remember what it looks like. Choose one child to tell you what letters make the grapheme. Turn the flashcard over to show the grapheme and stick it on the board.
- Repeat for "naughty in autumn" and "it's got an awful claw".
- On the board display the three graphemes and all the picture cards. Ask children to work with their chatting chums to discuss which picture cards contain which grapheme.
- Discuss with them and check if they are correct by revealing the grapheme on the reverse of each picture card.
- Move the picture cards next to the correct graphemes.

Blend /or/, /au/ and /aw/

- Using the green sentence "It was an awful storm for August", practise blending each word individually and then the whole phrase. Do this by asking children to say the sounds as you press the sound buttons, and then blend the sounds together as you sweep your hand underneath the word. Go through the whole phrase, then go back and point to each word for them to read.

Introduce /ore/

- Write the word "snore" on the board and circle the /ore/ at the end of the word.
- Explain that in the word "snore" the /ore/ at the end also makes an /or/ sound.
- Sound out the word with the children: /s/-/n/-/ore/.
- Give some more examples, such as sore, core, shore.

Tip

There are no rules to tell you which /or/ sound to use, but there are some helpful hints:
1. Never use *au* at the end of a word; use *ore* or *aw*, e.g. *shore, jaw*.
2. *aw* is often used before *n* and *l* e.g. *dawn, crawl*.

Sort your ors

Target graphemes: "or", "au", "aw"

Learning objectives

to learn to discriminate between the /or/, /au/ and /aw/ graphemes; to practise blending and segmenting words containing /or/, /au/ and /aw/

Resources

Carpet session

- Week 15: Teach software
- or, aw and au sections of the Song of Sounds classroom frieze
- A bag containing some real objects and/or pictures, some of which contain the or sound (e.g. cork, fork, horn, storm, shorts, torch, horse, corn, sauce, saw, straw, prawn, shawl, yawn) and some that don't (e.g. pencil, book, etc.)
- A mini whiteboard and pen for each chatting chum pair
- Three hoops (optional)

Are you sure of your or?

- or, aw and au sections of the Song of Sounds classroom frieze
- Song of Sounds audio CD

- Song of Sounds picture cards: or, aw and au
- A feely bag

I saw a paw

- Paw picture cards (Week 15: AS1–2)
- A mini whiteboard and pen for each child

Draw an aw

- Song of Sounds flashcards: or, aw and au
- Paper or exercise books
- A selection of different writing tools e.g. pencils, chalks, felt tips, glitter pens
- A feely bag with one of each of the above in

Revision

- Repeat the sorting activity from the carpet session.

Carpet session

- Gather the resources.
- Ask children to sit in a circle.
- [1] Explain that today they are learning about the different /or/ sounds.
- Begin the lesson by showing a bag of objects or pictures that you would like to sort.
- Place the /or/, /aw/ and /au/ sections of the Song of Sounds classroom frieze in the centre of the circle with space between them (place the frieze sections in the three hoops if using these).
- Give every child or every pair an object or picture.
- Ask children to take it in turns to come to the middle of the circle and place their object or picture next to the correct sign.
- Ask them to sit down in the circle again and give them some feedback on their choices.
- Pack the objects and/or pictures away and sit children with their chatting chums.

> Software
> Teach
> W15

2-4 • Play "Which of the four isn't an /or/?" Show four pictures on the software and tell children what each picture is to avoid confusion. Ask them to discuss with their chatting chums which picture isn't an /or/. After the count of three, ask them to tell you which picture is the odd one out.

5-7 • Give each pair a mini whiteboard and pen. A picture will appear on the screen together with the three graphemes. Children should discuss with their chatting chums which grapheme is in the word and write which one they think it is on their whiteboards. Reveal the answer and discuss. Then reveal the word and ask the class to read the word in unison, using the sound buttons to help them.

8-10 • Another picture will appear with the three graphemes. This time the sound buttons will appear first because the focus here is writing. Ask children to use the sound buttons to help them write the word, using the correct /or/ sound grapheme. The chatting chums should then reveal their whiteboards and you then should reveal the correct spelling of the word and discuss.

11 • Revise the session's learning objectives before moving off the carpet to begin their practical activities.

Practical activities

Are you sure of your or?

A game for a large group of 10–15 children

Aim: to listen to words that contain the /or/, /au/ and /aw/ graphemes and choose the correct grapheme

How to play:
• Gather the resources.
• Display the /or/, /aw/ and /au/ sections of the Song of Sounds classroom frieze around a large indoor or outdoor space and put your "or", "aw" and "au" Song of Sounds picture cards into a feely bag.
• Play the Song of Sounds CD and ask children to dance.
• When the music stops, they should run and choose an /or/ grapheme to stand next to.
• Pull a picture card out of the feely bag.
• Discuss whether the picture has an /or/, /aw/ and /au/ in it.
• Those who are standing next to the /or/ sound that is in the picture are out.
• Keep playing until you have a winner.

Support
To make this game easier for less-able children, use the Song of Sounds flashcards and sing the song and do the actions as you pull each flashcard out of the feely bag.

Challenge
When the music stops, pull a picture card out of the bag. Children should run to the corresponding grapheme and the last one there is out. You could also discuss spellings.

I saw a paw

A game for a small group of 5–6 children

Aim: to practise segmenting words for writing containing /or/, /aw/ and /aw/ and choosing the correct grapheme

How to play:
• Gather the resources.
• Prior to the lesson, print the paws and hide them all around a large space.
• Give each child a mini whiteboard and pen.
• Children should walk around the space with an adult as a group. When the group find a paw, they should look at the picture on the paw, and on their whiteboards write whether it has an /or/, /au/ or /aw/ in it.
• Reveal the answer and discuss, before beginning the hunt for the next paw.
• Repeat until they have found all the paws.

Support
Sing the corresponding part of the song and do the action of the correct /or/ grapheme.

Challenge
Encourage more-able children to write the whole word independently.

Draw an aw

An activity for a small group of 5–10 children

Aim: to practise correct formation of the /or/, /aw/ and /au/ graphemes

How to play:

- Gather the resources.
- Give each child a piece of paper or exercise book.
- Put one of each writing implement in a feely bag.
- Choose a flashcard ("or", "aw" or "au").
- Model writing it on the board in a cursive script using the correct grapheme explanation.
- Pull a writing implement out of the feely bag.
- Ask children to practise writing the appropriate grapheme lots of times.
- Repeat the activity writing the different graphemes using different writing implements.

Support

Use the Song of Sounds flashcards and sing the song and do the actions prior to writing each grapheme.

Challenge

Ask more-able children to finish by writing a few words.

Revision

Repeat the sorting activity from the carpet session.

Now read...

Feelings, *Red B, Band 2B*

Hansel and Gretel, *Blue, Band 4*

Target grapheme: /ou/

Learning objective

to learn to say, read and write /ou/

Resources

- Song of Sounds flashcard: ou
- Song of Sounds picture cards: mouse, house, trousers
- Song of Sounds green words: cloud, mouth

Starter

Sing /ou/

> ♪ **Song text:** "mouse in a house ou ou ou"

- Gather the children on the carpet.
- Sing the Song of Sounds all the way through.
- Explain that this week they are going to be learning about different graphemes that make the /ou/ sound.
- Explain that today they are going to practise the /ou/ sound that they have already learned before going on to learning some new ones
- Show the class the "ou" flashcard and sing "mouse in a house ou ou ou".
- Remind them of the action and ask the class to perform it together.

Main lesson

Say /ou/

- Remind children how to say /ou/ – say /ou/ to me, say /ou/ to your friend, say /ou/ to the ceiling, say /ou/ to the floor, say /ou/ to the book corner etc.
- Show them the "ou" picture cards and ask them to repeat after you, using the "I say, you say" technique, so they can hear the /ou/ sound in the words: /m/-/ou/-/s/, /h/-/ou/-/s/, /t/-/r/-/ou/-/z/-/er/-/z/.

Read /ou/

- Show children the grapheme side of the card and remind the class what an "ou" looks like.
- Hide the flashcard behind your back – if you bring it out and show the picture side they must sing "mouse in a house ou ou ou", if you bring it out and show the grapheme side they must say /ou/. Bring the card out in different ways from either side of your body.

Write /ou/

- Show children how to form an "ou" on the board using the explanation "Start at the top and go around the orange" and "Start at the top, go down, around the puddle, back up, down and flick".
- Ask them to follow you and sky-write the "ou" grapheme – don't forget you need to write backwards.
- Ask them to stand next to their chatting chums, and to write an "ou" on their partner's back and then swap over. Write a big "ou" and a small "ou" and swap over.

Blend /ou/

- For the Song of Sounds green words "cloud" and "mouth", practise reading and blending the graphemes to make the word. Do this by asking the children to say the sounds as you press the sound buttons, and then blend the sounds together as you sweep your hand underneath the word.

Revision

Add the "ou" flashcard to the stack you have already taught. Ask the children to sit in a circle. Give out a few flashcards to random children. Play the Song of Sounds CD and pass the flashcards round the circle. When you stop the music, the children holding the flashcards should sing the corresponding parts of the song. Repeat lots of times, asking them to either sing the song/do the actions or say the sounds. As you produce the grapheme side, can they say the different sounds? Repeat throughout the day. **149**

Target grapheme: /ow/

Learning objective

to learn to say, read and write /ow/ , and to
recognise that it is an alternate grapheme of /ou/

Resources

- Song of Sounds
  flashcard: ow
- Song of Sounds picture
  cards: cow, clown, owl
- Song of Sounds green
  words: brown, crowd

Starter

Sing /ow/

> ♪ **Song text:** "clown upside down ow ow ow"

- Gather the children on the carpet.
- Sing the Song of Sounds all the way through.
- Explain that today they are going to a learn a new grapheme.
- Show the class the "ow" flashcard and sing "clown upside down ow ow ow".
- Show them the action and ask the class to perform it together.

Main lesson

Say /ow/

- Point out that /ow/ makes exactly the same sound as "mouse in a house ou ou ou".
- Show children how to say /ow/ – ask them to say /ow/ to each of their fingers and finally to
  look at you and say the /ow/ sound.
- Show them the "ow" picture cards and ask them to repeat after you, using the "I say, you say"
  technique, so they can hear the /ow/ sound in the words: /c/-/ow/, /c/-/l/-/ow/-/n/, /ow/-/l/.

Read /ow/

- Explain that although this phoneme makes the same sound as "mouse in a house ou ou ou", it
  looks different.
- Show children the grapheme side of the card and explain what this "ow" looks like.
- Hide the flashcard behind your back – if you bring it out and show the picture side they must sing
  "clown upside down ow ow ow", if you bring it out and show the grapheme side they must say
  /ow/. Bring the card out in different ways from either side of your body.

Write /ow/

- Sit the children in their chatting chum pairs.
- Show them how to form an "ow" on the board using the explanation "Start at the top and go
  around the orange" and "Go over the stormy waves – down, up, down, up and flick".
- Ask them to follow you and sky-write the "ow" grapheme – don't forget you need to write backwards.
- Ask them to write an "ow" on the carpet with their finger. Ask their chatting chums to check their formation.

Blend /ow/

- Using the Song of Sounds green words "brown" and "crowd", practise reading and blending the
  graphemes to make the words. Do this by asking the children to say the sounds as you press the
  sound buttons, and then blend the sounds together as you sweep your hand underneath the word.

Revision

Add the "ow" flashcard to the stack you have already taught. Show the class the flashcards one at a
time, picture-side up, and ask them to sing each sound. Give a selection of flashcards, including "ow",
to some of the children and ask them to come to the front of the class – they should take it in turns
to either sing/do the action or say their sound in front of the class. They can then give their flashcard
to another child so they can have a turn. Repeat for each child in the class. As you produce the
grapheme side, can they say the different sounds? Repeat throughout the day.

Target graphemes: /ou/, /ow/

Learning objective

to learn to say, read and write /ou/ and /ow/, and to recognise that it is an alternate grapheme of /ow/

Resources

- Song of Sounds flashcards: ou, ow
- Song of Sounds picture cards: mouse, house, trousers, cow, clown, owl
- Green sentences: The clown shouts out to the crowd. I found myself down in the mouth.

Starter

Sing /ou/ and /ow/

- Gather the children on the carpet.
- Sing the Song of Sounds all the way through.
- Explain that today they are going to practise all the /ou/sounds they have learned this week.
- Show the class the "ou" and "ow" flashcards and sing the correct parts of the song as you hold up each card. Ask children to perform the actions at the same time.

Main lesson

Say /ou/ and /ow/

- Remind children that all of these make exactly the same sound.
- Ask them to say /ou/ as you show them each flashcard, picture-side up.
- Stick all the picture cards on the board. Point to a few at random and using the "I say, you say" technique, ask the children to repeat the word after you, stressing the /ou/ sound in the word.

Read /ou/ and /ow/

- Sit the children with their chatting chums.
- Remind them that although they all make the same sound, they look different.
- Hold up the "mouse in a house ou ou ou" flashcard picture-side up. Ask children if they can remember what it looks like. Choose one child to tell you what letters make the grapheme. Turn the flashcard over to show the grapheme and stick it on the board.
- Repeat for "clown upside down ow ow ow".
- On the board, display the two graphemes and all the picture cards. Ask children to work in their chatting chum pairs to discuss which picture cards contain which grapheme.
- Discuss with children and check if they are correct by revealing the grapheme on the reverse of each picture card.
- Move the picture cards next to the correct grapheme accordingly.

Blend /ou/ and /ow/

- Using the green sentence "The clown shouts to the crowd", practise blending each word individually and then the whole phrase. Do this by asking children to say the sounds as you press the sound buttons and then blend the sounds together as you sweep your hand underneath the word. Go through the whole phrase, then go back and point to each word for children to read.
- Repeat for "I found myself down in the mouth."

Revision

At different points during the day, produce your "ou" and "ow" flashcards and ask children to sing the song, do the actions and/or say the sound. Remind them that this week they will be learning different graphemes for the phoneme /ou/.

Target graphemes: /ou/, /ow/

Learning objective

to learn to say, read and write /ou/ and /ow/

Resources

- Song of Sounds flashcards: ou, ow
- Song of Sounds picture cards: mouse, house, trousers, cow, clown, owl
- Song of Sounds green sentences: The clown shouts out to the crowd. I found myself down in the mouth.

Starter

Sing /ou/ and /ow/

- Gather the children on the carpet.
- Sing the Song of Sounds all the way through.
- Explain that today they are going to practise all the /ou/ sounds they have learned this week and that you are going to show the children a special trick to help them with their spelling.
- Show the class the "ou" and "ow" flashcards and sing the correct parts of the song as you show each card. Ask children to perform the actions at the same time.

Main lesson

Say /ou/ and /ow/

- Remind children that both of these make exactly the same sound.
- Ask them to say /ou/ as you show them each flashcard, picture-side up.
- Stick all the picture cards on the board. Point to a few at random and, using the "I say, you say" technique, ask children to repeat the word after you, stressing the /ou/ sound.

Read /ou/ and /ow/

- Now take the picture cards away and stick the "ow" and "ou" flashcards on the board, grapheme-side up. Underneath each grapheme write three words: "out", "loud", "count" and "cow", "now", "how".
- Point to each word and ask children to read them in unison.
- Tell them that these words can help us to work out when to use /ou/ in a word and when to use /ow/.
- Circle the "ow" grapheme in the words. Ask children what they notice (the "ow" is at the end of the word in each of these words). Explain that you never find /ou/ at the end of words, so if the /ou/ sound is at the end it must be /ow/.
- Circle the "ou" grapheme in each word – what do the children notice? It is in the middle or at the start of the word?
- Explain that at the beginning or in the middle of a word it can be /ou/ or /ow/, but /ou/ is the most common.

Blend /ou/ and /ow/

- Stick the green sentences "The clown shouts out to the crowd" and "I found myself down in the mouth" on the board. Ask children to check where the "ou" and "ow" graphemes are in the words and see if this rule works.

Tip

There is a firm rule to help you decide which /ou/ sound goes in a word.

If the /ou/ sound is at the end of a word, it is always spelled /ow/. Helpful hints for other words:

- In the middle of a word, it can be /ou/ or /ow/ but "ou" is the most common.
- Before n and l, it is usually /ow/ e.g. down, howl.
- Before nd, use /ou/, e.g. round, found.

Revision

At different points during the day, produce your "ou" and "ow" flashcards and ask children to sing the song, do the actions and/or say the sound. Remind them that this week they will be learning different graphemes for the phoneme /ou/.

Croc returns

Target graphemes: /ou/, /ow/

Learning objective

to learn to discriminate between the /ou/ and /ow/ graphemes; to practise blending and segmenting words containing /ou/ and /ow/

Resources

Carpet session

- Week 16: Teach software
- A crocodile puppet or soft toy
- A mini whiteboard and pen for each chatting chum pair

I found an ou

- Crocodile picture cards (Week 16: AS1–5)
- A mini whiteboard and pen for each child

Snap up a word

- Crocodile cards (Week 16: AS6)
- A set of /ou/ word cards (Week 16: AS7–8)

- An empty water tray or washing-up bowl
- A sock for each child (optional)

Tick tock handwriting

- Song of Sounds flashcards: ou and ow
- Feely bag
- A spinner or dice with different time limits on – for example, 10 seconds, 20 seconds, 30 seconds and 1 minute
- Paper or exercise books
- Pencils
- Song of Sounds picture cards: ou and ow (optional)

Carpet session

- Gather the resources.
- Sit children in their chatting chum pairs.

- Ask them which sounds they have been learning about this week: /ou/ and /ow/ graphemes, which both make the /ou/ sound.
[1]
- Bring out your puppet or soft toy, and/or play the software. Explain that "Croc" has come to help us learn about the /ou/ sound today.
- Remind children that he is just a baby and, although he can talk, he can't say whole words yet so it might be difficult for them to understand him.

Software
Teach
W16

- Ask the puppet a series of questions. The puppet will talk in sound-talk and the children should blend the words together to reveal what he is saying.
  - "What is your name?" "/C/-/r/-/o/-/c/"
  - "How old are you?" "/W/-/u/-/n/" (one)
  - "Where do you live?" "/P/-/o/-/n/-/d/"
  - "What do you like to do in the pond?" "/S/-/n/-/a/-/p/, /s/-/w/-/i/-/m/"
  - "What is your favourite colour?" "/G/-/r/-/ee/-/n/"
  - "What do you like to eat?" "/F/-/i/-/sh/, /c/-/r/-/a/-/b/"

Congratulate children on being able to understand Croc.

- Explain that Croc knows we are learning about words with an /ou/ sound and he has been searching for things in his pond that could help us. He has *found* all sorts of things and would like to tell us about them. Make Croc say a few /ou/ sound words in sound-talk: /c/-/ow/, /ow/-/l/, /m/-/ou/-/s/-/e/, /c/-/r/-/ow/-/n/. Again, children should blend the words together to reveal what he is saying.
- Explain that it is time for Croc to go, but he is leaving us some games to play to help us practise our /ou/ sounds. Make Croc say "bye bye" in sound-talk and put him away.

2 • Play "Croc talk". On the screen, display a picture of Croc's pond with all the items that Croc found. Children should work with their chatting chums and take it in turns to use their hand to imitate a crocodile talking and sound-talk one of the /ou/ sound words for their chatting chums to guess. Repeat a few times.

3 • Play "Snap". When you press play, a selection of graphemes flash into Croc's mouth on the screen. Every time the children see an /ou/ sound grapheme, the children should "snap" their arms like crocodile jaws.

4-7 • Play "Mouthy sounds". Give each chatting chum pair a mini whiteboard and pen. Press play to make a picture of Croc appear on the screen with a picture of an /ou/ sound word, for example, owl. Ask: "Which /ou/ sound is in owl and how do you write it?" They should try to write the word before he eats it. Repeat a few times.

8 • Revise the learning objectives before moving off the carpet and beginning practical activities.

> ### Support
> Give less-able children a Song of Sounds phoneme finder and ask them to write the correct grapheme. Alternatively, sing the song to give them a clue.

> ### Challenge
> Ask more-able children to write the word more than once before Croc eats it. Can they think of a word that rhymes, e.g. owl, howl?

Practical activities

I found an /ou/

A game for a small group of 6–8 children

Aim: to practise segmenting words containing /ou/ and /ow/ for writing and choosing the correct grapheme

How to play:
- Gather the resources.
- Before the lesson, place the crocodile cards around the classroom, playground or the whole school.
- Give each child or pair in the group a mini whiteboard and pen.
- Ask them to divide their whiteboards in half and write /ou/ at the top of one side and /ow/ at the top of the other side.
- Ask them to walk around the area until they see a crocodile card.
- They should then have a look at the picture in Croc's mouth and decide if the word contains an /ou/ sound. If it does, they should have a go at writing the word on the corresponding side of their whiteboard. If the picture does not contain an /ou/ sound, they should put the card back.

> ### Support
> Ask less-able children to focus on hearing whether it is an /ou/ word or not and tick on the correct side of their board.

> ### Challenge
> Ask more-able children to come back and discuss the words they have found. By thinking of rhyming families, can they think of any more /ou/ words, e.g. pound – round, hound, mound, ground, found etc?

Snap up a word

An activity for a small group of 5–6 children

Aim: to practise blending words for reading containing /ou/ and /ow/

How to play:
- Gather the resources.
- Give each child a sock to represent a crocodile, or ask them to make a snapping crocodile mouth with their hand.

> ### Support
> Say the sounds for the less-able children to help them blend.

- Put the word cards and crocodile cards face down in the empty water tray or washing-up bowl.
- Children should take turns to use their Croc to snap up a word. If they can read the word, they can keep it. However, if they "snap up" a Croc card they must put it back. The child with the most cards at the end of the game is the winner.

Tick tock handwriting

An activity for a small group of 5–10 children

Aim: to practise the correct formation of graphemes learned so far

How to play:
- Gather the resources.
- Gather the children on the carpet.
- Place the "ou" flashcards in a feely bag.
- Ask a child to pick out a letter from the bag. All children in the group must say the phoneme.
- Demonstrate how to write the grapheme correctly.
- Spin the spinner or roll a dice to decide how many seconds the children have to write the grapheme as many times as they can.

Revision

Play "Knock ou-t". The whole class should stand up. Call out an /ow/ sound word in sound-talk, such as /ou/-/ch/, /l/-/ou/-/d/, /p/-/r/-/ou/-/d/, /h/-/ou/-/l/, /g/-/r/-/ou/-/l, /s/-/c/-/ou/-/l/. The first child to shout out the answer can choose to knock out (eliminate) another child and that child is /ou/-/t/ and must sit /d/-/ou/-/n/. The last child standing is the winner. This game, although competitive, normally ends up with an average-ability winner, as they tend to choose the fastest children to knock out.

Now read...

Feelings, *Red, Band 2B*

Horse Up a Tree, *Yellow, Band 3*

Target phoneme: /oy/

Learning objective

to learn to read, write and say /oy/

Resources

- Song of Sounds flashcard: oy
- Song of Sounds picture cards: boy, toy, oyster
- Song of Sounds green words: annoy, enjoy

Starter

Sing /oy/

> ♪ **Song text:** "boy with a toy oy oy oy".

- Gather the children on the carpet.
- Sing the Song of Sounds all the way through.
- Explain that this week they are going to be learning about different graphemes that make the /oy/ sound.
- Explain that today they are going to practise the /oy/ sound that they have learned before going on to learning some new ones.
- Show the class the "oy" flashcard and sing "Boy with a toy oy oy oy".
- Remind them of the action and ask the class to perform it together.

Main lesson

Say /oy/

- Remind children how to say /oy/ – they should take turns saying /oy/ as you point to them.
- Show them the "oy" picture cards and ask them to repeat after you, using the "I say, you say" technique, so they can hear the oy sound in the words: /b/-/oy/, /t/-/oy/, /oy/-/s/-/t/-/er/.

Read /oy/

- Show children the grapheme side of the card and remind the class what an "oy" looks like.
- Hide a flashcard behind your back – if you bring it out and show the picture side they must sing "boy with a toy oy oy oy", if you bring it out and show the grapheme side they must say /oy/. Bring the card out in different ways from either side of your body.

Write /oy/

- Show children how to form an "oy" on the board using the explanation "Start at the top and go around the orange" and "Go down and around, down the yoyo's string and add a curl."
- Ask children to follow you and sky-write the "oy" grapheme – don't forget you need to write backwards.
- Ask them to use their hand as a pad and their finger as a pencil and practise writing an "oy" several times.

Blend /oy/

- For the Song of Sounds green words "annoy" and "enjoy", practise reading and blending the graphemes to make the word. Do this by asking children to say the sounds as you press the sound buttons, and then blend the sounds together as you sweep your hand underneath the word.

Revision

Add the "oy" flashcard to the stack you have already taught. In front of the children, display last week's flashcards together with /oy/ in different places around the classroom. Point to a flashcard and ask children to all point and say the sound. Repeat a few times. Now you should either sing the song, do the actions or say the sound and see if the children can point to the correct flashcard. Can they do it with their eyes closed?

Target grapheme: /oi/

Learning objective

to learn to read, write and say /oi/

Resources

- Song of Sounds flashcard: oi
- Song of Sounds picture cards: oil, toilet, point
- Green words: coin, spoil

Starter

Sing /oi/

♪ **Song text:** "don't be noisy oi oi oi".

- Gather the children on the carpet.
- Sing the Song of Sounds all the way through.
- Explain that today they are going to a learn a new grapheme.
- Show the class the "oi" flashcard and sing "don't be noisy oi oi oi".
- Show them the action and ask the class to perform it together.

Main lesson

Say /oi/

- Point out that /oi/ makes exactly the same sound as "boy with a toy oy oy oy".
- Show children how to say /oi/ – ask them to whisper /oi/, sing /oi/, shout /oi/.
- Show them the "oi" picture cards and ask them to repeat after you, using the "I say, you say" technique, so they can hear the /oi/ sound in the words: /oi/-/l/, /t/-/oi/-/l/-/e/-/t/, /p/-/oi/-/n/-/t/.

Read /oi/

- Explain that although this phoneme makes the same sound as "boy with a toy oy oy oy", it looks different.
- Show children the grapheme side of the card and explain what this "oi" looks like.
- Hide the flashcard behind your back – if you bring it out and show the picture side they must sing "don't be noisy oi oi oi", if you bring it out and show the grapheme side they must say /oi/ . Bring the card out in different ways from either side of your body.

Write /oi/

- Show children how to form an "oi" on the board using the explanation "Start at the top and go around the orange" and "Go down the insect's body, add a flick for his tail and a dot for his head."
- Ask them to follow you and sky-write the "oi" grapheme – don't forget you need to write backwards.
- Ask them to write an "oi" on each of their fingers.

Blend /oi/

- For the Song of Sounds green words "coin" and "spoil", practise reading and blending the graphemes to make the words. Do this by asking the children to say the sounds as you press the sound buttons, and then blend the sounds together as you sweep your hand underneath the word.

Revision

Add the "oi" flashcard to the stack you have already taught. Ask one child to suggest a number between 1 and 10. Turn over that number of flashcards from the pack and sing the flashcard you reach. Repeat lots of times either singing/doing the actions or saying the sounds.

Target graphemes: /oy/, /oi/

Learning objective

to learn to read, write and say /oi/

Resources
- Song of Sounds flashcards: oy, oi
- Song of Sounds picture cards: oil, toilet, point, boy, toy, oyster
- Song of Sounds green sentences: The boy had a new toy to enjoy, I enjoy it if Mum spoils me with toys.

Starter

Sing /oy/ and /oi/

♪ **Song text:** "don't be noisy oi oi oi".

- Gather the children on the carpet.
- Sing the Song of Sounds all the way through.
- Explain that today they are going to practise all the /oy/ sounds they have learned this week.
- Show the class the "oy" and "oi" flashcards and sing the correct parts of the song as you show each card. Ask children to perform the actions at the same time.

Main lesson

Say /oy/ and /oi/

- Remind children that all of these make exactly the same sound.
- Ask them to say /oy/ as you show them each flashcard picture-side up.
- Display all the picture cards on the board. Point to a few at random and, using the "I say, you say" technique, ask children to repeat the word after you, stressing the /oy/ sound in the word.

Read /oy/ and /oi/

- Sit the children with their chatting chums.
- Remind them that although /oy/ and /oi/ make the same sound, they look different.
- Hold up the "boy with a toy oy oy oy" flashcard picture-side up. Ask the children if they can remember what it looks like. Choose one child to tell you what letters make the grapheme. Turn the flashcard over to show the grapheme and stick it on the board.
- Repeat for "don't be noisy oi oi oi".
- On the board, display the two graphemes and all the picture cards. Ask children to work with their chatting chums to discuss which picture cards contain which grapheme.
- Discuss with the children and check if they are correct by revealing the grapheme on the reverse of each picture card.
- Move the picture cards next to the correct graphemes.

Blend /oy/ and /oi/

- For the green sentence "The boy had a new toy to enjoy", practise blending each word individually and then the whole phrase. Do this by asking the children to say the sounds as you press the sound buttons, and then blend the sounds together as you sweep your hand underneath the word. Go through the whole phrase, then go back and point to each word for the children to read.
- Repeat for "I enjoy it if Mum spoils me with toys".

Revision

At different points during the day, produce your "oy" and "oi" flashcards and ask children to sing the song, do the actions and/or say the sound. Remind them that this week they will be learning different graphemes for the phoneme /oy/.

Target graphemes: /oy/, /oi/

Learning objective

to learn to read, write and say the graphemes /oy/ and /oi/

Resources

- Song of Sounds flashcards: oy, oi
- Song of Sounds picture cards: boy, toy, oyster, oil, toilet, point
- Song of Sounds green word cards: annoy, enjoy, coin spoil
- Song of Sounds green sentences: The boy had a new toy to enjoy, I enjoy it if Mum spoils me with toys.

Starter

Sing /oy/ and /oi/

♪ **Song text:** "don't be noisy oi oi oi".

- Gather the children on the carpet.
- Sing the Song of Sounds all the way through.
- Explain that today they are going to practise all the /oy/ sounds they have learned this week and that you are going to show them a special trick to help them with their spelling.
- Show the class the "oy" and "oi" flashcards and sing the correct parts of the song as you show each card. Ask them to perform the actions at the same time.

Main lesson

Say /oy/ and /oi/
- Remind children that /oy/ and /oi/ make exactly the same sound.
- Ask them to say /oy/ as you show them each flashcard, picture-side up.
- Stick all the picture cards on the board. Point to a few at random and, using the "I say, you say" technique, ask them to repeat the word after you, stressing the /oy/ sound.

Read /oy/ and /oi/
- Now take the picture cards away and stick the green words all over the board.
- Point to each word and read in unison. Do this by asking children to say the sounds as you press the sound buttons, and then blend the sounds together as you sweep your hand underneath the word.
- Tell them that these words can help us to work out when to use /oi/ in a word and when to use /oy/.
- Circle the "oy" and "oi" graphemes in each word – what do children notice? The "oi" grapheme is in the middle of the words but the /oy/ grapheme is at the end of words.
- Explain that in words of one syllable this is almost always the case.

Blend /oy/ and /oi/
- Display on the board the green sentences "The boy had a new toy to enjoy" and "I enjoy it if Mum spoils me with toys." Ask children to check where the "oy" and "oi" graphemes are in the words and see if this rule works.
- They will notice that it works for all the words except "toys" where the /oy/ is in the middle. Explain that this is because this is a plural version of the word "toy".

Revision

At different points during the day, produce your "oy" and "oi" flashcards and ask children to sing the song, do the actions and/or say the sound. Remind them that this week they will be learning different graphemes for the phoneme /oy/.

The noisy boy

Target graphemes: "oy" and "oi"

Learning objective

to learn to discriminate between the "oy" and "oi" graphemes; to practise blending and segmenting words containing /oy/ and /oi/

Resources:

Carpet session

- Week 17: Teach software
- A toy picture card for each child or pair hidden around the room prior to the lesson (Week 17: AS1–4)
- A "noisy boy" outfit, e.g. jeans, leather jacket and a drum or similar (optional)

Noisy words

- Song of Sounds green words: oy and oi
- Song of Sounds picture cards: oy and oi
- A selection of musical instruments, one per child

Noisy toys

- Eight small cones

- Four large sheets of paper
- Two marker pens
- Two travelling toys, e.g. scooter, trike, bouncer, etc.
- A list of oy and oi words – boy, toy, joy, annoy, enjoy, oyster, oil, coin, point, boil, soil, foil, spoil, etc.

Noisy handwriting

- Song of Sounds flashcards: oy and oi
- Song of Sounds picture cards: oy and oi
- Paper or an exercise book for each child
- A pencils or pen for each child
- A drum

Revision

- Song of Sounds flashcards: oy and oi

Carpet session

- Gather the resources.
- Hide the toy picture cards around the classroom, one per child or chatting chum pair. .
- Gather the children on the carpet.
- This lesson includes an option to teach in role as a "noisy boy", as an alternative you can use the software. Enter the classroom making lots of noise.

1 • Introduce yourself and explain why you are here, for example, "Oi you lot. I'm the noisy boy and I love making lots of noise. Now listen – I am annoyed because some of my noisy toys have gone missing. Without my noisy toys, how I am supposed to enjoy myself? My day is spoiled. So I need to find my noisy toys and I want you to help me."

> **Software**
> Teach
> **W17**

2 • Explain that you want the children to look for your /oy/ sound toys but to do this you want to check that they know what they are looking for. Ask them if they know that there are two graphemes that make the /oy/ sound. Ask them what they look like. Play "Everybody shout /oy/". On the screen, different graphemes appear and children should shout /oy/ when they see an "oy" and "oi" grapheme.

- Ask them individually or in pairs, to go and find one of your /oy/ sound toy picture cards from around the classroom. When they have found one, they should bring it back to the carpet.

- Ask them to hold up their flashcards and shout /oy/. Sing "boy with a toy oy oy oy" and ask children holding the corresponding "oy" to hold it up. Sing "don't be noisy oi oi oi" and ask those holding the corresponding "oi" to hold it up.

3 • Ask if there is special way to know which words use "boy with a toy oy oy oy" and which use "don't be noisy oi oi oi". Children will remember the rule you taught them during the week, so let them explain and be impressed. Show slide 3 and explain that this word is "boy". Which grapheme do they think makes the /oy/ sound in this word? Ask those holding the correct /oy/ to hold it up.

- Repeat for slides 4–7.

8 • Reveal a picture of an oyster. Explain that we know to use /oi/ in the middle of a word and to use /oy/ at the end, but what do they think goes at the beginning of this word? Ask children to show their flashcards for their guess. Reveal the answer.

9 • Repeat using slide 9. Conclude that either /oy/ or /oi/ can go at the beginning of words.

10 • Revise the learning objectives before moving off the carpet to begin the practical activities.

Practical activities

Noisy words

An activity for a small group of 5–6 children

Aim: to practise blending words for reading containing the "oy" and "oi" grapheme and then segmenting words into phonemes to music

How to play:
- Gather the resources.
- Give each child a muscial instrument.
- Hold up an /oy/ or /oi/ green word.
- Show children how to beat out the different phonemes in the word and say them out loud at the same time e.g. /a/-/n/-/oy/.
- Ask the group to do this in unison.
- Repeat for all green words.
- Hold up a picture card.
- First ask children to segment the word into phonemes and then beat out the different phonemes as before.
- Repeat for all picture cards.

Support
For less-able children, ensure that you work together as a group and model carefully.

Challenge
For more-able children, allow them to choose the words and pictures independently, practise and then perform to the group.

Noisy toys

A game for a large group of 6–10 children

Aim: to practise segmenting words for writing containing /oy/ and /oi/ and choosing the correct grapheme

How to play:
- Gather the resources.
- This game should be played in a large space.
- Split the group into two teams.
- From a starting line, for each team place four cones in a row that lead to two pieces of paper on the wall with an /oi/ on one and an /oy/ on the other. They also need a travelling toy per team, such as a scooter.
- Ask the first child in each team to get ready.
- Call out a word, for example, "point".
- The two children must race on their toy, zigzagging through the cones to their large pieces of paper.
- They should then write "point" on the paper, depending on whether they think it is an /oy/ or /oi/ word, and race back.
- The child who is first back to the line with the correct answer is the winner.

Support
Sing the corresponding part of the song and do the action, and support children with segmenting.

Challenge
More-able children should be challenged to write the whole word independently.

Noisy handwriting

An activity for a small group of 5–10 children

Aim: to practise correct formation of the "oy" and "oi" graphemes

How to play:

- Gather the resources.
- Give each child a piece of paper/exercise book and a pencil/pen.
- Choose a flashcard.
- Model writing it on the board in a cursive script using the correct patter.
- Now bang the drum several times to indicate how many times children should write the grapheme.
- Repeat a few times.

Support

Less-able children can use the flashcards and sing the song and do the actions prior to writing the grapheme.

Challenge

Use the picture cards with more-able children. Work together as a group to segment the word, model writing it in a cursive script and then ask the children to write it a few times.

Revision

Gather the children back on the carpet. Back in role as the noisy boy, use the Song of Sounds flashcards. Hide the "oy" and "oi" flashcards in the pack. Show the flashcards one at a time, picture-side up. Children should not make a sound until they see "don't be noisy oi oi oi" or "boy with a toy oy oy oy", when they should sing it. Repeat. Next show the flashcards one at a time, grapheme-side up. The children should not make a sound until they see "oi" or "oy", when they should shout it. Repeat multiple times.

Now read...

Feelings, *Red, Band 2B*

Hansel and Gretel, *Blue, Band 4*

Target phoneme: /air/

Learning objective

to learn to read, write and say /air/

Resources

- Song of Sounds flashcard: air
- Song of Sounds picture cards: fairy, hair, chair
- Song of Sounds green words: pair, stairs

Starter

Sing /air/

♪ **Song text:** "a hairy fairy air air air".

- Gather the children on the carpet.
- Sing the Song of Sounds all the way through.
- Explain that this week they are going to be learning about different graphemes that make the /air/ sound.
- Explain that today they are going to practise the /air/ sound that they have already learned, before going on to learning some new ones.
- Show the class the "air" flashcard and sing "a hairy fairy air air air".
- Remind them of the action and ask the class to perform it together.

Main lesson

Say /air/

- Remind children how to say /air/ – say /air/ with a happy face, angry face, sad face.
- Show them the /air/ picture cards and ask them to repeat after you, using the "I say, you say" technique, so they can hear the /air/ sound in the word: /f/-/air/-/y/, /h/-/air/, /ch/-/air/.

Read /air/

- Show children the grapheme side of the card and remind the class what an "air" looks like.
- Hide the flashcard behind your back – if you bring it out and show the picture side, they must sing "a hairy fairy air air air"; if you bring it out and show the grapheme side they must say /air/. Bring the card out in different ways from either side of your body.

Write /air/

- Show children how to form an "air" on the board using the explanation "Go around the apple, down and flick" and "Go down the insect's body, add a flick for his tail and a dot for his head" and "Start at the top, go down, back up and over the rabbit's floppy ear."
- Ask them to follow you and sky-write the "air" grapheme – don't forget you need to write backwards.
- Write a tiny "air" in the air, then repeat getting increasingly bigger.

Blend /air/

- For the Song of Sounds green words "pair" and "stair", practise reading and blending the graphemes to make the word.
- Do this by asking children to say the sounds as you press the sound buttons, and then blend the sounds together as you sweep your hand underneath the word.

Revision

Add your "air" flashcard to the stack you have already taught. Show the class the flashcards one at a time, picture-side up, and ask them to sing each sound. Ask the class to do the actions to the song silently as you show them the flashcards one at a time. As you produce the grapheme side, let them say the different sounds. Repeat continually throughout the day.

Target grapheme: /are/

Resources

- Song of Sounds flashcard: are
- Song of Sounds picture cards: bare, stare, care
- Song of Sounds green words: bare, stare, scare

Learning objective

to learn to read, write and say /are/

Starter

Sing /are/

🎵 **Song text:** "share if you care are are are".

- Gather children on the carpet.
- Sing the Song of Sounds all the way through.
- Explain that today they are going to a learn a new grapheme.
- Show the class the /are/ flashcard and sing "share if you care are are are".
- Show them the action and ask the class to perform it together.

Main lesson

Say /are/

- Point out that /are/ makes exactly the same sound as "a hairy fairy air air air".
- Show children how to say /air/ /are/ – ask them to say /are/ ten times with their eyes closed.
- Show them the "are" picture cards and ask them to repeat after you, using the "I say, you say" technique, so they can hear the /air/ /are/ sound in the words: /b/-/are/, /s/-/t/-/are/, /s/-/c/-/are/.

Read /are/

- Explain that although this phoneme makes the same sound as "a hairy fairy air air air", it looks different.
- Show children the grapheme side of the card and explain what an "are" looks like.
- Hide the flashcard behind your back – if you bring it out and show the picture side they must sing "share if you care are are are", if you bring it out and show the grapheme side they must say /air/. Bring the card out in different ways from either side of your body

Write /are/

- Show children how to form an /are/ on the board using the explanation "Go around the apple, down and flick" and "Start at the top, go down, back up and over the rabbit's floppy ear" and "Go around the elephant's head and add his curly trunk."
- Ask them to follow you and sky-write the "are" grapheme – don't forget you need to write backwards.
- Ask them to look up to the ceiling and write an "are" in the air.

Blend /are/

- For the Song of Sounds green words "care" and "square", practise reading and blending the graphemes to make the words. Do this by asking the children to say the sounds as you press the sound buttons, and then blend the sounds together as you sweep your hand underneath the word.

Revision

Add the "are" flashcard to the stack you have already taught. Show the class the flashcards one at a time picture-side up and ask them to sing each sound but in a whisper, until they see the "share if you care" flashcard when they should sing it out loudly. Repeat a few times. Ask the class to silently do the actions to the song as you show them the flashcards one at a time. As you produce the grapheme side, let them whisper the different sounds until they see the "are", when they should shout it. Repeat the flashcard work throughout the day.

Target graphemes: /air/, /are/

Learning objective

to learn to read, write and say /air/ and /are/

Resources

- Song of Sounds flashcards: air, are
- Song of Sounds picture cards: fairy, hair, chair, bare, stare, scare
- Song of Sounds green sentences: I don't care if you stare at my hair. It is not fair if you will not share.

Starter

- Gather the children on the carpet.
- Sing the Song of Sounds all the way through
- Explain that today they are going to practise all the /air/ sounds they have learned this week.

Sing /air/ and /are/

- Show the class the "air" and "are" flashcards and sing the correct parts of the song as you show each card. Ask them to perform the actions at the same time.

Main lesson

Say /air/ and /are/

- Remind children that both of these make exactly the same sound.
- Ask them to say /air/ and /are/ as you show them each flashcard, picture-side up.
- Stick all the picture cards on the board. Point to a few at random and, using the "I say, you say" technique, ask children to repeat the word after you, stressing the /air/ sound in the word.

Read /air/ and /are/

- Remind children that although /air/ and /are/ make the same sound, they look different.
- Hold up the "a hairy fairy air air air" flashcard, picture-side up. Ask them if they can remember what it looks like. Choose one child to tell you what letters make the grapheme. Turn the flashcard over to show the grapheme and stick it on the board.
- Repeat for "share if you care are are are".
- On the board, display the two graphemes and all the picture cards. Ask children to work with their chatting chums to discuss which picture cards contain which grapheme.
- Discuss with the children and check that they are correct by revealing the grapheme on the reverse of each picture card.
- Move the picture cards next to the correct graphemes accordingly.

Blend /air/ and /are/

- Using the green sentence "I don't care if you stare at my hair", practise blending each word individually and then the whole phrase. Do this by asking children to say the sounds as you press the sound buttons, and then blend the sounds together as you sweep your hand underneath the word. Go through the whole phrase, then go back and point to each word for children to read.
- Repeat for "It is not fair if you will not share".

Revision

At different points during the day, produce your "air" and "are" flashcards and ask children to sing the song, do the actions and/or say the sound. Remind them that this week they will be learning different graphemes for the phoneme /air/.

Target graphemes: /air/ and /are/

Learning objective

to revise the /air/ and /are/ phonemes

Resources

- Song of Sounds flashcards: air, are
- Song of Sounds picture cards: fairy, hair, chair, bare, stare, scare
- Song of Sounds green word cards: pair, stairs, care, square
- Song of Sounds green sentences: I don't care if you stare at my hair. It is not fair if you will not share.
- Song of Sounds tricky word cards: there, where

Starter

- Gather the children on the carpet.
- Sing the Song of Sounds.
- Explain that today they are going to practise all the /air/ sounds they have learned this week.

Sing /air/ and /are/

- Show the class the "air" and "are" flashcards and sing the correct parts of the song as you show each card. Ask them to perform the actions at the same time.

Main lesson

Say /air/ and /are/

- Remind children that all of these make exactly the same sound.
- Ask them to say /air/ as you show them each flashcard, picture-side up.
- Stick all the picture cards on the board. Point to a few at random and, using the "I say, you say" technique, ask children to repeat the word stressing the /air/ sound.

Read /air/ and /are/

- Now take the picture cards away and stick the green words all over the board.
- Point to each word and read in unison. Do this by asking children to say the sounds as you press the sound buttons, and then blend the sounds together as you sweep your hand underneath the word.
- Tell children that you are going to give them a spelling tip about /air/ and /are/ words. Explain that although there are no rules to help you work out where to use /air/ and /are/, the most common is /are/.

Blend /air/ and /are/

- Display the green sentences "I don't care if you stare at my hair" and "It is not fair if you don't share." Ask children whether there are more "air" graphemes or more "are" graphemes.

Introduce /ear/

- Write the word "bear" on the board and circle the "ear" at the end of the word.
- Explain that in the word "bear", the "ear" at the end also makes an /air/ sound.
- Sound-talk the word with the children: /b/-/ear/. Give more examples: /t/-/ear/, /w/-/ear/, /p/-/ear/.

Introduce "there" and "where"

- Show children the tricky words "there" and "where" flashcards.
- Ask them what is tricky about these two words: the /air/ sound at the end sounds like it should be "a hairy fairy air air air" or a "share if you care are are are". However, it is spelled "e-r-e".

Revision

At different points during the day, produce your "air" and "are" flashcards and ask children to sing the song, do the actions and/or say the sound.

Felicity's favourite phoneme

Learning objective

to learn to discriminate between the "air" and "are" graphemes; to practise blending and segmenting words containing /air/ and /are/

Resources

Carpet session

- Week 18: Teach software
- Song of Sounds "air" and "are" green word cards (all)
- A fairy bag containing Felicity's flashcards (Week 18: AS1)
- A mini whiteboard and pen for every chatting chum pair
- A Felicity the Phoneme Fairy outfit, including wings, wand and fairy dust (optional)
- A print-out of slide 2 for every chatting chum pair (optional)

Find the fairies

- Fairy cards (Week 18: AS2–3)
- A mini whiteboard and pen for each child
- An outside area, preferably with trees and hidden areas (optional)

Read with Felicity

- Word cards (Week 18: AS4–5)
- A playing board for each child (Week 18: AS6)
- A feely bag or box
- Counters

Felicity's formation

- Felicity's flashcards from the carpet session (Week 18: AS1)
- Paper or an exercise book for each child
- A pencil or pen for each child
- A feely bag
- Glitter
- Gold pen or pink pencil

Revision

- Felicity's flashcards from the carpet session (Week 18: AS1)

Carpet session

- Gather the resources.
- Sit the children in their chatting chum pairs.
- Enter the classroom as Felicity the Phoneme Fairy. Explain that you are very excited because you have heard the children are learning about your favourite sound this week. Ask children if they know what your favourite sound. Let them discuss with their chatting chums and tell you what they think.

1
- Reveal to children that your favourite sound is the /air/ sound because you are a /f/-/air/-/y/.

> **Software**
> Teach
> **W18**

- Give each chatting chum pair a mini whiteboard and a pen.

2
- Explain that some of the pictures on the slide have the /air/ sound in them and some don't. Ask them to work with their chatting chums and decide which have the /air/ sound and which do not. Tell them to write down on their print-out the number of the images that have the /air/ sound. Discuss their answers.

3
- Reveal the answers.
- Ask children to write on their whiteboards two graphemes that make the /air/ sound: "air" and "are".

4
- Reveal slide 4 to show both sounds. Sing the part of the Song of Sounds for each grapheme on the board.
- Ask children to sit in a fairy circle. Tell them that they are going to practise reading words with the different graphemes in.
    - Give one child a green word.
    - Sing (to the tune of London Bridge is Falling Down) with children "pass the word around the ring, around the ring, around the ring, pass the word around the ring, around the ring, around the ring, what does it say?"
    - The child holding the word must stand up and read it.
    - Add another green word and repeat. Each time, add another green word until all four green words are going around the circle. You could then add a picture card and whoever ends up holding the word, must stand up and spell it. Repeat a few times.
- Play "Fairy dust". Use the cards from the resource CD. Put them in a bag. Sit the children with their chatting chums and give each pair a mini whiteboard and pen. Pull a card out of the bag. If the card shows /air/ or /are/, ask them to write a word that they think has that grapheme. If the card has a fairy on, they must wave their arms in a fairy style. If the card has yellow fairy dust on, Felicity sprinkles fairy dust over the children. (You could pretend, or be daring and use real glitter.) Repeat lots of times.

5
- The presentation finishes by inviting children to play some games to practise /air/ and /are/.

Practical activities

Find the fairies
A game for a group of 10–12 children

Aim: to practise segmenting words for writing containing /air/ and /are/ and choosing the correct grapheme

How to play:
- Gather the resources.
- Prior to the lesson, hide the fairy cards around your outside area.
- Invite children to search for the fairies independently. The supervising adult should stand where they can see all the children.
- When they find a fairy, they must try to write the correct /air/ or /are/ word on their whiteboards. After they have written the word, children must go back to the adult to discuss their spelling of the word.

Support
Walk with less-able children and ask them to just record which "air" or "are" sound they think it is.

Challenge
Ask more-able children to try to put their /air/ or /are/ word into a simple sentence.

Read with Felicity
An activity for a small group of 5–6 children

Aim: to practise blending words for reading containing /air/ and /are/

How to play:
- Gather the resources.
- Give each child a playing board and counters.
- Children should take it in turns to pull a word card out of the bag.
- If they can read the word, they should cover the corresponding grapheme on their playing board with a counter.
- If they can't read it, they cannot cover up a grapheme.
- If they can read a word but don't have the corresponding grapheme blank, they miss a turn.
- The first child to cover all their graphemes is the winner.

Support
Help less-able children to read the words by orally blending and ask them to match the grapheme in the word to their board.

Challenge
Ask more-able children to read independently and tell you what a words means by putting it into a sentence.

Felicity's formation

An activity for a small group of 5–10 children

Aim: to practise correct formation of the /air/ and /are/ graphemes

How to play:

- Gather the resources.
- Put the flashcards in a feely bag.
- Pull out a flashcard. If it is the "air" or "are" flashcard, model writing the grapheme using a cursive script and the correct explanation. Children should then write it several times.
- If you pull out Felicity's fairy dust card, Felicity should give children a bit of magic dust (e.g. glitter on their cheeks).
- If you pull out the fairy card, they can write both graphemes using a gold pen or pink pencil.

Revision

Use the flashcards to sing the Song of Sounds with the class and give out sparkle dust for good singing. Invite the boys to sing a part of the song on their own and then the girls. You could pick several children to sing the song on their own.

Now read...

Gorillas, *Blue, Band 4*

The Rainforest at Night, *Blue, Band 4*

Target tricky words: "when", "what"

Learning objective

to practise reading and spelling tricky words

Resources

- Song of Sounds tricky word cards: when and what

Introducing "when" and "what"

- Gather the children on the carpet.
- Explain that today they are going to learn two new tricky words.
- Before you show children the "when" and "what" flashcards, ask them if they can remember what makes some words trickier than others: they don't follow Felicity's phoneme rules.
- Hold up the flashcards – ask children why these words are red and spiky: they are red because, like a red traffic light, red means stop and you need to stop and think about them.

Read "when" and "what"

- Show children the tricky word "when" and read it to them.
- Give a few examples of when "when" might be used in sentences, for example, "I love it when my mummy cuddles me" and "When is it time to go to the park?"
- Display the word "when". Explain to children that in this word it is the /wh/ that is tricky because it is made by a "w" and an "h" and together they make the /w/ sound but you cannot hear the /h/. Explain that the "e" and the "n" are not tricky because you can hear them. To remember this word they must remember that there is a silent /h/ and the /w/ sound is made by a "w" and an "h" together.
- Show the children the tricky word "what" and read it to them. Give a few examples of when "what" might be used in sentences, for example, "What time is it?" and "What are you doing?"
- Display the word "what". Explain that this has the same tricky /w/ sound at the beginning, which is made by a "w" and a silent "h". Can children spot anything else that is tricky (the "a" in this word makes an /o/ sound. To remember this tricky word, they need to remember it has a silent "h" and the "a" makes the /o/ sound. Explain that the "t" is not tricky as it makes the correct sound.

Write "when and what"

- Show children how to write the word "when" on the board. As you write each grapheme say it out lloud: "w"-"h"-"e"-"n". You could say the letters and whisper the "h" to show that it is silent.
- Repeat for "what": "w"-"h"-"a"-"t". Practise saying the word as it looks: wh-a-t.

Revision

Tell children that you will keep testing them to see if they can remember the words because they are so tricky. Throughout the day, keep producing the "when" and "what" flashcards and ask children to read them on sight. Repetition is the key.

Target tricky words: "why", "which"

Resources

- Song of Sounds tricky word cards: why, which
- Previously-taught Song of Sounds tricky word cards: when, what

Learning objective

to practise reading and spelling tricky words

Introducing "why" and "which"

- Gather the children on the carpet.
- Explain that today they are going to learn two new words.
- Ask them if they can remember what makes some words trickier than others (they don't follow Felicity's phoneme rules).
- Hold up the "why" and "which" flashcards. Ask children why these words are red and spiky (they are red because, like a red traffic light, red means stop and you need to stop and think about them).

Read "why" and "which"

- Show children the tricky word "why" and read it to them.
- Give a few examples of when "why" might be used in sentences, for example, "Why do I have to go to bed?" and "Why is the sea blue?"
- Display the word "why". Explain that just like the words they learned yesterday, in "why" the /w/ sound is made by a "w" and a silent "h". Also, the /y/ in "why" sounds like "soar up high igh igh igh" but it is in fact a "y". Conclude that *all* of the word "why" is tricky. You must remember the silent "h" and that the "y" makes an /igh/ sound like in "sky" and "cry".
- Display the word "which". Give a few examples of when "which" might be used in sentences, such as "Which is your favourite?" and "Which teddy is yours?" Explain that there is only one tricky bit in "which". Ask if anybody knows what it is: in the same way as "why", the "w" and the "h" together make the /w/ sound. You must remember that the "h" is silent.

Write "why" and "which"

- Show children how to write the word "why" on the board. As you write each grapheme, say it out loud: "w"-"h"-"y".
- Repeat for "which": "w"-"h"-"i"-"c"-"h".
- To help them remember, you could say the word as you write it, but whisper the silent "h".

Revision

Add the "why" and "which" flashcards to those you taught yesterday. Throughout the day, keep producing the flashcards and ask children to read them on sight. Repeat continually throughout the day.

Target tricky words: "where", "were"

Learning objective

to practise reading and spelling tricky words

Resources

- Song of Sounds tricky word cards: where, were
- Previously-taught Song of Sounds tricky word cards: when, what, why, which

Introducing "where" and "were"

- Gather children on the carpet.
- Explain that today they are going to a learn two new words.
- Ask them if they can remember what makes some words trickier than others (they don't follow Felicity's phoneme rules).
- Hold up the "where" and "were" Song of Sounds flashcards. Remind children why these words are red and spiky: they are red because, like a red traffic light, red means stop and you need to stop and think about them.

Read "where" and "were"

- Show children the tricky word "where" and read it to them.
- Give a few examples of when "where" might be used in sentences, such as "Where are you going?" and "Where is my coat?" Explain that the "wh" is tricky in exactly the same way as the other words they have learned this week – the "w" and the "h" go together to make the /w/ sound. Furthermore, "ere" is tricky as it makes the /air/ sound as in "a hairy fairy air air air". The tricky bits of "where" are that you have to remember the silent "h" and that that the "ere" at the end makes an /air/ sound.
- Display the word "were" and read it to them. Explain that this word sounds similar to "where" but it looks different and it has a different meaning. Give a few examples of when "were" might be used in sentences, for example "Were you looking for me?" and "They were playing football." Explain that the "w" in "were" is not tricky as it makes the /w/ sound and there is no silent "h". Also, the /er/ is not tricky as it makes the correct "flower in a shower er er er" sound. However, the tricky bit in the word "were" is that you have to remember it has a silent "e" on the end.

Write "where" and "were"

- Show children how to write the word "where" on the board. As you write each grapheme, say it out loud: "w"-"h"-"e"-"r"-"e". Draw sound buttons underneath to emphasis that the "ere" is all one sound.
- Repeat for "were": "w"-"e"-"r"-"e". You could whisper the silent "e".

Revision

Add the "where" and "were" flashcards to those you have already taught this week. Throughout the day, keep producing the flashcards and ask the children to read them on sight. Repeat continually throughout the day.

Target tricky words: "who", "how"

Learning objective

to practise reading and spelling tricky words

Resources

- Song of Sounds tricky word cards: who, how
- Previously-taught Song of Sounds tricky word cards: when, what, why, which, where, were

Introducing "who" and "how"

- Explain that today you are going to a learn two new words.
- Ask children if they can remember what makes some words trickier than others (they don't follow Felicity's phoneme rules).
- Hold up the "who" and "how" Song of Sounds flashcards. Remind children that they are red because, like a red traffic light, red means stop. Because it is a tricky word, you need to stop and think about it.

Read "who" and "how"

- Show children the tricky word "who" and read it to them.
- Give a few examples of when "who" might be used in sentences, for example "Who are you? and "Who lives there?"
- Explain that the word "who" is *really* tricky as it is the complete opposite of the other words they have learned this week. There is a "w" and an "h" at the beginning but they don't make the /w/ sound. In fact in this word it is the "w" that is silent and so the "w" and the "h" together make a /h/ sound. Ask children what is tricky about the "o": it makes an /oo/ sound from "zoom to the moon oo oo oo". So to remember this word, you have to remember that the "w" is silent and the "o" goes /oo/.
- Show the word "how" and read it to the children. Give a few examples of when "how" is used in sentences, for example "How long till we get there? and "How did you do that?" Explain that "how" shouldn't really be a tricky word as the "h" makes the correct sound and the /ow/ makes the "clown upside down ow ow ow" sound. However, LOTS of people spell "how" incorrectly because it has the same letters as "who". The trick to remembering how to read and spell "how" is to remember which word it is. To help you, read the whole sentence to make sure you have got the correct word or think of the whole sentence that you are writing.

Write "who" and "how"

- Show children how to write the word "who" on the board. As you write each grapheme say it out loud: "w"-"h"-"o". Whisper the silent "w" at the beginning.
- Repeat for "how" on the board: "h"-"o"-"w". Make sure you draw sound buttons underneath before you read it to highlight that the "o" and the "w" are all one sound.

Revision

Add the "who" and "how" flashcards to those you have already taught this week. Throughout the day, keep producing the flashcards and asking children to read them on sight. Repeat continually throughout the day.

Tricky words

Target Song of Sounds tricky words: "when", "what", "why", "which", "where", "were", "who", "how"

Learning objective

to practise reading and spelling tricky words

Resources

Carpet session

- Week 19: Teach software
- Song of Sounds tricky word cards: when, what, why, which, where, were, who, how
- Song of Sounds green words
- Three coloured cards or a coloured fan (blue, green, purple) for each child
- Briefcase/bag
- A Tricky Trevor costume (optional)

Tricky hide and seek

- Song of Sounds tricky words: when, what, why, which, where, were, who, how
- A mini whiteboard and pen for each child (optional)

Tricky tear it up bingo

- Song of Sounds tricky word cards: when, what, why, which, where, were, who, how
- A strip of paper for each child, folded into eight equal sections
- A pen or pencil for each child

Tricky time

- Song of Sounds tricky word cards: when, what, why, which, where, were, who, how
- A timer
- A mini whiteboard and pen for each child

Homework

- Homework sheet (on Resource CD)

Revision

- Song of Sounds tricky word cards : when, what, why, which, where, were, who, how

Carpet session

- Gather the resources.
- Gather children on the carpet.
- This lesson has the option of teaching in role as Tricky Trevor, a wise old man with grey hair, a walking stick and a briefcase/bag. Another option is to use a Tricky Trevor teddy or receive a letter enclosing the tricky words from Trevor, or simply use the software.
- Depending on the option you have chosen, enter the classroom as Tricky Trevor or hold up your teddy or letter.

[1]
- Play the software. Remind children that you are an incredibly clever man and that you have come here today to teach them some more tricky words.
- From your briefcase/bag produce a selection of green words and tricky words. Ask them the difference between "green" words and "tricky" words.

> **Software**
> Teach
> **W19**

[2]
- Explain that before you teach them any more tricky words this year, you would like to check that they can remember all the tricky words they have learned so far. Press play on the software. On the second slide, the tricky words that the class learned on Trevor's last visit will appear – check that they can read them.

- From your briefcase/bag produce the tricky word cards that they are going to learn about today.
- Show children the tricky words and asks them to repeat the words after you. Ask them to whisper the words, shout the words, say the words and sing the words.

 3-4
- Reveal the words one at a time. Ask them to identify the green and tricky parts of each word and offer advice to help them remember each word as you have done in the daily sessions.

 5-11
- Play "Trevor's trick". Give each child cards of three different colours or a coloured fan corresponding to the colours of the words on the software game. Show the three different versions of each word, only one of which has the correct spelling, for example "what", "wot", "whot". They must work with their chatting chums to choose the correct spelling and reveal the card of that colour.

12
- Revise the session's learning objective before dividing children into their differentiated groups for the practical activities.

Practical activities

Tricky hide and seek
A game for a large group of 6–10 children

Aim: to practise reading and spelling tricky words

How to play:
- Gather the resources.
- Sit children in a circle.
- Practise reading and spelling today's tricky words using the Song of Sounds tricky word cards.
- Choose one child to be the "seeker" and send them to wait outside the classroom.
- Choose a tricky word, for example, "what", and make sure all the children know how to read and spell it. Discuss the tricky part(s) of the word.
- Choose one child to go and hide the word somewhere around the classroom.
- Ask the seeker to come back in, and tell them which word they are looking for.
- The seeker should look for the word while the other children in the group chant how to spell the word, for example, w-h-a-t. When the seeker is far away from the hidden word the children should chant very quietly, getting louder as the seeker gets close to the word, chanting loudly when the seeker is near it.
- Repeat for a different word.

> **Support**
> Less-able children could chant the whole word (e.g. what, what, what), instead of breaking it down into phonemes.

> **Challenge**
> More-able children could write a sentence containing the word on a mini whiteboard.

Tricky tear it up bingo
An activity for a small group of 5–6 children

Aim: to practise reading and spelling tricky words

How to play:
- Gather the resources.
- Give a strip of paper and a pen/pencil to each child.
- Use the Song of Sounds tricky word cards to practise reading and spelling this week's tricky words before you begin.
- Display the tricky words on a board or in the middle of a table so that all children can see them.
- Give each child a strip of paper (with eight equal sections) and a pencil.
- Ask them to write a different tricky word in each section of their paper, in any order they like.

> **Support**
> Hold up the tricky word card as you say the word so that less-able children can match the words.

- Call out a tricky word, for example, where.
- The children must look at their strip of paper. If the word "where" is on either end, they may tear it off.
- Keep calling out different tricky words. You may repeat words several times.
- The first to tear off all their words is the winner.

Tricky time

An activity for a small group of 5–10 children

Aim: to practise spelling tricky words

How to play:
- Gather the resources.
- Give each child a mini whiteboard and pen.
- Set the timer to 30 seconds or one minute.
- Call out a tricky word.
- The children should see how many times they can write that word on their whiteboards in the given time.

Homework (optional)

On the resource CD is a letter for parents that you might choose to send home with each child. The letter explains the concept behind tricky words and has the tricky words that you have taught today on the reverse to practise reading and spelling with their child.

Challenge

Ask more-able children to spell the words independently without using the tricky word cards, but check that they are correct. As an extension, ask them to write a sentence on each section of paper containing each tricky word.

Support

Display the tricky word card as you say the word for less-able children to copy if they need to.

Challenge

Ask more-able children to write a sentence containing the tricky word.

Revision

Play "Pass the tricky word". Sit children in a circle and give them one tricky word card each. Pass the cards around the circle while singing (to the tune of London Bridge is Falling Down), "Pass the tricky words around the ring, around, the ring, around the ring, pass the tricky words around the ring, what do they say?" Those holding the tricky words should stand up and say the word, and the others should repeat it. Play several times.

Now read...

Sheep to Jumper, *Yellow, Band 3*
Feeling Things, *Yellow, Band 3*
Zog and Zebra, *Yellow, Band 3*
Peas, please!, *Yellow, Band 3*
The Small Bun, *Blue, Band 4*
Buzzy Bee, *Blue, Band 4*

Target skill: Revise all graphemes learned so far

Learning objective

to practise using all graphemes learned so far

Resources

- Song of Sounds IWB version
- Song of Sounds flashcards taught so far
- Whiteboards and pens for each chatting chum pair

Starter

- Sing the Song of Sounds using the IWB version.
- Gather the children on the carpet.

Main lesson

Reading graphemes

- Show the class the flashcards one at a time, picture-side up, and ask them to sing each sound.
- Ask them to silently do the actions to the song as you show them the flashcards.
- As you produce the grapheme side, can they say the different sounds? Ask the class to say them in unison as you get faster and faster.

Writing graphemes

- Give each chatting chum pair a whiteboard and pen.
- Show the class a flashcard picture-side up and ask them to write the grapheme on their whiteboards. Repeat a few times.
- Then demonstrate an action from the song – as you do the action ask children to write the corresponding grapheme. Repeat a few times.
- Finally, say a sound and ask them to write a grapheme that makes that sound, for example, if you said /a/ they could write any of the /a/ graphemes: "ay", "ai" or "a-e".

Support

Give less-able children a Song of Sounds phoneme finder to help them.

Challenge

Ask more-able children to write all the alternative graphemes you have learned for each sound.

Revision

At different points during the day, produce your flashcards and ask children to sing the song, do the actions and/or say the sound.

Target skill: Practise reading green and tricky words

Learning objective

to recognise the difference between decodable and non-decodable words

Starter

- Sit children in their chatting chum pairs.
- Sing the Song of Sounds using the IWB version.

Resources

- Song of Sounds IWB version
- A selection of Song of Sounds green words that you have taught so far, e.g. day, pair, feet, tooth, horn, fright, toast, spoil, cloud, sister
- A lolly stick labelled with each child's name, in a pot (optional)
- Song of Sounds tricky word cards: when, what, why, which, where, were, who, how

Main lesson

Reading green words

- On your board, display two green words that contain two homophone graphemes, for instance, "day", "pair". Explain to the class that you are going to practise reading words with two phonemes.
- Ask children to work with their chatting chums to practise reading the green words.
- Choose a lolly stick from your pot with a child's name on. Ask that child to stand up, choose a green word and read it out loud.
- Ask the class to read the word together in unison. Do this by asking them to read each grapheme as you press the sound button, and then read the whole word as you sweep your hand underneath. Remove the word from the board. Repeat for the second word.
- Then display three green words on the board that contain three phonemes, such as "feet", "teeth", "horn". Explain that now you are going to practise reading words with three phonemes. Repeat the steps above.
- Then display four green words on the board that contain four phonemes, such as "fright", "toast", "spoil". Explain that now you are going to practise reading words with four phonemes. Repeat the steps above.
- Finally, display a green word on the board, such as "sister". Explain to the class that this word has five phonemes. Repeat the steps above.

Reading tricky words

Ask children to explain to you the difference between green words and tricky words.

Revision

Show the class the Song of Sounds tricky word cards one at a time and ask them to read them.

Target skill: Practise writing green words

Learning objective

to practise decoding green words

Starter

- Sit children in their chatting chum pairs.
- Sing the Song of Sounds using the IWB version.

Main lesson

Writing green words

- Explain to children that today they are going to practise writing some green words.
- Give each chatting chum pair a mini whiteboard, pen and a Song of Sounds phoneme finder.
- Choose a two-phoneme word to say out loud, for example, "eat". Ask children to sound-talk the word with their chatting chums to segment the word into the correct phonemes. They should then write the word on their whiteboards, using their Song of Sounds phoneme finder to help them.
- Pull a lolly stick with a child's name on out of your pot. Ask that child to stand up and sound-talk the word they have written on their whiteboard. As they sound-talk, you should write it on the board so that you are modelling the correct handwriting to the class. Discuss which grapheme is used to represent the phoneme /e/.
- Repeat the above steps choosing a three-phoneme word, such as "might".
- Repeat the above steps choosing a four-phoneme word, such as "float".
- Display your selection of picture cards on the board. Give children a time limit, for instance, two minutes, to write as many words as they can on their whiteboards. Discuss.

Writing tricky words
- Ask children to explain to you the difference between green words and tricky words.
- Finish the session by practising writing the tricky words that they learned last week. Say a tricky word out loud and ask them to write it on their mini whiteboards.

Resources

- Song of Sounds IWB version
- A mini whiteboard and pen for each chatting chum pair
- Song of Sounds phoneme finders for each chatting chum pair
- A selection of Song of Sounds picture cards: snail, sheep, kite, chair, goat, screw, fork, skirt, clown, trousers, oyster
- A lolly stick labelled with each child's name, in a pot (optional)
- Song of Sounds tricky word cards: when, what, why, which, where, were, who, how

Support

To support less-able children, give them the Song of Sounds phoneme finder with the tricky words on the back so they have to find the correct tricky word and write it.

179

Target skill: Practise reading and writing a sentence

Resources

- Song of Sounds tricky word cards: when, what, why, which, where, were, who, how
- Song of Sound green sentence cards for each chatting chum pair of your choice
- A Song of Sounds phoneme finder for each chatting chum pair
- A mini whiteboard and pen for each chatting chum pair

Learning objective

to begin to use sentences correctly

Starter

- Sit children in their chatting chum pairs.
- Ask them to explain to you the difference between green words and tricky words.
- Practise reading the tricky words that they learned last week. Show the class the tricky words one at a time and ask them to read them, increasing in speed.

Main lesson

Reading a sentence

- Give each chatting chum pair a green sentence card. Explain to them that their sentence includes some green words and tricky words.
- Give them a time limit, e.g. one minute, to practise reading their sentence with their chatting chums.
- Ask each pair in turn to stand up and read their sentence out loud to the class.

Writing a sentence

- Give each chatting chum pair a mini whiteboard and pen and a Song of Sounds phoneme finder.
- Explain that you are going to write a sentence that contains both green words and tricky words.
- Call out: "I like dressing up in my monster costume."
- Ask children to repeat the sentence. Repeat a few times, adding a few actions, for instance, I (point to yourself), like (draw smile on your face with your finger), dressing up (act putting sleeves on), monster (show your claws).
- Model writing the sentence on the board. Explain your thought processes to the children as you write.
  - Use sound-talk to write the green words.
  - Find tricky words on your Song of Sounds phoneme finder.
  - Make sure you use finger spaces.
  - Read back your sentence to work out which word comes next.
- When the sentence is complete, read it back as a class. Then rub the sentence off the board and ask children to work with their chatting chums to write the sentence independently.
- To finish this session, ask children to rub out the word "monster". Discuss what their favourite dressing up costume is. On their whiteboards, ask them to change the sentence so it has a different ending.
- Ask each chatting chum pair to read their sentence out loud and all have fun reading the sentences.

Felicity returns

Target phonemes: all phonemes learned so far

Learning objective

to assess each child's phonic ability on a one-to-one basis

Resources

Carpet session

- Week 20: Teach software
- The Song of Sounds IWB version
- Song of Sounds phoneme finders
- A certificate for each child (Week 20: ASI)
- A mini whiteboard and pen for every chatting chum pair
- A fairy/wizard outfit and wand, a Felicity puppet, or a letter (optional)
- Glitter to reward children with a fairy sparkle on their cheek if they are being good/clever (optional)
- A lolly stick for each pair (optional)

Splat the sounds

- IWB version of Song of Sounds phoneme finder
- Two chairs
- Two fly swatters (optional)

Song of sounds lotto

- Song of Sounds lotto game

Felicity's formation

- Song of Sounds phoneme stars
- Song of Sounds phoneme finders (optional)
- A dice for each child
- A mini whiteboard and pen for each child

Revision

- A mini whiteboard and pen for each child

Carpet session

- Gather the resources.
- This lesson has the option of teaching in role as Felicity the Phoneme Fairy in a fairy costume. Alternatively, you could use a fairy puppet or receive a letter from Felicity.
- Depending on the option you have chosen, enter the classroom as Felicity or hold up your puppet or letter.
- [1] Play the software. Explain that you are very excited because the children have now finished learning all of the phonemes in the Song of Sounds.

  Software
  Teach
  W20

- Remind children that your favourite phoneme is /air/ because it is in the word "fairy".
- Ask children to tell you, after the count of three, what their favourite phoneme is. Ask them to show you the action of their favourite and to sing it.
- Tell them that today you are going to practise all the phonemes they know.
- Use the software to sing the Stage 2 song with children all the way through.
- Give each chatting chum pair a photocopied phoneme finder sheet or display the digital version on the IWB. Ask them to take turns with the lolly stick to point to a phoneme and the other child should say it out loud. Swap over and repeat a few times.

2
- Graphemes appear on the screen from all directions – children should say them out loud as they see them.
- Give each chatting chum pair a mini whiteboard and pen.

3
- Phoneme images will appear on the screen. Children should discuss and write the corresponding grapheme on their whiteboards.

4
- Two pictures appear and children should write two graphemes.

5
- Three pictures appear and children should write three graphemes.

6
- Tell them you will now practise reading and writing all the phonemes and graphemes they have learned.

> **Tip**
> At the end of the session you could present children with a certificate to celebrate them finishing the Song of Sounds (Week 20: AS1).

Practical activities

Splat the sounds

A game for a large group of 6–10 children

Aim: to recognise phoneme–grapheme correspondences at speed

How to play:
- Gather the resources.
- Display the IWB version of the Song of Sounds phoneme finder.
- Divide the children into two teams.
- At the front of each team place a chair facing away from the IWB.
- One child from each team should take it in turns to sit on the chair holding their fly swatter (or use their hand).
- Call out a phoneme. Children should get up from their chairs and race to splat or touch the correct picture and grapheme.

> **Tip**
> Ensure there are no obstacles between the children and the board.

> **Support**
> To help less-able children, say the phoneme and show the picture flashcard at the same time so that the children have to match them. They should focus on the easier sounds, e.g. /ay/, /ee/, /igh/.

> **Challenge**
> For more-able children, say a word that contains one of the graphemes, e.g. short. Children should splat the correct grapheme e.g. "or". They should focus on the trickier sounds e.g. /er/, /ou/ and /air/.

Song of sounds lotto

A game for a small group of 5–6 children

Aim: to recognise phoneme–grapheme correspondences

How to play:
- Play The Song of Sounds lotto game according to the instructions.

Felicity's formation

An activity for a small group of 5–10 children

Aim: to practise correct letter formation

How to play:
- Gather the resources.
- Gather the children around a table.
- Scatter Felicity's phoneme stars on the table, face down.
- Children should choose a star, roll their dice and write the corresponding grapheme that many times.
- Work with them and focus on their letter formation, rewarding individuals with glitter if they are working hard.

> **Support**
> Less-able children can use the Song of Sounds phoneme finder to support them.

Revision

 Gather children back on the carpet and give each child a mini whiteboard and pen. Challenge them to guess the phonemes – ask them to sing the corresponding part of the song as you mime the action, then call out the correct phoneme. Finally, ask them to write the correct grapheme on their whiteboards.

Now read...

Real Monsters, *Yellow, Band 3*

Frog or Toad?, *Yellow, Band 3*

Your Nose, *Blue, Band 4*

A Day Out, *Blue, Band 4*

Buzzy Bee, *Blue, Band 4*

Target skill: Reading and writing CVC words

Learning objective

to practise reading and writing CVC words

Resources

- Song of Sounds flashcards taught so far
- Song of Sounds green word cards: read, food, might, throw, feet, tooth, horn, hurt, coin, mouth
- A mini whiteboard and pen for each chatting chum pair

Starter

- Gather the resources.
- Sit children in their chatting chum pairs.
- Show the class the flashcards one at a time, picture-side up, and ask them to sing each sound.
- Ask them to silently do the actions to the song as you show them the flashcards.
- As you produce the grapheme side, can they say the different sounds? Ask the class to say them in unison as you get faster and faster.

Main lesson

Reading CVC words

- Explain that today they are going to practise reading words with a tricky phoneme in the middle.
- Using the Song of Sounds green word "read", practise reading and blending the graphemes to make the word. Do this by asking them to say the sounds as you press the sound buttons, and then blend the sounds together as you sweep your hand underneath the word
- Repeat using the words "food", "might" and "throw".

Reading and writing CVC words

- Stick all your green words on the board.
- Give each chatting chum pair a whiteboard and pen.
- Tell children that you are going to mime a word and they must guess your word as you do it and write it on their whiteboards.
- Mime one phoneme at a time without making a sound. Pause between each sound to allow the chatting chums to talk to each other and write the grapheme down. Ask them to read their word to work out the answer.
- On the count of three, they should all tell you the answer.
- Repeat a few times.
- After a few turns, ask the pairs to work together to play the game. One child should mime the word while the other writes it.
- Give them five minutes to play. You can observe while they are playing.

Support

Give less-able children a Song of Sounds phoneme finder to support them in writing the graphemes.

Challenge

For more-able pupils, take the whiteboard and pen away so they have to "see" the spelling in their head.

Target skill: Reading and writing CVC words

Learning objective

to practise reading and writing CVC words

Starter

- Gather the resources.
- Sit children in their chatting chum pairs.
- Show the class the flashcards one at a time, picture-side up, and ask them to sing each sound.
- Ask them to silently do the actions to the song as you show them the flashcards.
- As you produce the grapheme side, can they say the different sounds? Ask the class to say them in unison as you get faster and faster.

> **Resources**
> - Song of Sounds flashcards taught so far
> - Song of Sounds green word cards: make, shape, even, these, smile, like, home, joke, tune, rude
> - A mini whiteboard and pen for each chatting chum pair

Main lesson

Reading split digraph words
- Explain that today you are going to practise reading words with a split digraph.
- Using the Song of Sounds green word "make", practise reading and blending the graphemes to make the word. Do this by asking the children to say the sounds as you press the sound buttons, and then blend the sounds together as you sweep your hand underneath the word
- Repeat using the words "shape", "smile", "these" and "even".

Reading and writing split digraph words

- Stick the green words "make", "like", "home", "joke", "tune" and "rude" on the board.
- Give each chatting chum pair a mini whiteboard and pen.
- Tell them that you are going to mime a word and that they must write it down on their whiteboards as you do it, to see if they can guess your word.
- Show children that all the words have the same sound buttons. Ask them to draw sound buttons on their whiteboards so they are ready to help them remember that in a split digraph the two letters go either side of another letter and hold hands.
- Mime one sound at a time without making a sound. Pause between each to allow the chatting chums to talk to each other and write the grapheme down. Then ask them to read their word to work out the answer.
- On the count of three, they should all tell you the answer.
- Repeat a few times.
- Give the children five minutes to play. You can observe while they are playing.

> **Support**
> Give less-able pupils a Song of Sounds phoneme finder to help them write the graphemes.

> **Challenge**
> Ask more-able children to rub out their sound buttons and to mime more complex words, e.g. even, these, smile, shape etc.

Target skill: Reading and writing words with adjacent consonants

Learning objective

to practise reading words with two consonants in a row

Resources

- Song of Sounds flashcards taught so far
- Song of Sounds green word cards: slug, crab, twig, tent, hand
- Song of Sounds green sentence: I held a slug in my hand.

Starter

- Gather the resources.
- Sit children in their chatting chum pairs.
- Sing the Song of Sounds using the IWB version.
- Show the class the flashcards one at a time, picture-side up, and ask them to sing each sound.
- Ask them to do the actions to the song silently as you show them the flashcards.
- As you produce the grapheme side, can they say the different sounds? Ask the class to say them in unison as you get faster and faster.

Main lesson

Reading CVCC words

- Explain that today they are going to practise reading words with four graphemes.
- Using the Song of Sounds green word "slug", practise reading and blending the graphemes to make the word. Do this by asking the children to say the sounds as you press the sound buttons, and then blend the sounds together as you sweep your hand underneath the word.
- Repeat for the words "crab", "twig", "tent" and "hand".
- Put the green sentence "I held a slug in my hand" on the board. Ask the chatting chums to work together to read the sentence.
- Read the sentence together as a class.
- Display a selection of graphemes on the board, for example, /w/, /e/, /n/, /t/, /d/, /l/, /o/, /s/, /h/, /a/, /u/. Ask children to close their eyes. While their eyes are closed, you should use the graphemes to make a CVCC word. It could be a real word such as "went", "wind", "lost", "hand", "hunt" or it could be a nonsense word such as "wolt".
- When children open their eyes, they should decide whether it is a real word or a nonsense word.

Target skill: Reading and writing words with adjacent consonants

Learning objective

to practise reading words with two consonants in a row

Resources

- Song of Sounds flashcards cards taught so far
- Song of Sounds green word cards: paint, toast, first, fright, crowd, float, storm, prawn, spoil, cloud
- Song of Sounds picture cards in a feely bag: train, spoon, screw, skirt, clown, point

Starter

- Sit children in their chatting chum pairs.
- Sing the Song of Sounds using the IWB version.
- Give each chatting chum pair a whiteboard and pen.
- Sing a part of the song, for instance, "train in the rain ai ai ai" and ask them to write the grapheme on their whiteboards. Repeat a few times, with the chatting chums taking turns and helping each other.
- Perform actions from the song and ask children to write the grapheme on their whiteboards.
- Finally say a phoneme on its own and ask them to write one of its graphemes on their whiteboards.

Main lesson

Reading CVCC and CCVC words

- Explain that today you are going to help them read and write *harder* words with four phonemes.
- Using the Song of Sounds green word "paint", practise reading and blending the graphemes to make the word. Do this by asking the children to say the sounds as you press the sound buttons. Draw the children's attention to the longer sound button underneath the /ai/ and ensure that they read it as /ai/ not "a" and "i". Then blend the sounds together as you sweep your hand underneath.
- Repeat with the words "toast", "first" and "storm".

Writing CVCC and CCVC words

- Draw four large sound buttons on your board.
- Pull one of the picture cards out of the feely bag, for example, train.
- Say the word out loud to the children, and then say it in sound-talk, accentuating the consonant that is difficult to hear, for example, the "r" in /t/-/r/-/ai/-/n/.
- Repeat with another word, such as "spoon", and ask them to sound-talk it to their chatting chums.
- Make the word on your boards, placing each of the graphemes above one of your sound buttons.
- Discuss which grapheme is represented by two letters, for example, "oo", and change your sound button to a long sound button accordingly.
- Read the word with them.
- Choose a picture card. Ask children to tell their chatting chums what the word would be in sound-talk.
- Ask them to tell you which graphemes to place on each sound button.
- Ask them to write the graphemes on their whiteboards.
- Repeat with the other words, and as children become more confident, ask them to write the word first and then demonstrate the correct answer.

Writing CVCC words

- Jumble up the graphemes on the board again.
- Say a CVCC word, such as "golf", "band", "belt", "sink", "hump". Ask children to talk to their chatting chums and decide which four phonemes spell that word.

Meet the wordbuilder

Target words: wordbuilding CVC and CCVC/CVCC words

Learning objective

to practice reading and spelling a range of CVC, CCVC and CVCC words

Resources:

Carpet session

- Week 21: Teach software
- A mini whiteboard and pen for each chatting chum pair
- Bert the Wordbuilder costume (optional)
- A wheelbarrow of phoneme bricks – plastic building bricks with pictures from the song on one side of the brick and graphemes on the other (optional)
- Plastic hammer (optional)
- Giant picture cards – night, cake, slug, prawn (optional)

Build a word wall

- CVC and CCVC/CVCC words (Week 21: AS1–3) stuck to plastic building bricks

- Three bricks with a bulldozer picture stuck on (Week 21: AS2)
- A feely bag or box

Bulldozer bowling

- Song of Sounds picture cards
- A "cement mixer" e.g. a bin or bucket
- Ten plastic skittles/plastic bottles/tin cans
- A mini whiteboard and pen for each team
- A soft ball

Wordbuilding cards

- CVC and CCVC/CVCC words (Week 21: AS1–3)
- A mini whiteboard and pen for each child
- A dice for each child
- Song of Sounds phoneme finders (optional)

Revision

- CVC and CCVC/CVCC words (Week 21: AS1–3) stuck to plastic building bricks

Carpet session

- Gather the resources.
- Gather children on the carpet.
- This session has the option to teach in role as "Bert the Wordbuilder". If you do not wish to teach in role, use the software as an alternative.
- If you have plastic bricks in your classroom, you could attach pictures from the song on one side of the brick and graphemes on the other and put them in a wheelbarrow. It works well to physically build the words with the bricks. However, this is just an option and if you have no plastic bricks, the slide numbers are given below as an alternative.

1 • Explain that you are not just a builder who builds houses, but you can also build words.

2-3 • Explain that to build words you need to know your sounds. Pull a brick out of your wheelbarrow and show it to the children with the picture showing (or show slide 2) and ask children to sing the corresponding part of the song. The children will sing and you should act amazed. Repeat with four or five more bricks. Then turn the bricks around and ask children if they know what sounds these letters make (or show slide 3).

> **Software**
> Teach
> **W21**

188

- Explain that if they know their phonemes, they can not only read but they can also write words.

 • From your wheelbarrow, get out the bricks for the word "foot". Place them one at a time on your word wall. Use your plastic hammer to knock them closer together and then show children that you have "built" a word (or show slide 4). Ask children to read the graphemes as you touch the bricks, and when you sweep your hand underneath, to read the whole word.

 • Sit children in their chatting chum pairs.

- Give each pair a mini whiteboard and a pen. Explain that you are going to build another word and that you would like the pairs to read it and draw a picture of the word on their whiteboards. Put on the wall the phoneme bricks to spell "nine". Ask them to reveal their pictures . Repeat for the words "c-r-a-b" and "t-r-ai-n" (or show slides 5–7).

 • Explain that if they know their phonemes, not only can they read words but they can write words too. Pull a picture of "night" out of your wheelbarrow (or show slide 8). Model how to write this on a whiteboard. Show how, if they listen carefully to the word, they can hear the sounds – choose the correct sounds to make the word.

 • Pull further pictures out of your wheelbarrow, such as cake, belt, prawn (or show slides 9–11). Ask children to work with their chatting chums to write the words.

 • Finish by explaining that today they are going to practise wordbuilding by reading and writing words.

Practical activities

Build a word wall

A game for a small group of 5–6 children

Aim: To practise blending CVC and CVCC/CCVC words for reading

How to play:
- Gather the resources.
- Put the building bricks with the words stuck on in a feely bag or box.
- Sit the children in a circle.
- They children should take it in turns to pull a brick out of the feely bag or box.
- They should use the sound buttons to help them read the word. If they can read it correctly, they can keep it.
- The child who builds the highest word wall by the end of the game is the winner.
- However, if a child pulls out a brick with a bulldozer on, their word wall should be knocked down and they must put their bricks back in the feely bag or box and start again.

> **Support**
> Help less-able children to read the words by saying the sounds with them and encouraging them to blend the sounds together.

> **Challenge**
> Encourage more-able children to read the words at speed rather than using the sound buttons.

Bulldozer bowling

A game for a small group of 6–10 children

Aim: To practise segmenting CVC and CVCC/CCVC words for writing

How to play:
- Gather the resources.
- Put the picture cards in a "cement mixer", for example, a large bin.
- Set up the skittles in a V formation.
- Divide children into two teams and give each team a mini whiteboard and pen.
- One member of the first team should bowl the ball at the skittles. They should count how many skittles they have knocked down and then pick the corresponding number of picture cards out of the "cement mixer".

> **Support**
> Give less-able children a Song of Sounds phoneme finder to help them. You could also use the simpler words e.g. bee, play, moon etc.

- Collaboratively, the team should see if they can use their wordbuilding techniques to write the words on the whiteboards. For every word they write correctly they win a point.
- Repeat with the other team until the cards are all taken.
- At the end of the game, the team with the most points is the winner.

Wordbuilding cards

An activity for a small group of 5–10 children

Aim: To practise segmenting CVC and CVCC/CCVC words for writing

How to play:
- Gather the resources.
- Sit the children around a table and give each child a mini whiteboard and pen.
- Scatter the wordbuilding cards all over the table.
- Ask each child to pick a card and using the sound buttons to help them, write the word on their whiteboard.
- They could roll the dice to decide how many times to write the word (optional).
- They should then continue choosing cards until they have attempted to write them all. Discuss any misconceptions.

Challenge
Put more complex words, e.g. athlete, trousers, in the "cement mixer".

Support
Give less-able children a Song of Sounds phoneme finder to help them. Choose a word as a group and work on it together, helping the children to hear the sounds in the word. You could also use the simpler wordbuilding cards.

Challenge
Challenge more-able children to write a sentence containing the word.

Revision

Gather the children back on the carpet. Still in role as Bert (if applicable), use your bricks to make some nonsense words and ask them to read them. Begin with simpler words and use increasingly difficult words as the children progress.

Now read...

Hand Play, *Yellow, Band 3*

The Sun and the Moon, *Yellow, Band 3*

The Small Bun, *Yellow, Band 3*

Target skill: Reading and writing words that contain digraphs

Resources

- Song of Sounds flashcards
- Song of Sounds green word cards: stand, crisp

Learning objective

to practise reading and wirting words containing digraphs

Starter

- Show the class the flashcards one at a time, picture-side up, and ask them to sing each sound.
- Ask them to silently do the actions to the song as you show the flashcards one at a time.
- As you produce the grapheme side, can they say the different sounds? Ask the class to say them in unison as you get faster and faster.

Main lesson

Reading words containing digraphs

- Explain that today they are going to learn to practise reading words that contain five simple phonemes.
- Using the green word "stand", practise reading and blending the graphemes to make the word. Do this by asking children to say the sounds as you press the sound buttons, and then blend the sounds together as you sweep your hand underneath the word.
- Repeat for the words "crisp".

Reading and writing words containing digraphs

- Display the flashcards "f", "r", "o", "s", "t", "a", "m", "p", "d", "i", "n" and "k" on the board, grapheme-side up.
- Ask children to close their eyes. While their eyes are closed, you should use the graphemes to make a CCVCC word on the board. It could be a real word such as frost, stamp, drink, stink or it could be a nonsense word such as dramp.
- When they open their eyes, they should decide whether it is a real word or nonsense word. If it is a real word, they should give a thumbs-up. If it is a nonsense word, they should give a thumbs-down.
- Read the word together as a class. Repeat a few times.
- Jumble up the graphemes on the board again.

- Say a CCVCC word out loud. Ask children to talk to their chatting chums and decide which five phonemes spell that word.
- Choose a chatting chum pair to stand up and tell the class what the sounds are. Then ask every child to hold up five fingers and spell out the word in unison, saying the sounds as they touch each finger in turn.
- Repeat using a mixture of real words and nonsense words for children to spell.

Target skill: Reading and writing words that contain digraphs

Learning objective

to practise reading and writing words containing digraphs

Resources

- Song of Sounds flashcards
- Song of Sounds green word cards: street, splash, thrust, tooth, throw, storm, enjoy, cloud, fright, stairs
- Song of Sounds green sentence: I stamp down the street in my strong boots.
- A mini whiteboard and pen for each chatting chum pair

Starter

- Gather the resources.
- Sit children in their chatting chum pairs.
- Show the flashcards one at a time, picture-side up, and ask them to sing each sound.
- Ask the class to do the actions to the song silently as you show them the flashcards.
- As you produce the grapheme side, can they say the different sounds? Ask the class to say them in unison as you get faster and faster.

Main lesson

Reading words containing digraphs

- Explain that today they are going to practise reading words that contain a digraph.
- Using the green word "splash", practise reading and blending the graphemes to make the word. Do this by asking children to say the sounds as you press the sound buttons, and then blend the sounds together as you sweep your hand underneath the word.
- Repeat using the words "tooth", "cloud" and "street".
- On the board, display the green sentence "I stamp down the street in my strong boots." Ask the chatting chums to work together to read the sentence.
- Read the sentence together as a class.

Reading and writing words containing digraphs

- Display the green words "street", "splash", "tooth", "throw", "storm", "enjoy", "cloud", "brown", "mouth" and "crowd" on the board.
- Give each chatting chum pair a whiteboard and pen.
- Tell children that you are going to mime a word. They must try to guess the word and write their guess on their mini whiteboards.
- Using the actions from the song, mime one sound at a time without making a sound. Pause between each to allow the chatting chums to talk to each other and write the grapheme down. Then ask them to read their word to work out the answer.
- On the count of three, they should all tell you the answer.
- Repeat a few times.

> **Tip**
> Give the children five minutes to play. You can observe while they are playing.

> **Support**
> To support less-able pupils, give them a Song of Sounds phoneme finder to support them with writing the graphemes. Alternatively you may ask them to work with a teaching assistant to play the same game but with simpler words.

> **Challenge**
> To challenge more-able pupils, take the whiteboard and pen away so they have to "see" the spelling in their head.

Target skill: Reading and writing words that contain split digraphs

Learning objective

to learn how to spell difficult words correctly

Resources

- Song of Sounds flashcards
- Song of Sounds green word cards: brown, crowd, paint, float, toast, straw, haunt, first, spoil, square
- A mini whiteboard and pen for each chatting chum pair

Starter

- Sit children in their chatting chum pairs
- Show the class the flashcards one at a time, picture-side up, and ask them to sing each sound.
- Ask the class to do the actions to the song silently as you show them the flashcards.
- As you produce the grapheme side, can they say the different sounds? Ask the class to say them in unison as you get faster and faster.

Main lesson

Reading words containing split digraphs

- Explain that today they are going to practise reading words that contain some of the graphemes they learned in the Song of Sounds.
- Using the green word "paint", practise reading and blending the graphemes to make the word. Do this by asking children to say the sounds as you press the sound buttons, and then blend the sounds together as you sweep your hand underneath the word
- Repeat with the words "fright", "toast" and "first".

Reading and writing words containing split digraphs

- Stick the green words "paint", "fright", "float", "toast", "straw", "haunt", "first", "spoil", "stairs" and "square" on the board.
- Give each chatting chum pair a mini whiteboard and pen.
- Tell children that you are going to mime a word and they must write it down on their whiteboards as you do this to see if they can guess your word.
- Using the actions from the song, mime one sound at a time without making a sound. Pause between each to allow the chatting chums to talk to each other and write the grapheme down. Then ask them to read their word to work out the answer.
- On the count of three, they should all tell you the answer.
- Repeat a few times.
- After a few turns, ask children to work together to play the game. One child should mime the word while the other writes it.
- Give them five minutes to play. You can observe while they are playing.

Support

Give less-able pupils a Song of Sounds phoneme finder to support them with writing the graphemes. Alternatively you may ask them to work with a teaching assistant to play the same game but with simpler words.

Challenge

To challenge more-able pupils, take the whiteboard and pen away so they have to "see" the spelling in their head.

Target skill: Reading and writing words with split digraphs

Learning objective

to learn to read and write difficult words

Starter

- Sit children in their chatting chum pairs.
- Give each chatting chum pair a whiteboard and pen.
- Sing a part of the song for example, "throw the snow ow ow ow" and ask children to write the grapheme on their whiteboards. Repeat a few times with chatting chums taking turns and helping each other.
- Perform an action from the song and ask them to write the grapheme on their whiteboards. Repeat a few times.
- Finally say a phoneme on its own and ask children to write one of its graphemes on their whiteboards. Repeat a few times.

Resources

- Song of Sounds flashcards
- Song of Sounds green words: shape, these, smile
- Song of Sounds picture cards: flute, snake, throne
- A mini whiteboard and pen for each chatting chum pair

Main lesson

Reading words containing split digraphs

- Explain that today you are going to help them to read and write words that have a split digraph.
- Using the green word "shape", practise reading and blending the graphemes to make the word. Do this by asking children to say the sounds as you press the sound buttons. Draw their attention to the longer sound button underneath the "a" and "e" and remind them that the two letters might be split up but they are holding hands and together make the sound /a-e/. Then blend the sounds together as you sweep your hand underneath the word.
- Repeat with the words "these" and "smile".

Writing words containing split digraphs

- Display the picture card "flute".
- Say the word and then say it in sound-talk for example, /f/-/l/-/oo/-/t/.
- Ask them to tell their chatting chums what it is in sound-talk.
- Write the word on the board and draw the appropriate sound buttons to remind them visually that the "u" and the "e" are holding hands to make the /oo/ sound.
- Read the word with the children.
- Show them the word "snake" and the sound buttons in the word, asking them to draw them on their mini whiteboard.
- Ask them to write the graphemes on their whiteboards on top of the corresponding sound buttons.
- Then demonstrate the correct answer.
- Repeat for "throne".
- Finish by calling out a CCVCC word that contains a split digraph, such as "slide", "stroke", "crane", "spade". They should race to write the word as quickly as they can on their mini whiteboard and stand up. The first to write it correctly is the winner. Repeat a few times.

The wordbuilder returns

Target words: Wordbuilding CCVCC/CCCVC and CCCVCC words

Learning objective

to practise reading and spelling a range of CVC, CCVC/CVCC, CCVCC/ CCCVC and CCCVCC words

Resources

Carpet session
- Software (Week 22: Teach)
- A whiteboard and pen for each child
- A builder costume (optional)
- A wheelbarrow of phoneme bricks (optional)

Ten bricks tall
- Wordbuilding cards (Week 22: ASI)
- Plastic building bricks (blank)
- A feely bag or box

Wall of words
- IWB game screen

- A word wall – twelve pieces of paper pinned on a board to make a brick wall
- A mini whiteboard and pen for each team
- A fly swatter for each team

Wordbuilding cards
- Wordbuilding cards (Week 22: ASI)
- A mini whiteboard and pen for each child
- A dice for each child
- Song of Sounds phoneme finders (optional)

Revision
- Plastic building bricks

Carpet session

- Gather the resources.
- Gather the children on the carpet.
- This session has the option to teach in role as "Bert the Wordbuilder". If you do not wish to teach in role, use the software as an alternative.
- Depending on the option you have chosen, enter the classroom as Bert, or press play on the software.

1 • Tell children you are back to help them build some difficult words, but first you are going to give them a test to check that they have remembered the wordbuilding skills you taught them last week.

Software
Teach
W22

2 • Show the children a CVC word. Demonstrate how to read the word by wordbuilding: blend the sounds together to read the word. Ask them if this word is a real word or a nonsense word. Ask them to read the next CVC word on the slide independently and to decide whether it is real or a nonsense word. If it is a real word they should show you a thumbs-up and if it is a nonsense word they should show you a thumbs-down. Repeat for two more words.

3 • Repeat for CVCC/CCVC words.

4 • Tell children they have remembered their wordbuilding skills well and so you are going to show them how to wordbuild some really difficult words. Use slide 4 to demonstrate how to read the word "frost" by blending the sounds to read the word. Ask them to then read "drink" and "stroke".

Ensure that you stress the sound button for the split digraph in "stroke" and revise that the "o" and the "e" are holding hands to make the /o/ sound.

- Give each chatting chum pair a mini whiteboard and pen.

5
- Show a picture of a stamp and display the appropriate sound buttons. Revise with children how to segment the word into the five phonemes and then how to write the corresponding graphemes. Reveal the correct answer. Ask them to work with their chatting chums to write the words "crisps" and "grapes". Discuss any misconceptions.

6-8
- Finish by challenging children to a game of "Odd one out". Display slide 6 which shows three CVC words. Explain that two of the words are real words and one is a nonsense word. Ask children to read the words with their chatting chum pair and write the nonsense word on their whiteboards. On a signal, the children should show their whiteboards to you. Discuss their answers. Repeat for slides 7 and 8.

9
- Finish by explaining that today they are going to practise their wordbuilding skills by reading and writing words.

Practical activities

Ten bricks tall

A game for a small group of 5–6 children

Aim: to practise blending real and nonsense CCVC/CVCC and CCVCC/CCCVCC words for reading

How to play:
- Gather the resources.
- Print the word cards and put them in a feely bag or box.
- Give each child five building bricks to make into a tower.
- The children should take it in turns to pull a wordcard out of the feely bag or box and read it.
- If it is a real word, they win a brick for their wall and can start building a tower. If it is a nonsense word, they lose a brick from their tower.
- The first pair to build a tower of 10 bricks is the winner.

Wall of words

A game for a small group of 6–10 children

Aim: to practise segmenting CCVC/CVCC and CCVCC/CCCVC words for writing

How to play:
- Gather the resources.
- Clear a space in the classroom for children to run to and from the IWB (make sure this game is played safely).
- Divide the children into two teams. Sit them with their "word wall" with the IWB opposite.
- On the IWB, display the screen made up of twelve pictures of CCVCC words.
- On a given signal, the first child from each team should run to the IWB, touch a picture and run back and write it on a "brick" in their word wall. They should then give the pen to the next person on their team who does the same.
- The first team to fill in all of their bricks with the twelve words with no repeats is the winner.

Support

Help less-able children to read the words by saying the sounds with them and encouraging them to blend the sounds together.

Challenge

Encourage more-able children to read at speed rather than using the sound buttons.

Support tip

Give less-able children a Song of Sounds phoneme finder to help them. You may also choose to make another screen using simpler words, e.g. man, flag etc.

Challenge tip

More-able children should work independently and spell words correctly.

Wordbuilding cards

An activity for a small group of 5–10 children

Aim: to practise segmenting CVC and CVCC/CCVC and CCVCC/CCCVCC words for writing

How to play:

- Gather the resources.
- Sit the children around a table and give each a mini whiteboard and pen.
- Scatter the wordbuilding cards all over the table.
- Ask each child to pick a card and, using the sound buttons to help them, write the word on their whiteboard.
- They could roll the dice to decide how many times to write the word (optional).
- They should then continue choosing cards until they have attempted to write them all. Discuss any misconceptions.

Support

Give less-able children a Song of Sounds phoneme finder to help them. Choose a word as a group and work on it together, helping the children to hear the sounds in the word. You could also use the simpler wordbuilding cards.

Challenge

Challenge more-able children to write a sentence containing the word.

Revision

Gather the children back on the carpet. Still in role as Bert (if applicable), use your bricks to make some nonsense words and ask children to read them. Begin with simpler words and use increasingly difficult words as they progress.

Now read...

The Hat Maker and the Chimps, *Blue, Band 4*

The Rainforest At Night, *Blue, Band 4*

Target skill: Reading and writing words with two syllables

Learning objective

to discriminate syllables in multi-syllabic words

Resources

- Song of Sounds flashcards
- Song of Sounds green words: mushroom, lunchbox, morning, napkin
- List of one-, two-, three- and four-syllable words (Week 23: AS1-7)

Starter

- Sit children in their chatting chum pairs.
- Show the class the flashcards one at a time, picture-side up, and ask them to sing each sound.
- Ask them to do the actions to the song silently as you show them the flashcards one at a time.
- As you produce the grapheme side, can they say the different sounds? Ask the class to say them in unison as you get faster and faster.
- Play "Sound tennis". Children should sit so they are facing their chatting chums. One child should say a sound, for example, /ai/, then spell the version they mean using the letter names, for instance, "a", "i". Their chatting chums should then do exactly the same for a different sound, for example, /i-e/, "i split e". They should keep going backwards and forwards (like a game of tennis.) until one of them falters. Then they should start again. Encourage them to look around the classroom at the Song of Sounds classroom frieze or poster for help.

Main lesson

Reading two-syllable words

- Explain that today they are going to practise reading longer words and that you are going to show them an easy way to do it.
- Show children the green word "mushroom". Explain that to make it easier to read you are going to cut it up into syllables, and they are going to read one syllable at a time, then put them together to read the whole word.
- Draw a slash between the two syllables: mush/room.
- Sound-talk the first syllable and blend it: /m/-/u/-/sh/.
- Sound-talk the second syllable and blend it: /r/-/oo/-/m/.
- Say both syllables: /mush/-/room/. Repeat and ask the children to join in.
- Repeat with the green words "lunchbox", "morning" and "napkin".

Syllable practice

- Play "Show your syllables". Choose a word from the list of one-, two-, three- and four-syllable words on the resource CD and say it out loud.
- Children should work individually to decide how many syllables are in that particular word. Say "Ready, steady, show your syllables" and ask them to hold up the appropriate number of fingers to show how many syllables are in that word. You should reveal your fingers at the same time to show the correct answer. Show them how to clap the syllables in the word.
- Repeat many times with words of one, two, three and four syllables.

Target skill: Reading and writing words with two syllables

Learning objective

to discriminate syllables in multi-syllabic words

Resources

- Song of Sounds flashcards
- Song of Sounds green word cards: dentist, sandpit, lightning, scooter
- List of one-, two-, three- and four-syllable words

Starter

- Sit children in their chatting chum pairs.
- Show the class the flashcards one at a time, picture-side up, and ask them to sing each sound.
- Ask them to do the actions to the song silently as you show them the flashcards.
- As you produce the grapheme side, can they say the different sounds? Ask the class to say them in unison as you get faster and faster.
- Play "Song tennis". Choose a chatting chum pair to stand at the front of the class. Pick one of the pair to sing a phrase from the Song of Sounds, such as "busy busy bee ee ee ee" – their partner should listen and do the corresponding action. They should then swap over, and keep going, singing different parts of the song and performing the different actions.

Main lesson

Reading two-syllable words

- Explain that today they are going to read some longer words. Ask children if they remember the special trick they practised yesterday to help with reading long words.
- Show them the green word "dentist". Explain that to make it easier to read you are going to cut it up into syllables, to read one syllable at a time and then put them all together to read the whole word.
- Draw a slash between the two syllables: den/tist.
- Sound-talk the first syllable and blend it: /d/-/e/-/n/.
- Sound-talk the second syllable and blend it: /t/-/i/-/s/-/t/.
- Say both syllables: /den/-/tist/. Repeat and ask the children to join in.
- Repeat for the green words "sandpit", "lightning" and "scooter".
- Add these to the green words practised yesterday and practise reading by sound-talking and blending each syllable.

Syllable practice

- Play "Syllable people" Choose a word from the list of one-, two-, three- and four-syllable words on the resource CD and say out loud.
- Children should work individually to decide how many syllables are in that particular word. They should then find that number of classmates to stand in a group with. Anybody without a group is out and must sit down. They should then practise breaking the word into the correct number of syllables and saying a syllable each. Perform the word altogether as a class.
- Repeat many times with words of one, two, three and four syllables.

Target skill: Reading and writing words with three syllables

Learning objective

to discriminate syllables in multi-syllabic words

Resources

- Song of Sounds flashcards
- Song of Sounds green word cards: chimpanzee, kangaroo, zookeeper, Saturday
- A percussion instrument for each chatting chum pair
- Syllable picture cards (Week 23: AS2)
- Song of Sounds IWB version

Starter

- Sit children in their chatting chum pairs.
- Show the class the flashcards one at a time, picture-side up, and ask them to sing each sound.
- Ask the class to do the actions to the song silently as you show them the flashcards.
- As you produce the grapheme side, can they say the different sounds? Ask the class to say them in unison as you get faster and faster.
- Use the IWB version of the song . Ask a child to choose a number between one and five. Move the IWB presentation on that number of slides, so that if they say four, you move the song on four slides. The class should sing the corresponding part of the song. Repeat several times. For more of a challenge, you could ask children to tell you words that begin with that sound (or have that sound in them).

Main lesson

Reading three-syllable words

- Explain that today they are going to read some longer words. Ask children if they remember the special trick they have been practising this week to help read long words.
- Show children the green word "chimpanzee". Explain that to make it easier to read you are going to cut it up into syllables and then read one syllable at a time and then put them together to read the whole word.
- Draw a slash between each syllable: chim/pan/zee.
- Sound-talk the first syllable and blend it: /ch/-/i/-/m/.
- Sound-talk the second syllable and blend it: /p/-/a/-/n/.
- Sound-talk the third syllable and blend it: /z/-/ee/.
- Say all three syllables: /chim/-/pan/-/zee/. Repeat and ask them to join in.
- Repeat for the green words "kangaroo", "zookeeper" and "Saturday". Point out the capital letter at the beginning of the word "Saturday" and discuss.
- Add these words to the green words you have already practised this week and practise reading by sound-talking and blending each syllable.

Syllable practice

- Give each chatting chum pair a percussion instrument to share.
- Print a selection of the syllable picture cards (Week 23: AS2) and display them on the board.
- Ask the pairs to take turns with their instrument to practise beating out the syllables in each word.
- Ask each chatting chum pair to choose a word to perform.
- Each pair should perform a word and the rest of the class should echo the word using their own instruments.

Target skill: Reading and writing words with two syllables

Learning objective

to discriminate syllables in multi-syllabic words

Starter

- Sit children in their chatting chum pairs.
- Show the class the flashcards one at a time, picture-side up, and ask them to sing each sound.
- Ask them to do the actions to the song silently as you show them the flashcards.
- As you produce the grapheme side, can they say the different sounds? Ask the class to say them in unison as you get faster and faster.
- Use the IWB version of the song. As you play it, challenge children to sing it silently in their heads and to just sing out loud the target phoneme, for example: "ay ay ay", while doing the action. They must do it in time to the song.

Resources

- Song of Sounds flashcards
- Song of Sounds green word cards: yesterday, September, helicopter, holiday
- Objects (or picture cards) to represent multi-syllabic words in a feely bag or box, e.g. crayon, paintbrush, rubber, napkin, caterpillar etc.
- A mini whiteboard and pen for each chatting chum pair

Main lesson

Reading three-syllable words

- Explain that today they are going to read some longer words. Ask them if they remember the special trick they have been practising this week to help read long words.
- Show children the green word "yesterday". Explain that to make it easier to read you are going to cut it up into syllables and then read one syllable at a time and then put them together to read the whole word.
- Draw a slash between the two syllables: yest/er/day.
- Sound-talk the first syllable and blend it: /y/-/e/-/s/-/t/.
- Sound-talk the second syllable: /er/.
- Sound-talk the third syllable: /d/-/ay/.
- Say all the syllables: /yest/-/er/-/day/. Repeat and ask them to join in.
- Repeat for the green words "September", "helicopter" and "holiday". Ensure that you point out the capital letter at the beginning of September and discuss why.
- Add these words to the green words you have already practised this week and practise reading by sound-talking and blending each syllable.

Syllable practice

- Give each chatting chum pair a whiteboard and pen.
- Pull an object out of your feely bag or box, for example, a paintbrush.
- Ask children to talk to their chatting chums and decide how many syllables are in the word.
- Clap out the syllables together and chant the word.
- Now ask them to segment the first syllable into phonemes, for example, /p/-/a/-/i/-/n/-/t/. Model it writing on the board.
- Then ask them to segment the second syllable into phonemes, for example, /b/-/r/-/u/-/sh/. Model writing it on the board.
- Pull another object out and repeat, counting the syllables in the word.
- This time ask children to segment the first syllable and write it on their whiteboards. Repeat for the second syllable and third syllable.
- Repeat a few times.

Sally Syllable

Target words: one-, two- and three-syllable words

Learning objective

to discriminate syllables in multi-syllabic words

Resources

Carpet session

- Software (Week 23: Teach)
- A selection of percussion instruments
- A "syllable sack" (or bag) containing a variety of objects with I or 2 or 3 syllables, or pictures of those objects (Week 23: ASI–3)
- Five A4 sheets of paper numbered I–5
- A mini whiteboard and pen for each child
- A girl costume for Sally Syllable (optional)

Syllable charades

- Pictures of multi-syllabic words (Week 23: AS2)
- A feely bag or box

Secret syllables

- Syllable cards (Week 23: AS4–8)
- A mini whiteboard and pen for each child

Syllable cards

- Syllable cards (Week 23: AS4–8)
- A mini whiteboard and pen for each child
- A dice for each child (optional)

Carpet session

- Gather the resources.
- Before the lesson gather some percussion instruments.
- This lesson has the option of teaching in role as Sally Syllable, carrying a selection of percussion instruments. Alternatively, use the software.
- Depending on the option you have chosen, enter the classroom in role as Sally Syllable or press play on the software.
- [1] Ask children if they remember who you are. Remind them that you came to visit them earlier. Explain that you are really clever at spelling words because you can break words down into little chunks that make it easier when spelling. Explain that these chunks are called syllables.

  Software
  Teach
  W23

- Pull an object out of the "syllable sack" that contains one syllable. Show children how to say this word, for example, book. Remind them that your mouth only moves once and this means it only has one syllable. Repeat with words that contain two or three syllables. Beat out the syllables using your instruments.
- Ask children to stand up and make a circle. Demonstrate how to clap out and say the syllables in a name, for example, Sa-lly. They should take it in turns to clap out the syllables in their names. Discuss any misconceptions or help any children with tricky names.
- Place five A4 sheets numbered 1–5 in the middle of the circle, evenly spread out. Give six children in the circle an instrument. Ask them to beat out the syllables in their name and go and stand next to the correct sign according to the number of syllables. Ask those children to give their instruments to other children and repeat a few times.

2

- Ask these children to sit back down facing you. Explain that you are now going to show them how syllables can help you to read and write words easily.
- Using the software, reveal the word "lunchbox". Explain that splitting the word into syllables makes it easier to read. Split the word in two with a slash: den/tist. Sound-talk and blend the first part of the word, /d/-/e/-/n/ and then the second part of the word, /t/-/i/-/s/-/t/. Explain that splitting the word into syllables helps us to read it.

3–4

- Repeat for the words "scarecrow" and "sunflower".
- Explain that knowing your syllables is especially helpful when writing words.

5

- Use the software to show a picture of a picnic. Ask children how many syllables there are in the word and clap them out together. A slash will appear to show them that the word has two syllables. Model how to segment the first syllable p-i-c and then the second syllable n-i-c.

7–8

- Give children a mini whiteboard and pen and repeat for the words "sandwich" and "butterfly". This time, ask them to segment the syllables on their whiteboards.
- Revise the session's learning objective before dividing children into their differentiated groups for the practical activities.

Support
Give less-able children a Song of Sounds phoneme finder to help them.

Practical activities

Syllable charades
A game for a small group of 5–6 children

Aim: to chunk words into syllables and act out

How to play:
- Gather the resources.
- Put the picture cards in a feely bag or box and ask children to take it in turns to pull a picture card out.
- The object of the game is to mime the word to the rest of the group using the number of syllables it contains and by acting out either the whole word or the different syllables: for "lion" the child would mime two syllables (hold up two fingers) and then they could either roar or act out the first syllable by lying down.

Secret syllables
A game for a small group of 5–6 children

Aim: to practise using syllables to help them segment a multi-syllabic word for writing

How to play:
- Gather the resources.
- Scatter the syllable cards in the middle of a table and give each child a mini whiteboard and pen.
- Each card has a picture with the corresponding word broken up into syllables. On each card a syllable has been removed and replaced with a question mark.
- Each child should pick a card. They should read the card to find out which syllable is missing and use their phonic knowlege to segment the missing syllable and write the whole word on their whiteboard.
- Check their word. If it is correct, they should choose another. If not, discuss any misconceptions.

Support
Help less-able children to sound out the missing syllable by orally segmenting alongside them and allowing them to use a Song of Sounds phoneme finder.

Challenge
Ask more-able children to write the word in a sentence.

Syllable cards

An activity for a small group of 5–10 children

Aim: to practise using syllables to help them segment a multi-syllabic word for writing

How to play:

- Gather the resources.
- Give children a mini whiteboard and pen each.
- Scatter the syllable cards all over the table.
- Ask each child to pick a card and, using the sound buttons to help them, write the word on their whiteboard.
- Roll the dice to decide how many times they should write the word (optional).
- They should then continue choosing cards until they have completed them all. Discuss any misconceptions.

Support

For less-able children, support them by providing them with a Song of Sounds phoneme finder. Choose a word as a group and work on it together with the adult helping the children to hear the sounds in the word.

Challenge

If more-able children find it easy after a little while, challenge them to write a sentence using the word.

Revision

Gather the children back on the carpet. Play "Syllable fingers" using a mix of one-, two-, three- and four-syllable words. Ask them to hold up the appropriate number of fingers to show how many syllables are in that word. Show them how to clap the syllables in the word. Repeat a few times.

Now read...

Diggety Dog, *Yellow, Band 3*

Assessment week 3

Learning objective

to revise all phonemes learned so far

Resources

- IWB Song of Sounds song
- Song of Sounds flashcards

Starter

- Gather the resources.
- Sit children in their chatting chum pairs.
- Explain to them that this week they are going to practise everything they have learned so far so that you can see how well they are doing with their phonics.
- Explain that today they are going to practise their Song of Sounds.
- Using the IWB version of the Song of Sounds, sing the song all the way through with the class. Children should perform all the actions they know as they go along.

Main lesson

- Play "Song tennis". Choose a chatting chum pair to stand at the front of the class. Pick one of the pair to sing a phrase from the Song of Sounds, for example, "beans in your dreams ea ea ea" – their partner should listen and do the corresponding action. They should then swap over, and keep going, singing different parts of the song and performing the different actions.
- Next play "Sound tennis". Children should sit so they are facing their chatting chums. One child should say a sound, for instance, /ai/, then spell the grapheme they mean using letter names, for example, "a", "i". The other should then do exactly the same but it must be a different sound, for instance, /i-e/ then "i split e". They should keep going backwards and forwards (like a game of tennis.) until one of them falters. Then they should start again. Encourage them to look around the classroom at the Song of Sounds classroom frieze or poster to help them.

Revision

Finish this session with some flashcard work. Ask the class to do the actions to the song silently as you show them the flashcards one at a time. As you produce the grapheme side, can they say the different sounds?

Assessment week 3

Learning objective

to practise reading graphemes and blending to read words

Resources

- Song of Sounds flashcards
- Eight Song of Sounds green words
- Three Song of Sounds green sentences
- A lolly stick for each child in the class with their name written on (optional)

Starter

- Remind children that this week they are practising *everything* they have learned so you can see how well they are doing with their phonics.
- Explain that they are going to practise recognising letters and reading words.
- Use your flashcard pack to play "Speed sounds". Show the class the flashcards one at a time, grapheme-side up, getting faster and faster. As the children see the grapheme they should say the sound.

Main lesson

- Sit the children with their chatting chums.
- Display eight green words on the board. Give children two minutes to work with their chatting chums to blend the letters and read the words together.
- Pick a lolly stick out of a pot or bag. Read out the child's name. That child should stand up with their chatting chums and model to the class how to read the word. Discuss any errors. Repeat until all the words have been discussed.
- The whole class should then read the words together. Do this by asking children to say the sounds as you press the sound buttons, and then blend the sounds together as you sweep your hand underneath the word.

Revision

Finish this session by putting three green sentences on the board. Challenge the chatting chums to work together to read the sentences. Ask a chatting chums to demonstrate reading a sentence, then ask the whole to class read it. Repeat for each sentence.

Assessment week 3

Learning objective

to practise writing individual graphemes

Resources

- Song of Sounds flashcards
- Mini whiteboards and pens for each chatting chum pair
- Song of Sounds phoneme finders for less-able children

Starter

- Remind the children that this week they are practising *everything* they have learned so you can see how well they are doing with their phonics
- Explain that today they are going to practise writing letters.
- Use your flashcard pack to play "Speed sounds". Show the class the flashcards one at a time, grapheme-side up, getting faster and faster. As they see the grapheme, they should say the sound.

Main lesson

- Sit the children with their chatting chums and give each pair a mini whiteboard and pen.
- Reveal one of your flashcards, picture-side up, and ask children to sing the corresponding part of the song and write the correct grapheme on their whiteboards. Repeat multiple times.
- Finally, challenge them to listen to a word as you say it and write the correct version of the sound from the Song of Sounds. For example, if you say "prawn" they should write an /aw/. Ensure that you emphasise the sound so they can hear it.

Support
To support less-able children, give them a Song of Sounds phoneme finder so that they can find the correct letter and copy it.

Challenge
More-able children could write all three words.

Revision

Using the Song of Sounds flashcards, ask children to pick a card and practise writing the grapheme on that card five times.

Assessment week 3

Learning objective

to split words into phonemes

Starter

- Gather the children on the carpet.
- Remind them that this week they are practising *everything* they have learned so you can see how well they are doing with their phonics.

Main lesson

- Explain that today they are going to practise counting the phonemes in words by playing a game called "Phoneme fingers".
- Use words of one syllable that are phonetically regular and include only the sounds they have learned so far, for example, train, hay, moon, throw.
- Call out a word. The children must quietly count the phonemes in the word, for example, /s/-/ee/, /c/-/are/, /h/-/ur/-/t/, /b/-/r/-/ow/-/n/, /c/-/r/-/i/-/s/-/p/, /s/-/qu/-/are/. They should then put the corresponding number of fingers up on their hand but keep their answer hidden from the other children, and you. At the same time, get your fingers ready but also hidden so the children cannot see them.
- Then say "Ready, steady, phoneme fingers" and both you and the children should reveal your fingers to show the answer.
- You should then count the phonemes in the word together, by counting on your fingers, for example, /s/-/quare/ = 3.
- Now that they know their letter names, it is good practice to use these to explain the grapheme, for example, "it's 'a-r-e'" (using letter names).
- This activity is perfect for assessment because you can instantly scan the class to see who repeatedly is correct or who makes mistakes.
- Repeat many times.

Revision

Explain that if they can play "Phoneme fingers" they can write, because when you write you just listen to a word, count the phonemes and write the correct letters. Model this with two final words by writing the words on the board as you count out the phonemes.

Assessment week 3

Learning objective

to assess each child's phonic ability on a one-to-one basis

Resources

Carpet session

- Software (Week 24: Teach)
- An assessment sheet for each child (on Resource CD)
- A letter from Felicity to go inside the parcel
- A box addressed to the children (optional: covered in pink paper)

Assessment

- An assessment sheet for each child (on Resource CD)

Star sprint

- Song of Sounds phoneme stars (all previously-taught phonemes)
- A grapheme to match each phoneme star (magnetic, foam, carpet etc.)

- Song of Sounds picture cards
- Song of Sounds phoneme finders (optional)
- A whistle or bell (optional)
- A mini whiteboard and pen for each child (optional)

Blending bags

- Picture cards to attach to the front of zip bags (Week 24: AS1)
- 15 zip bags
- Magnetic letters to go inside each bag to spell out the picture on the bag, e.g. s-n-ai-l
- A mini whiteboard and pen for each child
- Dice (optional)

Revision

- Song of Sounds flashcards

Carpet session

- Gather the resources.
- Gather children on the carpet.
- Explain that you have received a parcel from Felicity and open it with the children to find a letter inside.
- The letter asks the children how they are getting on with their phonemes and says that Felicity has sent a special test for them to do with their teacher. It instructs the teacher to look at the screen.

Software
Teach
W24

1 • Start the software. Work through the slides to see if the children can:

2 • sing their sounds – pictures from the Song of Sounds flash up for children to sing.

3 • say their sounds – graphemes flash up for the children to say.

4–8 • read words – words come in for the children to read.

9–11 • write words – pictures appear on the screen for the children to write.

12 • Invite children to play some games to practise using all their sounds.

Practical activities

Assessment

An assessment activity for the teacher or teaching assistant to do individually with the children.

Aim: to assess children's progress so far

How to assess:
- This assessment should take about five minutes per child.
- Sit somewhere quiet so it is easy to concentrate and hear them.
- Follow the instructions on the assessment sheet, always ensuring that you are positive and encouraging. You could offer children a reward after the assessment.
- Check all children's knowledge of graphemes on the assessment sheet.

Star sprint

A game for a small group of 6–10 children

Aim: to identify the correct phoneme/grapheme correspondences

How to play:
- Play this game in the hall or a large indoor or outdoor space.
- Pin the phoneme stars up all round your large space.
- Scatter the graphemes all over the floor.
- On a given signal (such as a whistle or bell), children should run to a grapheme, pick it up and sprint to the correct star, for example, if they pick up a /a-e/ they should sprint to "bake a cake a-e a-e a-e". You should then check they have run to the correct star and discuss any errors.

Blending bags

An activity for a small group of 5–10 children

Aim: to segment words into the correct phonemes and order the graphemes accordingly to make the word

How to play:
- Gather the resources.
- Attach the pictures to the front of the zip bags.
- Scatter the zip bags on a table and give each child a mini whiteboard and pen.
- They should pick a zip bag, unzip it and take out the letters to see if they can make the picture word on the front with the magnetic letters.
- They should then write this word on their mini whiteboard.
- Repeat until they have completed all the bags.

Tip
You may find that less-able children are not yet able to blend their sounds for reading or attempting to write words. Ask them to try in case they surprise you – don't worry if they struggle, just move on.

Support
Less-able pupils can use a Song of Sounds phoneme finder to help them.

Challenge
To make this game more challenging you could scatter the selection of Song of Sounds picture cards on the floor, grapheme-side up. On a given signal the children should run to a grapheme, pick it up, run to the corresponding star and write on the whiteboard the word that the picture shows.

Support
Ask less-able pupils to find the initial letter of their picture and give them a Song of Sounds phoneme finder to help them.

Challenge
More-able pupils could roll a dice and write their word that many times or put the word in a sentence.

Revision

Play "Knock down". Divide the children into groups of 5–6 and stand them up a group at a time. Using the Song of Sounds flashcards, show the children a phoneme. The first child to say the sound remains in the game, the others sit down. Repeat with each group until you have a winner from each group. Repeat with the winning children and carry on playing until you have an overall winner.

Target tricky words: "of", "off"

Learning objective

to practise reading and spelling tricky words

Resources

- Song of Sounds tricky word cards: of, off

Starter

Introducing "of" and "off"

- Gather the children on the carpet.
- Explain that today they are going to learn two new tricky words.
- Before you show the tricky word cards, ask if they can remember what makes some words trickier than others, i.e. they don't follow Felicity's phoneme rules.
- Hold up the flashcards – ask the children why these words are red (they are red because, like a red traffic light, red means stop and you need to stop and think about them).

Main lesson

Read "of" and "off"

- Show children the tricky word "of" and read it to them.
- Give a few examples of when "of" might be used in sentences, for example, "I like the colour of his coat" and "Two of my friends are twins."
- Display the word "of". Explain that the "o" is not tricky as it follows the phoneme rules and makes the "octopus is orange o o o" sound. However, explain that the "f" sounds like "val has a violin v v v" and makes a /v/ sound. To remember this word, you must remember the tricky "f".
- Show children the tricky word "off" and read it to them.
- Give a few examples of when "off" might be used in sentences, for example, "Turn the light off" and "She fell off the swing."
- Display the word "off". Explain that again "o" is not tricky as it makes the correct sound and "ff" is not tricky as it makes the correct sound too. The tricky bit about this word is remembering that it is a double "ff" to make the /f/ sound. Also, lots of people get it muddled up with "of" because they are so similar and forget the second "f".

Write "of" and "off"

- Show children how to write the word "of" on the board. As you write each grapheme say it out loud: /o/-/f/.
- Show them how to write the word "off" the board. As you write each grapheme say it out loud: /o/-/ff/.

Revision

Tell children that you will keep testing them to see if they can remember the words because they are so tricky. Throughout the day, keep producing the tricky word cards and asking children to read them on sight. Repeat continually throughout the day.

Target tricky word: "house"

Learning objective

to practise reading and spelling tricky words

Resources

- Song of Sounds tricky word card: house
- Previously-taught Song of Sounds tricky word cards

Starter

Introducing "house"

- Gather the children on the carpet.
- Explain that today they are going to a learn a new word.
- Before you show them the "house" flashcard, ask if they can remember what makes some words trickier than others (they don't follow Felicity's phoneme rules).
- Hold up the "house" flashcard – remind children that it is red because, like a red traffic light, red means stop. Because it is a tricky word, you need to stop and think about it.

Main lesson

Read "house"

- Show children the tricky word "house" and read it to them.
- Give a few examples of when "house" might be used in sentences, for example, "My house has a red front door" and "I am going to my friend's house for tea."
- Display the word "house". Explain that most of the sounds in this word are not tricky at all. The phonemes /h/, /ou/ and /s/ all make the sounds that they are supposed to. Sing "hats on heads h h h", "mouse in a house ou ou ou" and "sausages are sizzling s s s". The tricky bit of this word is that you can't hear the "e" at the end – it is a silent "e".
- Write the word "house" on the board and ask children to guess how you might say the word "mouse". Explain that because these words rhyme, the only letter you need to change is the initial letter. Stress the fact that thinking of rhyming words is often a good way to help you read and spell words that you might be stuck on.

Write "house"

- Show children how to write the word "house" on the board. As you write each grapheme, say it out loud. Whisper the "e" to give the children an auditory clue that it is a silent "e".

Revision

Add the "house" flashcard to those you taught yesterday. Throughout the day, keep producing the flashcards and asking children to read them on sight. Repeat continually throughout the day.

Target tricky word: "because"

Learning objective

to practise reading and spelling tricky words

Resources

- Song of Sounds tricky word card: because
- Previously-taught Song of Sounds tricky word cards

Starter

Introducing "because"

- Gather the children on the carpet.
- Explain that today they are going to a learn a new word.
- Before you show children the "because" flashcard, ask them if they can remember what makes some words trickier than others (they don't follow Felicity's phoneme rules).
- Hold up the "because" flashcard – remind children that it is red because, like a red traffic light, red means stop. Because it is a tricky word, you need to stop and think about it.

Main lesson

Read "because"

- Show children the tricky word "because" and read it to them.
- Give a few examples of when "because" might be used in sentences, for example, "We can't go outside because it is raining" and "George was off school because he was ill."
- Explain that this is a very tricky word because when you sound it out it sounds nothing like the real word. Demonstrate by saying the individual graphemes and show how difficult it is to blend the word.
- Also show children that it is very difficult to spell, as it sounds like /b/-/c/-/o/-/s/.
- Tell them you have got a clever saying to help them remember the word "because" - big elephants can always understand small elephants" - and show how the initial letters spell the word "because".

Write "because"

- Show children how to write the word "because" on the board. As you write each grapheme, say the mnemonic out loud as you write the letters. Then point to each letter in turn and say them out loud.

Revision

Add the "because" flashcard to those you have already taught this week. Throughout the day, keep producing the flashcards and asking children to read them on sight.

Target tricky words: "looked", "called"

Learning objective

to practise reading and spelling tricky words

Resources

- Song of Sounds tricky word cards looked, called, all
- Previously-taught Song of Sounds tricky word cards

Starter

Introducing "looked" and "called"

- Gather the children on the carpet.
- Explain that today they are going to a learn two new words.
- Before you show the children the "looked" and "called" flashcards, ask them if they can remember what makes some words trickier than others (they don't follow Felicity's phoneme rules).
- Hold up the "looked" and "called" flashcards – remind children that they are red because, like a red traffic light, red means stop. Because it is a tricky word, you need to stop and think about it.

Main lesson

Read "looked" and "called"

- Show children the tricky word "looked" and read it to them.
- Give a few examples of when "looked" might be used in sentences, for example, "She looked and looked but she couldn't find it" and "He looked right and left before crossing the road."
- Explain that the first part of the word is not tricky at all as "look" follows all of Felicity's phoneme rules. Sound out the word, e.g. /l/-/oo/-/k/. Explain that the tricky part of the word "looked" is the ending as it sounds like "tiger on the TV t t t". Show children that to change the word from "look" to "looked" you have to add an "e" and a "d" on the end.
- Show children the tricky word "called" and read it to them.
- Give a few examples of when "called" might be used in sentences, for example, "My cat is called Fluffy" and "I called my friend for a chat."
- Display the tricky word "all" and explain how this word can help us with "called". Show the children how "call" is made up of a "c" and the word "all". Explain how the tricky part of the word "called" is the ending. It doesn't make a "t" sound like "looked", it just sounds like a "d". Explain that you can't hear the "e" but you must remember that the ending is a "e" and a "d".

Write "looked" and "called"

- Show children how to write the word "looked" on the board. Write the word in two halves and practise saying the word as /look/-/ed/ to help the children remember the "ed" ending.
- Show them how to write the word "called" on the board. Write the word in two halves and practise saying the word as /call/-/ed/ to help children remember the "ed" ending.

Revision

Add the "looked" and "called" flashcards to those you have already taught this week. Throughout the day, keep producing the flashcards and asking children to read them on sight.

Tricky words

Target Song of Sounds tricky words: "of", "off", "house", "because", "looked", "called"

Learning objective

to practise reading and spelling tricky words

Resources

Carpet session

- Software (Week 25: Teach)
- Song of Sounds tricky words: of, off, house, because, looked, called
- Song of Sounds green words of your choice
- A Tricky Trevor costume (grey hair, a walking stick and briefcase/bag) or toy (optional)
- Three coloured cards or a coloured fan (blue, purple, green) for each child

Higher or lower

- Song of Sounds tricky words
- An IWB or traditional whiteboard
- An IWB or traditional whiteboard pen

Sticky spelling

- Song of Sounds tricky words: of, off, house, because, looked, called

- Paper or exercise book for each child
- Old magazines and newspapers
- Scissors
- Glue

Tricky time

- Song of Sounds tricky words
- A timer
- A mini whiteboard and pen for each child

Homework

- Homework sheet (on Resource CD)

Revision

- Song of Sounds tricky word cards

Carpet session

- Gather the resources.
- This lesson has the option of teaching in role as "Tricky Trevor", a wise old man with grey hair and a walking stick. If you do not wish to do this, you could use a Tricky Trevor teddy or receive a letter enclosing the tricky words from a professor.
- Depending on the option you have chosen, enter the classroom as Tricky Trevor or hold up your teddy or letter.
- Remind children that Trevor is an incredibly clever man and that is why he has come here today, to teach children some more tricky words (of your choice).
- From your briefcase/bag produce a selection of green words and tricky words. Ask children to give you the differences between "green" words and "tricky" words.
- [1] Explain that before you teach them any more tricky words this year, you would like to check if they can remember all the tricky words they have learned so far. Press play on the software. On the first slide, the tricky words that the children learned on Trevor's last visit appear – check that the children can read them.

> **Software**
> Teach
> **W25**

- Then from your briefcase/bag produce the tricky word cards that they are going to learn about today: "of", "off", "house", "because", "looked, "called".
- Show children the tricky words and ask them to repeat the words after you. Ask them to whisper the words, shout the words, say the words and sing the words.

 2-7
- Reveal the words one at a time. Ask children to identify the green and tricky parts of each word and offer advice to help them remember each word.

8
- Play "Trevor's trick". Give each child cards of three different colours or a coloured fan corresponding to the colours of the words on the software game. Show the three different versions of each word, only one of which has the correct spelling, e.g. "of", "ov", "off". Children must work with their chatting chums to choose the correct spelling and reveal the card of that colour.

9-12
- Continue to play the game, focusing on the rest of the tricky words.

12
- Revise the session's learning objective before children begin their practical activities.

Practical activities

Higher or lower

A game for any-sized group

Aim: to practise reading tricky words

How to play:
- Gather the resources.
- Ask children to sit facing the board.
- Display your tricky word cards in a vertical line, one under the other, or write your words in a vertical line on the board.
- Explain that you are thinking of a tricky word and ask one child from the group to guess which word it is. The child should come out to the board, point to a word and read it to you.
- If they get it wrong, you should put a cross next to their incorrect guess and then tell them whether your word is "higher" or "lower".
- The children must keep guessing until the word is guessed correctly.
- The child who guesses the word successfully becomes the "teacher" and comes out to the front of the group and the game begins again.

Support
To support less-able children, read the words to them before they guess. e.g. "So do you think it is of, off, house, because, looked or called?" Point to each word as you read them to give a visual clue.

Challenge
Ask more-able children to close their eyes and spell the words.

Sticky spelling

An activity for a small group of 5–6 children

Aim: to practise spelling tricky words

How to play:
- Gather the resources.
- Display the tricky word cards on the board so that the children can see them, or write the words on the board.
- Give each child a piece of paper or an exercise book.
- Ask them to use the magazines to find the correct letters to spell the tricky words.
- They should cut out the letters and arrange them on the page to make a tricky word collage, then stick them onto the paper or into their book when they are happy with the spelling.

Support
Ensure that the tricky word cards are visible so that less-able children can match the letters.

Challenge
Remove the tricky word cards so that more-able children spell the words from memory. Extend further by asking them to write a sentence that includes that tricky word.

Tricky time

An activity for a small group of 5–10 children

Aim: to practise spelling tricky words

How to play:

- Gather the resources.
- Set the timer to 30 seconds or one minute.
- Call out a tricky word.
- Children should see how many times they can write that word on their whiteboards in the given time.

Support

Display the tricky word card as you say the word for less-able children to copy if they need to.

Challenge

Ask more-able children to write a sentence containing the tricky word.

Homework (optional)

On the resource CD is a letter for parents that you might choose to send home with each child. The letter explains the concept behind tricky words and has the tricky words that you have taught today on the reverse for parents to practise reading and spelling with their child.

Revision

Play "Pass the tricky word". Sit the children in a circle and give them tricky word cards. Pass the cards around the circle while singing "Pass the tricky words around the ring, around the ring, around the ring, pass the tricky words around the ring, what do they say?" to the tune of "London Bridge Is Falling Down". "The children holding the tricky words should stand up and say the word, and the others should repeat it. Play several times.

Now read...

Sheep to Jumper, *Yellow, Band 3*

The Sun and Moon, *Yellow, Band 3*

Rock Out, *Yellow, Band 3*

The Mouse and the Monster, *Red B Band 2B*

Thick and Thin, *Red B Band 2B*

Feelings, *Red B Band 2B*

We Are Not Fond of Rat!, *Red B Band 2B*

Bot on the Moon, *Red B Band 2B*

Pond Dipping, *Red B Band 2B*

Target skill: Revise all phonemes learned so far

Starter

- Gather the children on the carpet.
- Sing the Song of Sounds using the IWB version.

Main lesson

Reading graphemes

- Show the class the flashcards one at a time, picture-side up, and ask them to sing each sound.
- Ask them to do the actions to the song silently as you show them the flashcards.
- As you produce the grapheme side, can they say the different sounds? Ask the class to say them in unison as you get faster and faster.

Writing graphemes

- Give each chatting chum pair a whiteboard and pen.
- Show the class a flashcard, picture-side up, and ask them to write the grapheme on their whiteboards. Repeat this a few times.
- Then demonstrate an action from the song – as you do the action ask children to write the corresponding grapheme. Repeat a few times
- Finally, say a sound and ask them to write one of the alternative graphemes. Repeat a few times.

Support
Give less-able children a Song of Sounds phoneme finder to help them find the correct grapheme and copy.

Challenge
Challenge more-able children to write the alternatives, e.g. if you say /ay/, the children should write /ay/, /ai/ and /a-e/. You could even challenge them to write a word with each alternative grapheme in.

Target skill: Practise reading green words

Starter

- Gather the children on the carpet.
- Sing the Song of Sounds using the IWB version.

Resources

- Song of Sounds IWB version
- A selection of Song of Sounds green words, including three CVC words, four CCVC words and five CCVCC words
- A lolly stick for each child in the class with their name written on (optional)
- Song of Sounds tricky word cards: of, off, house, because, looked, called

Main lesson

Reading green words

- Sit the children in their chatting chum pairs.
- On the board, display three green words that contain three phonemes, for example, stir, like, horn. Explain to the class that you are going to practise reading words with three phonemes.
- Ask children to work with their chatting chums to practise reading the green words. Give them a time limit, perhaps one minute.
- Choose a lolly stick from the pot and read out the name of the child on the stick. The named child should stand up, choose a green word and read it out loud. Alternatively, just choose a child.
- The whole class should then read the words together. Do this by asking children to say the sounds as you press the sound buttons, and then blend the sounds together as you sweep your hand underneath the word.
- Repeat for all green words on the board.
- Then stick four words that contain four phonemes on the board, for example, paint, haunt, smile, enjoy. Explain that you are now going to practise reading words with four phonemes. Repeat the steps above.
- Finally, stick five green words that contain five or more phonemes on the board, for example, crisp, splash, morning, lunchbox, lightning. Explain that now you are going to practise reading words with five or more phonemes. Repeat the steps above.

Reading tricky words

- Ask children to explain to you the differences between green words and tricky words.
- Finish the session by practising reading the tricky words they learned last week. Show the flashcards one at a time and ask them to read them out loud.

Target skill: Practise writing green words

Starter

- Gather the children on the carpet.
- Sing the Song of Sounds using the IWB version.

Resources

- Song of Sounds IWB version
- Song of Sounds picture cards: play, train, snake, sheep, leaf, athlete, fight, pie, kite, snow, goat, throne, moon, screw, flute, torch, claw, letter, skirt, church, trousers, clown, poihnt, oyster, chair, stare
- A mini whiteboard and pen for each chatting chum pair
- A lolly stick for each child in the class with their name written on (optional)
- Song of Sounds phoneme finders for each chatting chum pair
- Song of Sounds tricky word cards: of, off, house, because, looked, called

Main lesson

Writing green words

- Sit the children in their chatting chum pairs.
- Explain that today they are going to practise writing some green words.
- Give each chatting chum pair a mini whiteboard, a pen and a Song of Sounds phoneme finder.
- Say a word with three phonemes, for example, bird. Ask children to sound-talk the word with their chatting chums in order to segment it into the correct phonemes. They should then write the word on their whiteboard, using their Song of Sounds phoneme finder to help them.
- Pull a lolly stick out of your pot. Ask that child to stand up and sound-talk the word they have written on their whiteboard. As they sound-talk it, you should write it on the board so that you are modelling the correct handwriting to the class.
- Repeat the above steps choosing a word with four phonemes, for example, snail.
- Repeat the above steps choosing a word with five phonemes, for example, street.
- Stick a selection of picture cards on the board. Give the children a time limit, for example, two minutes, to write as many words as they can on their whiteboards. Discuss.

Writing tricky words

- Ask children to explain to you the differences between green words and tricky words.
- Finish the session by practising writing the tricky words that they learned last week. Say a tricky word and ask children to write it on their whiteboards.

Support

To support less-able children, give them the Song of Sounds phoneme finder with the tricky words on the back so they have to find the correct tricky word and write it.

Target skill: Practise reading and writing a sentence

Starter

- Sit children in pairs with their chatting chums.
- Ask them to explain to you the differences between green words and tricky words.
- Practise reading the tricky words that they learned during the previous week. Show the class the tricky word cards one at a time and ask them to read them, increasing in speed.

Resources

- Song of Sounds tricky word cards: of, off, house, because, looked, called
- A Song of Sounds green sentence card for each chatting chum pair
- A Song of Sounds phoneme finder for each chatting chum pair
- A whiteboard and pen for each chatting chum pair

Main lesson

Reading a sentence

- Give each chatting chum pair a green sentence card. Explain to them that their sentence includes some green words and some tricky words.
- Give them a time limit, for example, one minute, to practise reading their sentences with their chatting chums.
- Ask each pair in turn to stand up and read their sentence to the class.

Writing a sentence

- Give each chatting chum pair a whiteboard and a pen and a Song of Sounds phoneme finder.
- Explain to the class that you are going to write a sentence that contains both green words and tricky words.
- Call out: "My dad gave me a treat because I was good."
- Ask children to repeat the sentence. Repeat a few times,
- Model writing the sentence on the board. Explain your thought processes as you write:
  - use "sound-talk" to write the green words
  - find tricky words on your Song of Sounds phoneme finder
  - make sure you use finger spaces
  - read back your sentence to work out which word comes next, etc.
- When the sentence is complete, read it back as a class. Then rub the sentence off the board and ask them to work with their chatting chums to write the sentence independently.
- To finish this session, ask children to rub out the word "treat". Discuss all the other things that a family member might give them, for example, a book, a toy, a computer game, a kitten. Include some silly ideas and have some fun with the sentence, for example, a crocodile.
- Ask children to change the sentence so it has a different treat.
- Ask each chatting chum pair to read their sentence out loud and all have fun reading the sentences.

Alphabetical order

Target skill: alphabetical order

Learning objective

to use letter names and to develop an understanding of the order of the alphabet

Resources

Carpet session

- Software (Week 26: Teach)
- Alphabet cards (Week 26: AS1–7)
- A mini whiteboard and pen for each chatting chum pair
- Letter from the Queen of the Letter Kingdom (optional)

Alphabetical relay

- Alphabet cards (Week 26: AS1–7)
- 2 large sheets of paper
- 2 pens

Alphabetical order cards

- Alphabetical order cards (Week 26: AS1–7)
- An exercise book for each child
- A pencil for each child

Magnetic alphabets

- A zip bag with a set of magnetic alphabet letters for each child
- A magnetic whiteboard and pen for each child

Revision

- A ball

Carpet session

- Gather the resources: software, alphabet cards, whiteboards and pens, letter (optional).
- Sit children in pairs with their chatting chums.
- Explain to the class that you have received a letter from the Queen of the Letter Kingdom (if you do not want to use a hard-copy letter, you can press play on the software, or just explain to children what is in the letter (see below).
- Explain that there is terrible trouble in the letter kingdom because the naughty knave has been causing havoc with the alphabet. He has muddled the whole alphabet up and some of the letters are missing. Can the children help?
- If using the software, press play.
1. - Ask children to turn to their chatting chums and tell them everything they know about the alphabet. Then ask children to put their hands up and tell you what they know.

   > **Software**
   > Teach
   > **W26**

2. - Use the software to revise facts about the alphabet – there are 26 letters, it begins with "a" and ends with "z", it includes vowels and consonants, it has a specific order.
   - Ask children if they know the order of the alphabet. Sing the traditional alphabet song and ask them to join in.
3. - As the alphabet appears on the software, ask children to say the letter names, re-singing the traditional alphabet song.
4. - Point out that it is clear they know their alphabetical order, so they can help the queen work out the correct order of the muddled alphabet. Look at slide 4 and ask the children what they notice (the whole alphabet is muddled up).

5-8 • Explain that the best way to sort out this muddled up alphabet is to tackle it a bit at a time. Give each chatting chum pair a mini whiteboard and a pen. One part of the muddled up alphabet appears on the screen at a time. Ask children to work with their chatting chums to put the letters in the correct order. Repeat until you reach "z".

9 • Show children that they have sorted out the whole alphabet.

10 • Remind them that the queen also said that the knave keeps taking letters away so that there are some letters missing from the alphabet. Invite them to have a look to see if they can help with that too. An alphabet will appear on the screen. When you click the slide, three letters disappear. Ask them to work with their chatting chums to work out the missing letters and write them on their whiteboard. Repeat several times.

> **Support**
> Give less-able children an alphabet card to help them.

11 • Challenge children to an "alphabet race". Give each chatting chum pair a mini whiteboard and a pen. Show the children a letter on the software. They must work together to write down the alphabet in alphabetical order as quickly as they can, starting from the letter on the screen. As soon as they have reached "z" they should stand up. The first pair to stand up is the winner. Repeat several times.

> **Challenge**
> Encourage more-able children to not use the alphabet cards and to work from memory.

12 • Finish by explaining that today they are going to practise their alphabetical order.

Practical activities

Alphabetical relay

A game for a small group of 6–10 children

Aim: to practise writing the alphabet in the correct order

How to play:
• Gather the resources.
• Stick a large piece of paper on a board/wall for each team.
• Divide the group into two teams.
• Sit the teams in a line a distance away from the board and give the first child in each team a pen.
• On a given signal (whistle, clap etc.), they should run to the board and write "a", they must then run back and give the pen to the next child who should run and write "b", and so on. The first team to write the whole alphabet with no mistakes is the winner.
• Play a few times, but in subsequent games show the teams a letter, for example, "m", and ask children to continue the alphabet from this letter. It is good fun to have a few quick races, e.g. start from "v".

> **Support**
> Encourage less-able children to use their alphabet cards to support them.

> **Challenge**
> Encourage more-able children to figure out the answers independently.

Alphabetical order cards

An activity for a small group of 5–6 children

Aim: to practise putting a selection of letters in alphabetical order

How to play:
• Gather the resources.
• Give each child an alphabetical order card and show them how all of these words have been jumbled up by the naughty knave and that we need to put them back into alphabetical order.
• Read the words with the children and look at the initial letters. Explain what it means to put words in alphabetical order.
• Ask them to write the alphabet vertically down the side of their exercise book.

> **Support**
> To support less-able children, repeat in the same way with the simpler cards.

- Show them how to find the letter the word begins with and write the word next to it.
- Repeat for all the words on their card.
- This way the children can visually see the words in alphabetical order in the context of their alphabet.

Magnetic alphabets

An activity for a small group of 5–10 children

Aim: to order the alphabet correctly and practise writing the alphabet in the correct order

How to play:
- Gather the resources.
- Give each child a bag of letters and ask them to put the letters in alphabetical order on their magnetic whiteboards.
- Ask them to say/sing the alphabet.
- Ask them to use their magnetic letters to help them write the alphabet in the correct order.

Challenge
Challenge more-able children to put the words in alphabetical order without writing down the alphabet first. Encourage them to use the song or say the alphabet as a strategy. For further extension, ask them to look at words where the initial letter is the same.

Support
Support less-able children by providing them with the alphabet card from the carpet session.

Challenge
Challenge more-able children by asking them to order and write the letters without any support.

Revision

Play "Alphabet hot potato". Ask the class to stand in a circle. Show everyone a ball. Ask them to imagine that it is a very hot potato and that they can't hold onto it for long (a second or two) or it will burn their fingers. They must pass the "potato" around the circle as quickly as they can, saying the alphabet in order as they go. If they make a mistake or take too long, the potato will burn their fingers and they are out. The children then start again from the beginning of the alphabet.

Now read

Choose a range of Big Cat Phonics readers that help children consolidate the skills they have learned so far.

Target skill: To practise using letter names

Starter

- Sit children with their chatting chums.
- Using the IWB version, sing the Song of Sounds.

Resources

- IWB version of the Song of Sounds
- Alphabet flashcards (a set is provided on resource CD (Week 27: AS1) but any set will do)

Main lesson

Practicing letter names

- Prior to the lesson, stick your alphabet flashcards up on the board in alphabetical order.
- Point to the alphabet flashcards as you sing the traditional alphabet song. Ask children to sing with you.
- Choose an alphabet flashcard from the board. Does anyone know the name of this grapheme? Ask the class to repeat the letter name after you.
- Sing the alphabet song and point to the letters as you do so, until you reach the correct letter. Say the letter name again.
- Repeat lots of times using different flashcards from the alphabet.
- Ask children to close their eyes. While their eyes are closed, remove a flashcard from the board. Ask them to turn to their chatting chums and discuss which letter is missing. Choose a chatting chum pair to answer and discuss how they worked it out, for example, using the letter before, or the letter after, or singing the alphabet song. Repeat lots of times.

Revision

Finish by taking all the flashcards off the board and shuffling them. Use the flashcards grapheme-side up and ask children to say the sound and the letter name as you show them. Tackle any misconceptions as you go along.

Target skill: To practise using letter names

Starter

- Sit the children with their chatting chums.
- Sing the traditional alphabet song.
- Play "Alphabet tennis". Ask children to work with their chatting chums. Explain that to begin today's session you would like them to practise their alphabetical order by playing. The first child should say "a", and the second says "b" etc. They should play this game standing up and act as if they are hitting a tennis ball to their partner as they say the letters in alphabetical order. If they go wrong, it means the ball is dropped and they have to start all over again.

Resources

- Alphabet flashcards (Week 27: AS1)
- Music e.g. Song of Sounds CD or alphabet song

Main lesson

Practising letter names

- Stick ten alphabet flashcards on the board, grapheme-side up.
- Ask children to work with their chatting chums to look at the flashcards and identify the sound each grapheme makes as well as its letter name.
- Point to a grapheme and ask the class to tell you, all together, the sound followed by the letter name. Repeat for all the graphemes.
- Give each chatting chum pair an alphabet flashcard. Play some music (if you have a CD version of the alphabet song, that would be perfect). When the music stops, each chatting chum pair should give their flashcard to another pair, telling them the sound it makes and its letter name. Repeat lots of times.

Revision

Finish by holding up the flashcards one at a time and asking children to say in unison the sound it makes and its letter name.

Target skill: To practise using letter names

Main lesson

Practising letter names

- Give each chatting chum pair an alphabet card and a lolly stick to share.
- Ask one child to use the lolly stick to point to each letter of the alphabet one-by-one. The other should say the alphabet as they point to the letters.
- Ask one child to hold the lolly stick and point randomly to a letter on the alphabet card. The other should then say the sound that letter makes and then its name. If they get stuck, their chatting chums should help them. Repeat five times. Then swap over so they both have a turn with the lolly stick. Repeat a few times.
- You should then say a letter name out loud. Children should work together – one should point to the correct grapheme with their lolly stick, the other should do the action from the Song of Sounds. Swap over. Repeat lots of times.

227

Target skill: To practise using letter names

Starter

- Gather the children on the carpet.
- Sing the traditional alphabet song.
- Play "Alphabet eliminate". Ask the class to make a circle. They should go around the circle saying the letters of the alphabet in order. If they make a mistake or take too long, the class should say "eliminate" and they are out. They should then start again from the beginning of the alphabet. Ensure you play long enough for the class to work their way through the alphabet.

Resources

- Alphabet cards from last week's lesson (Week 27: AS1)
- Mini whiteboards and pens

Main lesson

Practising letter names

- Ask the children to work with their chatting chums.
- Call out a letter name and ask them to sing the corresponding part of the Song of Sounds back to you.
- Call out a letter name and ask them to do the corresponding action from the Song of Sounds.
- Call out a letter name and ask them to say the sound it makes back to you.
- Give each chatting chum pair a mini whiteboard and pen and an alphabet card.
- Say a letter name out loud and ask children to write it on their whiteboards.
- Discuss any misconceptions as you go along.
- Then call out a section of the alphabet in order but miss out a letter. Ask them to work out the missing letter and write it on their whiteboards.

Upper and lower case

Target skill: upper and lower case letters

Learning objective

To be able to match lower and upper case letters and begin to be write upper case graphemes

Resources

Carpet session

- A letter from the Queen of the Letter Kingdom
- A set of upper and lower case letter cards (Week 27: AS1). Ensure that you have enough so that each child in the class has a letter. Choose the more complex letters e.g. R and r, B and b, A and a
- Upper case and lower case alphabet cards (Week 27: AS1–10)
- Cards that say "UPPER CASE" and "lower case" (Week 27: AS11)
- A mini whiteboard and pen for each chatting chum pair
- Two hoops (optional)

Playground pairs

- Upper case and lower case letter cards (Week 27: AS1–10)
- An envelope for every letter of the alphabet. Inside each envelope put a lower case letter

The Letter Kingdom

- A playing board for each child (optional: laminated) (Week 27: AS12)
- A dice that says "UPPER CASE" on two sides, "lower case" on two sides and a clown picture (to represent a 'naughty knave') on two sides (Week 27: AS14)
- Lower case and upper case alphabet cards (Week 27: AS1–10)
- A pencil for each child
- Mini whiteboards and pens (optional)

Royal writing

- Lower case letter cards (Week 27: AS2–6)
- A feely bag
- A pencil for each child
- A crown (optional)
- Crown-shaped paper (optional) or an exercise book for each child

Revision

- Upper and lower case letter cards (Week 27: AS1)
- A feely bag

Carpet session

- Gather the resources.
- Sit the children in their chatting chum pairs.
- Explain to the class that you have received another message from the Queen of the Letter Kingdom. Inside the parcel should be the upper case and lower case pairs and the cards that say "UPPER CASE" and "lower case". However, alternatively you could just do this lesson as a practical session using the cards.
- The letter explains that the naughty knave has been up to mischief again. This time he has muddled up all the upper case and lower case letters in the Letter Kingdom. Can the children help again by sorting the upper and lower case letters out? At this point, look in the envelope

and "discover" that the queen has sent you lots of letters to sort out. Some of them are upper case and some of them are lower case.

- Explain to children that today they are going to help sort out the upper case and lower case letters for the queen. Ask them to discuss with their chatting chums what upper case and lower case letters are. Pick a few children to explain to the class.

- Ask children to sit in a circle. Put the labelled hoops or A4 sheets in the middle of the circle. Give each child a lower case or upper case letter. Children should take it in turns to come and put their letter in the correct hoop or next to the correct sign. As they put it down, they should also say its letter name. Check what they have done and discuss any misconceptions.

- Go back to the letter and read the rest. The letter asks: "Can you also match the letters together to make pairs?" Explain that some of the letters are easy to match because the upper case letters are just bigger than the lower case letters, but some are very hard because they look completely different.

- Remove the hoops and/or labels from the circle. Give each child a card. Play some music. Children should move around the room silently showing each other their cards until they find their partner. When they find their partners, they should sit down together. When all the partners have found each other, stop the music. Point at each pair – when you point at them, they should stand up, hold up their cards and say their letter name. They should then come forward and you should display their letters on the board together so that everyone can see the upper case and lower case pairs.

- Give each chatting chum pair a mini whiteboard and pen and an alphabet card from last week's lesson (Week 26: AS1). Challenge them to write a lower case and an upper case alphabet. Encourage them to use the pairs on the board to help them if they forget what the harder upper case letters look like.

Practical activities

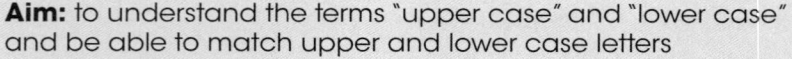

Playground pairs

A game for a small group of 6–8 children

Aim: to understand the terms "upper case" and "lower case" and be able to match upper and lower case letters

How to play:
- Gather the resources: upper case and lower case letter cards, envelopes, lower case letters.
- This game should be played in the playground.
- Scatter the lower case and upper case letters all over the playground.
- Ask each pair to sit down together on the ground.
- Give each pair an envelope.
- On a given signal, pairs should open their envelope and see which letter is inside.
- One child should run and find the lower case letter and the other should run and find the upper case letter.
- The first pair that finish and sit together again is the winner.
- Play lots of times.

> **Support**
> Ensure that a lower/upper case alphabet is available for less-able children to look at to help them.

> **Challenge**
> Concentrate on the harder upper/lower case combinations, e.g. Rr, Qq, Bb, Ee, Nn.

The Letter Kingdom

A game for a small group of 5–6 children

Aim: to understand the terms "upper case" and "lower case"; to match upper and lower case letters and begin to write them

How to play:
- Gather the resources: playing boards, dice, alphabet cards, pencils, mini whiteboards and pens.

> **Support**
> Ensure that a lower/upper case alphabet is available for less-able children to look at to help them.

- Make your dice and give each child a pencil and a playing board.
- Before beginning the game, ask children to write on each circle on the playing board, an upper case or lower case letter of their choice. They should all be different.
- Each child should take it in turns to roll the dice.
- If the dice says "UPPER CASE" they should rub one of their upper case letters off.
- If the dice says "lower case" they should rub one of their lower case letters off.
- If the dice lands on the naughty knave, they have to fill in one of their circles again with another lower case or upper case letter of their choice.
- The first child to rub off all their letters is the winner.

Royal writing

An activity for a small group of 5–10 children

Aim: to practise the correct formation of upper case letters

How to play:
- Gather the resources: lower case letter cards, a feely bag, pencils, exercise books or crown-shaped paper, a crown (optional).
- Give each child a crown-shaped piece of paper or an exercise book and a pencil.
- Put the lower case letter cards in a feely bag.
- Pull out a letter card, for example, "r". Ask children what sound it makes and its letter name. Model writing the corresponding upper case grapheme.
- Children should then copy it several times, focusing on the correct formation.
- Repeat several times.
- The child who does the neatest writing may wear the crown until someone wins it from them.

> ### Challenge
> Extend the game by asking more-able children to sit in a circle with a mini whiteboard and pen. Again, call out "lower case" or "upper case" but this time the children should write as many letters as they can in that case before you say "stop". They should win a point for every letter they write correctly.

> ### Support
> Leave the grapheme on the board for less-able children to look at.

> ### Challenge
> Concentrate on the harder upper/lower case combinations e.g. Rr, Qq, Bb, Ee, Nn.

Revision

Gather children back on the carpet. Play "Tops and tails". Put a selection of lower case and upper case letters into a bag or box. Explain that they are going to predict which sort of letter will be pulled out of the bag. If they think it will be an upper case letter, they put their hands on their heads and if they think it will be lower case they put their hands on their toes. Pull a letter out of a bag. If they are correct they stay standing, if they are incorrect they must sit down. Repeat until there is only one child left, who is the winner.

Now read

Choose any Big Cat Phonics readers that will help children to consolidate their knowledge of upper and lower case letters

Target skill: To practise letter names, alphabetical order and upper and lower case

Starter

- Gather the children on the carpet.
- Using the Song of Sounds flashcards, practise singing, performing the actions and saying sounds from the song.
- Sing the traditional alphabet song with the class.
- Play "Alphabet tennis". Ask children to work with their chatting chums. Explain that to begin today's session you would like them to practise their alphabetical order by playing a. The first child should say "a" and the second says "b", etc. Children should play this game standing up and act as if they are hitting a tennis ball to their partner as they say the letters in alphabetical order. If they go wrong, it means the ball is dropped and they have to start all over again.

Resources

- The Song of Sounds flashcards
- Lower and upper case alphabet cards from last week (Week 27: AS2)
- Music, e.g. the Song of Sounds CD or the traditional alphabet song
- Mini whiteboards and pens for each chatting chum pair

Main lesson

Practising alphabet skills

- Ask children to sit in a circle. Choose a lower case or an upper case flashcard. Play the Song of Sounds CD as you pass the flashcard around the circle. When the music stops, the child holding the flashcard should stand up and tell everyone the sound that letter makes and its letter name. Begin again, but this time pass two letters around the circle. Play lots of times adding more letters each time.

- Ask children to sit in their chatting chum pairs.
- Give each pair a mini whiteboard and a pen.
- Stick six upper case flashcards and six lower case flashcards on the board.
- Ask the pairs to draw a line down the middle of their whiteboard to divide it in half. They should work together to write the lower case letters on one side of the line and the upper case letters on the other.
- Discuss any misconceptions as you reveal the answers by moving the cards around on the board. Repeat a few times with different flashcards.

Target skill: To practise letter names, alphabetical order and upper and lower case

Starter

- Gather the children on the carpet.
- Using the Song of Sounds flashcards, practise singing the song, performing the actions and saying sounds from the song.
- Sing the traditional alphabet song.
- Play "Alphabet eliminate". Ask the class to make a circle. They should go around the circle saying the letters of the alphabet in order. If they make a mistake or take too long, the class should say "eliminate" and they are out. They should then start again from the beginning of the alphabet. Ensure you play long enough to work their way through the alphabet.

Main lesson

Practising alphabet skills

- Prior to the lesson, sort your upper case and lower case flashcards out so that you have enough flashcards to give one to every child and they can make upper/lower case pairs. You might want to choose pairs that include the more difficult upper case letters, for example, R, B, A, D etc.
- Give each child either a lower case or an upper case flashcard. Play some music. When the music stops, each child should give their flashcard to another child, telling them the sound it makes and its letter name. Repeat lots of times.
- Now tell the class that you would like them to find their upper case/lower case pairings but they must do it without talking. Ask them to move around the room in silence looking at each other's cards. When they have found their partner they should sit down. When all partners have been found, point to one pair at a time. They should jump up and tell you their letter name, and which one is the upper case grapheme and which one is the lower case grapheme.

Resources

- The Song of Sounds flashcards
- Lower and upper case alphabet cards: (Week 27: AS2)
- Music e.g. Song of Sounds CD or traditional alphabet song

Target skill: To practise letter names, alphabetical order and upper and lower case

Starter

- Using the Song of Sounds flashcards, practise singing/ performing actions/ saying sounds from the song.
- Sing the traditional alphabet song "a b c d e f g..."
- Play 'Alphabet Hot Potato'. Ask the class to make a circle. Use a ball and ask the children to imagine that it is burning hot and that they can't hold onto it for long or it will burn their fingers! They must pass the "potato" around the circle as quickly as they can, saying the alphabet in order as they go. If they make a mistake or take too long, the potato burns their fingers and they are out. The children then start again from the beginning of the alphabet.

Resources

- Song of Sounds Stage 2 flashcards
- Lower case alphabet cards (from Resource CD)
- A ball
- Mini whiteboards and pens for each chatting chum pair

Main lesson

Practising alphabet skills

- Prior to the lesson, display your lower case alphabet cards on the board in alphabetical order.
- Ask the children to close their eyes. While their eyes are closed, remove a flashcard from the board. Ask the children to turn to their chatting chums and discuss which letter is missing. Choose a chatting chum pair to answer and discuss how they worked it out, e.g. using the letter before, or the letter after, or singing the alphabet song. Repeat lots of times.
- Play 'Alphabet Anagrams'. Give each chatting chum pair a whiteboard and a pen. Remove 5 consecutive letters from the board, e.g. abcde and muddle them up, e.g. cadeb. Ask the chatting chum pairs to work together to unscramble them. Repeat a few times. When using letters from the middle of the alphabet you can support your less-able children by telling them which is the first letter, e.g. the first one is "r". They might also need an alphabet card to look at. To challenge more-able children, ask them to put non-consecutive letters in alphabetical order, e.g. fmbzt.

Target skill: Alphabet practice

Starter

- Gather the children on the carpet.
- Using the Song of Sounds flashcards, practise singing the song, performing the actions and saying sounds from the song.
- Sing the traditional alphabet song.
- Play "Alphabet bounce". Ask the class to make a circle. Bounce a ball across the circle and say "a". The child who catches it should bounce it to someone else and say "b", and so on. If they make a mistake, drop the ball or take too long, the game begins again from the beginning of the alphabet.

Resources

- The Song of Sounds flashcards
- A ball
- Mini whiteboards and pens for each chatting chum pair
- Lower and upper case alphabet cards: (Week 27: AS2)

Main lesson

Practising alphabet skills

- Ask children to work with their chatting chums.
- Give each chatting chum pair a mini whiteboard and a pen.
- Put five upper case letters on the board and ask the chatting chum pairs to work together to write the lower case letters to match them.
- Put five lower case letters on the board and ask the chatting chum pairs to work together to write the upper case letters to match them.
- Put a mixture of upper and lower case letters on the board and ask the chatting chum pairs to write the other case letters to match them.
- Now ask them to work together to test each other. One child should write a lower case letter and challenge their chatting chum to tell them the letter name and write the upper case letter to match it. They should then swap roles. Repeat a few times.

Alphabetical order

Target skill: dictionary skills

Learning objectives

to understand what a dictionary is and what it is used for, and to begin to develop the skills needed to use a dictionary effectively

Resources

Carpet session

- Software (Week 28: Teach)
- A children's dictionary for every chatting chum pair
- Alphabet cards (optional) (Week 28: AS1)
- A queen (or King) costume (optional)

Dictionary races

- Song of Sounds picture cards of words that are in your dictionary (check before hand as all dictionaries are slightly different)
- A dictionary for each child
- A mini whiteboard and pen for each child
- A bell (or similar)

Definition dilemma

- Song of Sounds green words of words that are in your dictionary (check beforehand as all dictionaries are slightly different)
- A mini whiteboard and pen for each child
- A feely bag or box

Alphabetical order cards

- Alphabet cards (Week 28: AS1)
- Alphabetical order cards (Week 28: AS2–7)
- An exercise book for each child
- A pencil for each child

Revision

- A dictionary for each chatting pair
- A bell

Carpet session

- Gather the resources.
- This lesson has the option of teaching in role as the Queen or King of the Letter Kingdom. Alternatively, you could use a thank-you letter from the queen or the software on its own.
- Depending on the option you have chosen, enter the classroom as the queen (or king), or bring your letter into the classroom.
- Explain to children that they have been very helpful in sorting out the kingdom's alphabet problems and that they have a thank-you gift.

1. - The gifts are books called dictionaries. Tell children that today you will show them what dictionaries are for, how to use them and then they can keep them in their classroom forever.

   > **Software**
   > Teach
   > **W26**

- Ask them to discuss with their chatting chums what they think a dictionary is and what it is for. Discuss the children's ideas.

2. - Tell them that a dictionary helps us in two different ways: (1) spell words and (2) understand what words mean.
- Demonstrate how a dictionary helps us to spell by using one to find the words "cat" and "house". Include a word that you know will not be there (for instance a dialect word) so that children understand that not all words are in a dictionary.

- Demonstrate how a dictionary helps us to understand what words mean by finding the word "dog" and reading the definition out loud.

- Ask children to turn to their chatting chums and discuss what the dictionary's definition for the word "school" might be. Ask a few of the pairs to feed back to you. Then look up the word "school" and read it out loud to see if they were right. Repeat the above steps for a word with several meanings, for example, "right".

3 • Explain to children that now they know what a dictionary is for, they need to learn how to use it. Use slide 3 to ask the question "How is a dictionary organised?" Explain that a dictionary is organised in alphabetical order. Ask them to chant the alphabet in order as it appears on the screen. Explain that all the "a" words are at the beginning of the dictionary and all the "z" words are at the end.

4 • Tell children that a dictionary gives us clues to help us find our way around. Give each child a dictionary. Ask them to look at how the dictionary is in alphabetical order. Show children by using the letters on the board, that the letters at the beginning of the alphabet (in red) are at the beginning of the dictionary, the letters in the middle of the alphabet (in green) are in the middle and the letters at the end of the alphabet (in blue) are at the end of the dictionary. Show that at the top of the dictionary and down the side of the dictionary there is a guide to where you are in the dictionary (how this is displayed will depend on the dictionaries your school uses).

> **Support**
> Provide less-able children with an alphabet card to refer to.

5 • Play "Discovering the dictionary". An "a" appears on the board. Ask children to find "a" in their dictionary. Now an "apple" appears – challenge them to race to find the word "apple". When they have found it, they should stand up. Repeat for the words "flower" and "shark".

6 • Finish by explaining that today they are going to practise using a dictionary.

> **Challenge**
> Encourage more-able children to work independently.

Practical activities

Dictionary races
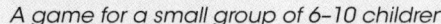
A game for a small group of 6–10 children
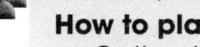
Aim: to practise using a dictionary to check spellings of words

How to play
- Gather the resources.
- Give each child a dictionary and a mini whiteboard and pen.
- Put the bell in the middle of the table.
- Choose a picture card, say the word out loud and ask children to write it on a whiteboard.
- When you have checked that they have spelled it correctly, check that all dictionaries closed and say "ready, steady, go".
- They should race to find the word in their dictionary and ring the bell when they have found it.
- The first to find the word and ring the bell is the winner.
- You should always start a race with dictionaries closed.

> **Support**
> Use simpler dictionaries and work together as a group instead of racing against each other, e.g. ask:
> - Which letter does this word begin with?
> - Can you point to this letter on your alphabet card?
> - Where does it come in the alphabet?
> - Let's see if we can find it. Now let's look for the word.

> **Challenge**
> Discuss with more-able children after the race how they found the word quickly. Which clues did they use to help them?

Definition dilemma

An activity for a small group of 5–10 children

Aim: to understand that dictionaries help us to find out what words mean through providing definitions of words

How to play:

- Gather the resources.
- Put the Song of Sounds green words in the feely bag or box and give each child a mini whiteboard and pen.
- Pick a word out and ask children to read it together.
- Ask them to write a definition of what this word means on their whiteboard, and in turn read their definition out loud.
- Read the definition in the dictionary and decide which definition was the closest.
- Repeat multiple times.

Support

Less-able children could do this activity orally by discussing their ideas.

Challenge

Discuss good elements and unclear elements in children's definitions and allow them time to improve them before you reveal the correct answer.

Alphabetical order cards

An activity for a small group of 5–6 children

Aim: to practise putting a series of words in alphabetical order

How to play:

- Gather the resources.
- Give each child an exercise book and pencil as well as an alphabet card.
- Show the group an alphabetical order card and write the words from the card on the board so that everyone can see them.
- Read the words with the children and look at the initial letters. Ask them what they notice: that they all begin with the same letter.
- Explain that when you are looking in a dictionary for a word, lots of words begin with the same letter.
- Show how to use the next letter in the word to put the words in alphabetical order.
- Put a few words in order together as a group and then ask them to each pick an alphabetical order card and work independently.

Support

Use the simpler alphabet cards from week 26 and put them in alphabetical order.

Challenge

Challenge more-able children to work out their alphabetical order without the help of an alphabet card. Encourage them to use the song or say the alphabet as a strategy. As an extension, move them on to looking at words where the first two letters are the same.

Revision

 Ask children to return to the carpet and sit in a circle. Give each chatting chum pair a dictionary and put the bell in the middle of the circle. Play more dictionary races. When children have found a word, they should race to the middle of the circle to ring the bell. The first pair are the winners and can go and get ready for lunch, hometime, or whichever activity follows the lesson.

Now read

Choose any Big Cat Phonics readers that will help children hone in on their problem areas

Target skill: Revise all phonemes learned so far

Starter

- Sit the children in their chatting chum pairs.
- Sing the Song of Sounds using the IWB version.

Resources

- Song of Sounds IWB version
- Song of Sounds flashcards
- Mini whiteboards and pens for each chatting chum pair
- Song of Sounds phoneme finders (optional)

Main lesson

Reading phonemes

- Show the class the flashcards, one at a time, picture-side up, and ask them to sing each sound.
- Ask them to silently do the actions to the song as you show them the flashcards.
- As you produce the grapheme side, can they say the different sounds? Ask the class to say them in unison as you get faster and faster.

Writing phonemes

- Give each chatting chum pair a mini whiteboard and pen.
- Show the class a flashcard picture-side up and ask the pairs to write the grapheme on their whiteboard. Repeat a few times.
- Then demonstrate an action from the song – as you do the action, ask children to write the corresponding grapheme. Repeat a few times.
- Finally, say a sound and ask them to write *all* the graphemes that make that sound, e.g. if you said /ay/ they should write all of the /ay/ graphemes: "ay", "ai", "a-e".

Support

Give less-able children a Song of Sounds phoneme finder to help them find the correct graphemes and copy.

Challenge

To challenge more-able children, ask them to write a word that has each alternative grapheme in.

Target skill: Practise reading green and tricky words

Starter

- Sit the children in their chatting chum pairs.
- Sing the Song of Sounds using the IWB version.

Resources

- Song of Sounds IWB version
- A selection of Song of Sounds green words of your choice
- A lolly stick for each child in the class with their name written on (optional)
- Song of Sounds tricky word cards (all)

Main lesson

Reading green words

- On the board, stick a selection of four green words that contain one syllable, for example, eat, paint, fright, toast etc. Explain to the class that you are going to practise reading words with one syllable.
- Ask children to work with their chatting chums to practise reading the green words.
- Choose a lolly stick from the pot. The named child should stand up, choose a green word and read it out loud.
- The whole class should then read the word together. Do this by asking children to say the grapheme as you press the sound buttons, and then read the whole word as you sweep your hand underneath.
- Remove the word from the board. Repeat for the other three words.
- Then stick four green words on the board that contain two syllables, for example, sister, enjoy, morning, lightning. Explain that now you are going to practise reading words with two syllables. Remind them that for a longer word it is easier to blend a chunk at a time, for example, l-igh-t/n-i-ng.
- Repeat for four green words that contain three phonemes, such as chimpanzee, holiday, Saturday, zookeeper.
- Finally, stick a green word on the board that has four syllables, for example, helicopter. Explain that this word has four syllables. Repeat the steps above.

Reading tricky words

- Ask children to explain to you the difference between green words and tricky words.
- Finish the session by practising reading the tricky words that you have learned during the programme. Show the class the tricky word cards one at a time and ask them to read them.

Target skill: Practise writing green words

Starter

- Sit the children in their chatting chum pairs.
- Sing the Song of Sounds using the IWB version.

Resources

- Song of Sounds IWB version
- Song of Sounds tricky word cards (all)
- A Song of Sounds phoneme finder for each chatting chum pair
- Mini whiteboards and pens for each chatting chum pair
- A lolly stick for each child in the class with their name written on (optional)

Main lesson

Writing green words

- Explain that today they are going to practise writing some green words.
- Give each chatting chum pair a whiteboard, pen and a Song of Sounds phoneme finder.
- Choose a one-syllable word with one of the alternative phonemes in to say out loud, for example, round. Ask children to sound-talk the word with their chatting chums in order to segment the word into the correct phonemes. They should then write the word on their whiteboards, using their Song of Sounds phoneme finder to help them.
- Pull a lolly stick out of your pot. Ask the named child to stand up and sound-talk the word they have written on their whiteboard. As they do, write it on the board so that you are modelling the correct handwriting to the class. Discuss which grapheme is used to represent the phoneme for example, /ou/.
- Repeat a few times for other unfamiliar one-syllable words.
- Repeat for two-syllable words, for example, playground.
- Repeat for three-syllable words, for example, caravan.
- Repeat for four-syllable words, for example, caterpillar.
- Play "Phoneme fingers" with two- or three-syllable words.

Writing tricky words

- Ask children to explain to you the difference between green words and tricky words.
- Finish the session by practising writing some of the tricky words that you have learned this year. Say a tricky word and ask children to write it on their whiteboards.

Support

To support less-able children, give them the Song of Sounds phoneme finder with the tricky words on the back so they have to find the correct tricky word and write it.

Target skill: Practise reading and writing a sentence

Starter

- Sit the children in their chatting chum pairs.
- Ask children to explain to you the difference between green words and tricky words.
- Practise reading the tricky words that you learned last week (of, off, house, because, looked, called). Show the class the flashcards one at a time and ask them to read them out loud, increasing in speed.

Resources

- Song of Sounds tricky word cards of, off, house, because, looked, called
- A Song of Sounds green sentence card for each chatting chum pair
- A Song of Sounds phoneme finder for each chatting chum pair
- A whiteboard and pen for each chatting chum pair

Main lesson

Reading a sentence

- Give each chatting chum pair a green sentence. Explain to them that their sentence includes some green words and some tricky words.
- Give them a time limit, for example, one minute, to practise reading their sentence with their chatting chums.
- Ask each pair in turn to stand up and read their sentence to the class.

Writing a sentence

- Give each chatting chum pair a whiteboard and pen and a Song of Sounds phoneme finder.
- Explain to the class that you are going to write a sentence that contains both green words and tricky words.
- Call out: "The chimpanzee ran away from the zookeeper."
- Ask children to repeat the sentence. Repeat a few times, adding a few actions, for example, chimpanzee (hands in armpits), ran (running action), zookeeper (turning a key).
- Model writing the sentence on the board. Explain your thought processes to them as you write:
  - use sound-talk to write the green words
  - find tricky words on your Song of Sounds phoneme finder
  - make sure you use finger spaces
  - read back your sentence to work out which word comes next, etc.
- When the sentence is complete, read it back as a class. Then rub the sentence off the board and ask children to work with their chatting chums to write the sentence independently.
- To finish this session, ask them to rub out the fullstop and add an "and", then they should write what happened next.
- Ask each chatting chum pair to read their sentence out loud and all have fun reading the sentences.

Felicity returns

Target phonemes: all phonemes learned so far

Learning objective

To practise blending and segmenting all phonemes learned so far

Resources

Carpet session

- Software (Week 29: Teach)
- IWB version of the song
- A fairy/wizard outfit and wand, fairy/wizard toy or a letter (optional)
- A mini whiteboard and pen for each chatting chum pair

Sprint and spell

- Song of Sounds phoneme stars
- Large sheets of paper
- A whiteboard and pen for each team
- Song of Sounds phoneme finders (optional)

- Hoop (optional)
- Whistle (optional)

Song of Sounds bingo

- A bingo playing board for each child (Week 29: AS1–6)
- IWB bingo game
- Six counters per child
- Song of Sounds lotto game (optional)

Felicity's formation

- Song of Sounds phoneme stars
- A dice for each child
- A mini whiteboard and pen for each child
- Song of Sounds phoneme finders (optional)

Carpet session

- Gather the resources.
- Sit the children in their chatting chum pairs.
- This lesson has the option of teaching in role as Felicity the Phoneme Fairy in a fairy costume and wand. Alternatively, you could use a fairy puppet or receive a letter from Felicity.
- Depending on the option you have chosen, enter the classroom as Felicity, hold up your puppet or letter, or simply play the software.

1
- Explain that Felicity wants to check how you are getting on with reading and writing your phonemes.

> **Software**
> Teach
> **W29**

- Play the Song of Sounds song. Challenge children to sing the song in a very clever way – they should sing the song in their head and do the actions for each part of the song, but sing the phoneme, e.g. /ai/, /ai/, /ai/.

2
- Stress how much children have learned since starting school. Ask them if they remember learning their simple phonemes and to call out the phonemes as the graphemes flash in on the board. Then ask they remember learning to read simple words using these phonemes? Ask them to read the words "bus" and "cat" as they appear.

3
- Remind children how they began to learn some trickier phonemes. Ask them to call out the phonemes as the graphemes flash in on the board. Then ask if they remember learning to read harder words using these phonemes. Ask them to read the words "fork" and "sleep" as they appear.

4 • Remind children how this year they have learned different ways of reading and writing the same sound. Show them the different alternatives they have learned for the phonemes /e/, /o/ and /er/. Explain that the tricky bit about these different alternatives is knowing when to use each one and that is what they are going to practise today. Give each chatting chum pair a mini whiteboard and pen.

5 • A picture of a bird will appear on the board. Ask children to spell "bird" out in sound-talk on their fingers, for example, b-ir-d. Explain that we know it is an /er/ sound but which /er/ is it? Is it /er/, /ir/ or /ur/? Explain that if you don't know which grapheme to use, a good strategy is to write them down and see which one looks right. On the screen, the words "berd", "bird" and "burd" appear. Ask them to write on their whiteboard what they think is the right way of spelling "bird" and to show their whiteboards on a given signal.

6–7 • Repeat the above steps for the words "snail" and "bone".

8 • Show three pictures that have the /ay/, /ai/ and /a-e/ sound. Ask children to discuss with their chatting chums which picture uses which /ay/ sound. Suggest that if they can't decide they might like to try writing the words down using the different /ay/ sounds to see which one looks right. Reveal the answers and deal with any misconceptions.

9–10 • Repeat the above steps for slides 9 and 10.

11 • Show children some pictures of words that have more than one harder phoneme. Ask them to see if they can write them on their whiteboards, trying out different alternatives if they are not sure.

12 • Finish by saying that they are are very clever and you think they should practise reading and writing all the phonemes and graphemes they have learned.

Practical activities

Sprint and spell

A game for a large group of 6–15 children

Aim: to practise writing all graphemes learnt so far at speed

How to play:
• Gather the resources.
• This game should be played in a large space.
• Divide the children into equal-sized teams.
• Stick a piece of paper on a board or wall for each teams, and each ask the teams to sit a distance away from their sheet of paper in a line.
• Give the first member of each team a whiteboard pen.

Game 1
• Between the pieces of paper and the teams, put a hoop on the floor and scatter the Song of Sounds phoneme stars inside it.
• Blow the whistle to start the game. The first member of each team should run to the hoop and pick a star. They should then run to their piece of paper and write the grapheme that corresponds with that star on their sheet of paper.
• They then run to the hoop, put the star back and run back to their team.
• Repeat for each member of the team.
• If they pick up a star that has already been used by their team, they can't write their letter on the sheet.
• Blow the whistle or shout to stop the game. The team who has written the most graphemes correctly wins the game.
• Play again.

> **Support**
> Give less-able children a Song of Sounds phoneme finder to help them.

> **Challenge**
> More-able children could write a word with that particular grapheme in. It has to be spelled correctly to count.

Game 2
- To make this game even harder, remove the phoneme stars.
- Call out a phoneme, for example, /ay/, and blow the whistle to start the game.
- The children should take it in turns to sprint to their piece of paper and spell a word with the phoneme in. They can spell words that use any of the alternatives, for example, /ai/, /ay/, /a-e/, but the word *must* be spelled correctly to count.
- Blow the whistle to stop the game and count up each team's correctly spelled words to find the winner.
- Play again but call out a different sound, for example, /or/.

Song of sounds bingo

A game for a small group of 5–6 children

Aim: to practise recognising graphemes and listening for phonemes in words

How to play:
- Gather the resources.
- Song of Sounds lotto game (optional)
- Sit the group in a semi circle in front of the IWB.
- Give each child a playing board and a pile of counters.
- Press play on the Song of Sounds bingo game.
- A grapheme appears on the screen. Children should look at their playing board. If they have a picture that contains that grapheme they should cover it up with a counter.
- The teacher should observe and discuss any misconceptions as they go along.
- The first child to cover all their pictures is the winner.
- There are a few alternatives of the game so you can play again and the graphemes will appear in a different order.

> **Support**
> To support less-able children, play "Song of Sounds Lotto" instead.

Felicity's formation

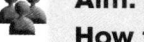

An activity for a small group of 5–10 children

Aim: to practise correct letter formation of all graphemes

How to play:
- Gather the resources.
- Gather the children around a table.
- Scatter Felicity's phoneme stars on the table, face down.
- Children should choose a star, roll their dice and write the corresponding grapheme that many times on their whiteboard.
- Felicity should work with the children and focus on their letter formation, rewarding them with glitter if they are working hard.

> **Support**
> Less-able children can use the Song of Sounds phoneme finder to support them.

Revision

Gather the children in a large space. Play a whole class game of "Sprint and spell".

Now read

> *Any Big Cat Phonics readers to consolidate children's decoding skills and knowledge of tricky words*

Target skill: To read real words without sound buttons

Starter

- Sit the children in their chatting chum pairs.
- Sing the Song of Sounds using the IWB version.

Resources

- Song of Sounds IWB version
- Song of Sounds flashcards
- Green words practice sheet 1 for each chatting chum pair
- A lolly stick for each chatting chum pair (optional)
- A pen and pencil for each chatting chum pair

Main lesson

Reading phonemes

- Explain to children that today they are going to practise reading words without any sound buttons. To start with, you are going to check that they know their sounds.
- Play "Speed sounds" with the Song of Sounds flashcards. As you produce the grapheme side, can they say the different sounds? Ask the class to say them in unison as you get faster and faster.

Reading without sound buttons

- Give each chatting chum pair a green words practice sheet and a pencil.
- Show children that none of the words have sound buttons.
- Explain that it is easier to read words if they have sound buttons.
- Write the word "moon" on the board. Show them how, if they read the word as m-o-o-n, it is not helpful because it doesn't help them to blend the word. Show children how they need to see the /oo/ as one sound, so they have to imagine the sound buttons.
- Ask them to work with their chatting chums to see if they can draw the sound buttons underneath each word.
- Once they have completed this, give each pair a lolly stick. They should take it turns using the lolly stick as a pointer to practise reading the words by breaking the words into sounds.
- Then ask children to read the words back to you in unison. They should sound out each word three times before saying the whole word.
- Then ask each pair to read out one word, again sounding the word out three times before saying the word as a whole word.

Target skill: To read real words without sound buttons

Resources

- Song of Sounds IWB version
- Song of Sounds flashcards
- Song of Sounds green words

Starter

- Sit the children in their chatting chum pairs.
- Sing the Song of Sounds using the IWB version.

Main lesson

Reading phonemes

- Explain that today they are going to practise reading words without any sound buttons. To start with you are going to check that they know their sounds.
- Play "Speed sounds" with the Song of Sounds flashcards. As you produce the grapheme side, can they say the different sounds? Ask the class to say them in unison as you get faster and faster.

Reading without sound buttons

- Explain that today the class are going to try reading some green words without any sound buttons at all. They must look carefully at each word and imagine the sound buttons in their head.
- Ask them to sit in a big circle with their chatting chums next to them. Give each chatting chum pair a word to read together.
- When they have all practised, ask them to pass their word to the next pair to the right and then practise reading their new word.
- Repeat a few times.
- Then go around the circle and ask each chatting chum pair to stand up and read the word they have out loud. They should use the same technique as yesterday, where they sounded it out three times before they read the whole word.
- When everyone has read their word, collect the words and ask the class to all face you again.

Revision

Use the green words as flashcards. Go through the pack a word at a time, asking the class to sound out each one three times and then reading the whole word.

Target skill: To read nonsense words without sound buttons

Starter

- Sit the children in their chatting chum pairs.
- Sing the Song of Sounds using the IWB version.

Resources
- Song of Sounds IWB version
- Song of Sounds flashcards
- Green words practice sheet 2 for each chatting chum pair
- A lolly stick for each chatting chum pair (optional)
- A pencil/pen for each chatting chum pair

Main lesson

Reading phonemes

- Explain that today they are going to practise reading some really hard words without any sound buttons. So it's extra important that they know their sounds.
- Play "Speed sounds" with the Song of Sounds flashcards. As you produce the grapheme side, can they say the different sounds? Ask the class to say them in unison as you get faster and faster.

Reading without sound buttons
- Give each chatting chum pair a green words practice sheet and a pencil.
- Ask children to look at the sheet and tell you what they notice: that these words are not real words, they are made-up nonsense words.
- Explain that nonsense words work in just the same way as real words, they just sound funny because they are not real.
- Show them that again none of the words have sound buttons.
- Ask them to work with their chatting chums to see if they can draw the sound buttons underneath each word.
- Once they have completed this, give each chatting chum pair a lolly stick. They should take it turns, using the lolly stick as a pointer, to practise reading the words by breaking them into sounds.
- Then ask children to read the words back to you in unison. They should sound out each word three times before saying the word as a whole word.
- Then ask each pair to read out one word, again sounding the word out three times before saying the word as a whole word.

Target skill: To read nonsense words without sound buttons

Starter

- Sit the children in their chatting chum pairs.
- Sing the Song of Sounds using the IWB version.

Resources
- Song of Sounds IWB version
- Song of Sounds flashcards
- Song of Sounds green words

Reading phonemes

- Explain that today they are going to practise reading nonsense words without any sound buttons. To start with, we are going to check those sounds again.
- Play "Speed sounds" with the Song of Sounds flashcards. As you produce the grapheme side, can they say the different sounds? Ask the class to say them in unison as you get faster and faster.

Main lesson

Reading without sound buttons

- Explain that today they are going to try reading some green nonsense words without any sound buttons at all. Explain to children that they must look carefully at each word and imagine the sound buttons in their head.
- Ask them to sit in a big circle with their chatting chums next to them. Give each chatting chum pair a word to read together.
- When they have all practised, ask them to pass their word to the pair to the right and then practise reading their new word.
- Repeat a few times.
- Then go around the circle and ask each chatting chum pair to stand up and read the word they have out loud. They should use the same technique as yesterday, where they sounded it out three times before they read the whole word.
- When everyone has read their word, collect the words and ask the class to all face you again.

Revision

Use the green words as flashcards. Go through the pack a word at a time, asking the class to sound out each one three times and then reading the whole word .

Phonics screening test

Target phonemes: all phonemes learned so far

Learning objective

to blend and read a mixture of real and nonsense words

Resources

Carpet session

- An alien costume (optional). You could wear green clothes, green face paint and deely boppers
- Week 30: Teach software
- Real and nonsense word cards
- 2 pairs of deely boppers (optional)

Roll and read

- A large space next to an IWB

- A large ball (a jingle ball if possible)
- IWB screen of real and nonsense words

Spacehopper sprint

- 2 large pieces of paper for each team, one with an alien on the top and one with a human on the top.
- 10 words, some should be real words and some should be nonsense words, for each team
- A hoop
- A spacehopper for each team (optional)

Carpet session

- Before the lesson, hide the real and nonsense cards around the classroom.
- If you would like to teach this lesson in character, enter the classroom dressed as an alien. Alternatively, use the software as normal.
- Speak to the children in alien language (lots of beeps!). Show the children that you are upset and agitated as you point to the nonsense word on the IWB. Hold your head, gesticulate wildly and look exasperated. The children will naturally try and work out what you are upset about. Keep pointing to the board until a child blends the word 'voo'. At that point, you should get very excited, make lots of beeping noises and jump up and down with excitement! Show the children the next word 'bim'. Point to the graphemes to encourage the children to sound out the word 3 times, then run your hand underneath to encourage the children to read the whole word. Repeat for all other words, beeping and being very excited at the children's success. When you get to the final word 'tentist' hold your face as if you have a toothache and point to your face as if to show the children that this word means 'dentist'. If a child says 'dentist' out loud, be very excited again to show the children that this means 'dentist' in alien! Jump up and down, beep a lot and then wave goodbye to the children. Exit the classroom.
- Re-enter the classroom as yourself again. (While you are gone, your teaching assistant should take over and talk to the children about what has just happened!) You should be very surprised that an alien has visited the children and ask what happened. They will explain to you that they have been reading words in alien language. You should tell them they are very clever at reading nonsense words so that must have been easy for them – well done! Tell children that it is time to get back to your lesson and read some REAL words you have prepared for them.

- When you press the button a mixture of real and nonsense words appear. Oh no! The alien has mixed his words up with yours. Ask the children to work with their chatting chums and discuss which words are real words (human words) and which words are nonsense words (alien words).

4
- Ask the children to feed back to you and reveal the correct answers on the IWB. Split the class into 2 teams. Tell the first team that they are the aliens and the second team that they are humans. Ask the aliens to read the nonsense words in unison, then ask the humans to read the real words in unison. Swap over.
- Play 'Walk for a word'. Explain to the children that around the room are lots of words – some of them are real and some of them are nonsense words. Challenge the children to walk around the room with their chatting chum and find a nonsense word. When they have found one, they should bring it back to the carpet.
- Ask the children to sit in a circle. Ask each chatting chum pair to stand up and read their nonsense word aloud. To make this a bit more exciting, the children who are reading the word aloud could wear a pair of deely boppers and when they have read their word, pass them to the next chatting chum pair.

Practical activities

Roll and read
A game for a large group of 6–15 children

Aim: to practise decoding a mixture of real and nonsense words

How to play:
- Sit the children in a circle.
- Display a mixture of real and nonsense words on the screen
- Give the jingle ball (or ball) to the first child
- Ask them to pick a nonsense word off the board, read it aloud and roll the ball to another child
- Keep going, asking children to read the words and dealing with any errors as they occur.

> **Support**
> Help less-able children to orally blend words by sounding out the words with them. Encourage them to choose the CVC words on the slide.

> **Challenge**
> Ask more-able children to sound-blend in their heads and read independently. Encourage them to choose the hardest words on the slide.

Spacehopper sprint
A game for a large group of 6–10 children

Aim: to practise distinguishing between real and nonsense words

How to play:
- This game is best played in a large indoor or outdoor space.
- Split the groups into two teams.
- Stick the two pieces of paper for each team on a wall or board.
- Sit each team a distance away from their pieces of paper in a line.
- Put their wordcards in a hoop between the team and the paper. Each team should have 10 words.
- On a given signal, the first person from each team should run to the hoop, pick a word and stick it on the alien sheet or human sheet, depending on whether it is a real word or a nonsense word. The child should run back to the team and tag the next player to go.
- The first team to empty their hoop and stick all the cards in the correct place is the winner.

> **Support**
> Ensure that the words in the less-able children's hoop are the simpler CVC and CCVC words.

> **Challenge**
> Ensure that the words in the more-able children's hoop are the harder CCVCC words.

Phonics screening check

A game for a large group of 6–10 children

Aim: An assessment activity to carry out individually with one child at a time (NB You may need more than one session for a complete check).

What to do:
- Carry out the test as per the instructions with one child at a time.

Tips:
- Encourage the children to sound-talk each word three times, before saying the word, to encourage accuracy.
- To differentiate between real and nonsense words, the child may put on the deely boppers when reading an 'alien' word.
- Give lots of praise and encouragement, and a reward at the end.

Revision

In silence, show the children a word at a time. If it is an "alien" word e.g. a nonsense word they should use their fingers to make alien antennae and say "bleep bleep". If it is a real word, they should sit smartly like smart humans!